ANTHROPOLOGICAL PAPERS

MUSEUM OF ANTHROPOLOGY, UNIVERSITY OF MICHIGAN

NO. 69

THE AIT AYASH OF THE HIGH MOULOUYA PLAIN: RURAL SOCIAL ORGANIZATION IN MOROCCO

BY JOHN CHIAPURIS

ANN ARBOR, MICHIGAN
1979

© 1979 Regents of The University of Michigan
The Museum of Anthropology
All rights reserved
Printed in the
United States of America

ISBN 0-932206-83-2

CONTENTS

List of Figures	iv
Lists of Maps	v
List of Plates	vi
Acknowledgements	vii
Introduction	ix
I. THE ETHNOHISTORICAL BACKGROUND	1
II. SOCIO-POLITICAL ORGANIZATION: THE TRADITIONAL PERIOD	37
III. REGIONAL ECOLOGY AND LOCAL GROUPS	63
IV. THE PROTECTORATE PERIOD	93
V. THE CONTEMPORARY PERIOD: GOVERNMENT AND THE VILLAGE ECONOMY	109
VI. DOMESTIC ORGANIZATION: HOUSEHOLDS, MARRIAGE, AND PROPERTY	135
VII. CONCLUSION	161
Bibliography	163
Glossary of Terms	171
Plates	177

LIST OF FIGURES

Figure 1a.	Age pyramids of two regions with different fertility rates.	
b.	Comparison of the age structures of the two regions with the population model for Morocco	88
Figure 2.	Social ascription and land property in an Ait Ayash village	122
Figure 3.	Irrigated field holdings of an Ait Ayash village	123
Figure 4.	Dry cultivation among the households of an Ait Ayash village	124
Figure 5.	Total cultivation of irrigated field and bour among the households of an Ait Ayash village	125
Figure 6.	Composition of households in Ait Akhatar	138
Figure 7.	Social ascriptions and household types in Ait Akhatar	139
Figure 8.	Joint households in Ait Akhatar	141
Figure 9.	Divorce and number of offspring	144
Figure 10.	Age at marriage in Ait Akhatar	147
Figure 11.	Marriage stability among the Ait Ayash men	148
Figure 12.	Marriage stability among the Ait Ayash women	149
Figure 13.	Age distribution and remarriages among the Ait Ayash	150
Figure 14.	Degree of kinship of wife in first and last marriage of 101 men in an Ait Ayash qsar	153
Figure 15.	Marital alliances in an extended family of Ait Akhatar	158

LIST OF MAPS

Map 1. Map of Morocco .... Facing page 1
Map 2. Map of Berber dialect distribution 3
Map 3. Location of Sanhaja tribal confederations 5
Map 4. Tribes in the High Molouya plain in the early 19th century 28
Map 5. Settlements and clans of the Ait Ayash 43
Map 6. Map of the High Molouya plain 62
Map 7. Populations of the High Molouya plain 67
Map 8. Cultivation with irrigation in the High Molouya plain 72
Map 9. Map of the collective land of the Ait Ayash 104

LIST OF PLATES

1.	Mausoleum of Sidi Abdullah ou Hamza	179
2.	Letter of qaid Mhand ou Talb	180
3.	Aerial photograph of two Ait Ayash villages	181
4.	Members of an extended family of the Ait Ayash	182
5.	Ait Ayash group circumcision	182
6.	Schoolboys standing beside an abandoned qsar	183
7.	Ait Ayash village houses	183
8a.	Threshing wheat	184
	b. Winnowing wheat	
9.	Measuring wheat	185
10.	Market at Kerroushen	185
11.	Construction of a mosque by cooperative village effort	186
12.	An Ait Ayash extended family	186

ACKNOWLEDGEMENTS

This book is a revised version of a doctoral dissertation submitted at the University of Michigan in 1977. I wish to thank the Center for Near Eastern and North African Studies, and its Director, Dr. William D. Schorger, for the financial support of the research for this study and for support of the publication of this monograph. The field research carried out in Morocco in 1968 and 1969 was also supported by a grant from the University of Michigan Project for the Study of Social Networks in the Mediterranean.

Many faculty members and fellow students have contributed directly or indirectly to the preparation of this study. I am grateful to all, particularly Eric Wolf, who encouraged me in the early part of my graduate work, Ernest Abdel-Massih for the language training in Tamazight Berber, and Wilfrid Rollman and Amal Rassam for sharing generously their knowledge and ideas during all the time I have known them. I feel a special debt of gratitude to William D. Schorger, who provided guidance and encouragement as my advisor throughout graduate training and field research.

During the sixteen months I lived in Morocco, between 1968 and 1969, many people gave me assistance and hospitality. Of these I would like to single out superqaid Nurredin al-Maati and qaid Ali Arara of the Bureau of Midelt Circle for their cooperation in making available for study papers in the Bureau's archives; also, Sheikh Madani of the Ait Ayash who was helpful throughout my stay in the villages. Most of all I owe a debt to all the people of the Ait Ayash who opened their homes to me with hospitality and warmth. I recall the friendship of Hmad, Lahsen, and Qssou with personal gratitude. I have deep regard for my field assistant, Youssef Hazmaoui, both for his work and for his friendship.

Two Moroccans gave me help while preparing for fieldwork. Muhammad Guerssel, while he attended the University of Michigan, and subsequently in Morocco in 1968, gave me many insights into his culture. Muhammad Raamouch, of the Ait Ayash, introduced me to his language while he was a student in Ann Arbor. In 1977, during a brief visit I made to Morocco and the Ait Ayash villages, I was pleased to find that Mr. Raamouch had been elected president of the council of the rural commune of the Ait Ayash.

I also wish to express my appreciation to Mary Shimizu and David Victor for the care they took in editing the typescript. Jane Mariouw drew the maps, and Margaret Van Bolt contributed the drawings of the kinship charts.

This work is dedicated to my wife, Camilla, who saw me through graduate study in my middle years, with encouragement, patience, and good humor.

INTRODUCTION

This study has two objectives. The first is to examine the social mechanisms by which rights over resources were allotted and maintained in rural Morocco. The second is to consider processes of change which affected land tenure, resource access, and the social relationships of production in the three political environments of the last seventy-five years: an archaic state system, a colonial interim (1912–1956), and a modernizing nation.

The study focuses on the Ait Ayash, a Berber-speaking community of irrigation agriculturalists, with a population of some 5,000 individuals. They occupy the Ansegmir valley in the High Moulouya plain, between the High Atlas chain and the Middle Atlas range. This is a region long dominated by semi-nomadic pastoralists. The account, rather than offering a complete ethnography, analyzes aspects of the relationships that organized production and maintained local groups with respect to each other and with respect to the state.

In the past, the dominant system that determined production and exchanges relied on membership and recruitment into kin-ascribed groups. This was never a discreet system but one which operated within a cash economy which was shared to different degrees by rural groups. One of the arguments developed in this study concerns the category of irrigated land in the tenure system of the Ait Ayash. Irrigated land was held in private or individual title as a function of specific ecological problems rather than direct involvement in a cash economy.

The study falls into three broad sections. The first deals with the ethnohistorical background of the Ait Ayash tribe and the sociopolitical organization of the tribe. The second focuses on the regional setting, on local group distribution, and the changes initiated by the French Protectorate in 1912. The third section deals with the contemporary period and focuses on a specific village with an analysis of domestic production, household organization and marriage patterns.

The sixteen month field research was carried out in 1968–1969. Ten months were spent living in an Ait Ayash village. I had to wait four months after application to obtain the authorization from the Ministry of Interior for rural research. The first five months were devoted to library research, language training, and travel to the area of study, but without prolonged stays which required a government permit.

Once the research permit was granted I was able to settle in one of the central villages of the valley. The regional government bureau suggested that I lodge with one of the three administrators of the Ait Ayash. I preferred to avoid identification with any particular household, especially that of an appointed chief. I set up living quarters in a market storehouse, a small room in a building constructed in the late fifties to serve as a market center. The market project had failed and the stalls of the building had remained vacant. I employed a field assistant for most of the stay. He was not an Ait Ayashi, but of another Berber speaking group, and had previously worked with other anthropologists. He was helpful to me in providing a comparative reference with respect to local institutions and practices. As a Berber companion, he facilitated travel outside the villages and eased acquaintance with unfamiliar households.

During the early months of the stay, data collection was confined to oral history for which many elders showed an unflagging enthusiasm. I had intended to collect household census data and household land holdings from all the villages of the Ait Ayash. Data collection was eventually limited to one village, the one in which I had become most familiar. Questions on property aroused wariness which took some time to dispel. The wariness was exacerbated because at this time a pilot program of range management was initiated on collective land of the Ait Ayash by the American organization International Volunteers Service (I.V.S.) under contract to U.S.A.I.D. The project failed in its early stages and had little impact on the villages except for the fears it raised about its purposes and the connection between my work and theirs. The purposes of the project were never properly explained to the local people. I believe I finally convinced them that my work was not tied to any government project, and in the later months of my stay I was able to collect the census data by interviews with the household heads of all but four of the 72 households in the village. This material is discussed in the last two chapters of the study.

I have tried to be reasonably accurate in transcribing Berber terms and names while retaining wherever practicable the French translation which is their accepted form in Morocco. In some cases changes have been made to conform to English orthography, but the variant forms will be readily recognizable. A case in point is the name Ait Ayash which is usually given in French transliteration as Ait

Ayache. A transliteration from the Arabic script, such as that of the International Journal of Middle East Studies, would give the name as Ayt ʿayyâ*sh*. I have left out diacritical marks in the text. Further notes on transliteration will be found in the Glossary section on p. 171).

A concession to accepted practice in European literature is the substitution of plurals of certain Arabic words with the singular form to which is added the plural morpheme {S}. The most frequently encountered examples are *qaids* for *quyyad, shaikhs* for *shioukh,* and *sharifs* for *shurfa*. I have followed this practice with the term *qaid*.

I use the term central Atlas in the text to refer to the area in the center of Morocco that includes the eastern High Atlas range, the high plain of the Moulouya river and the Middle Atlas mountains and plateaus.

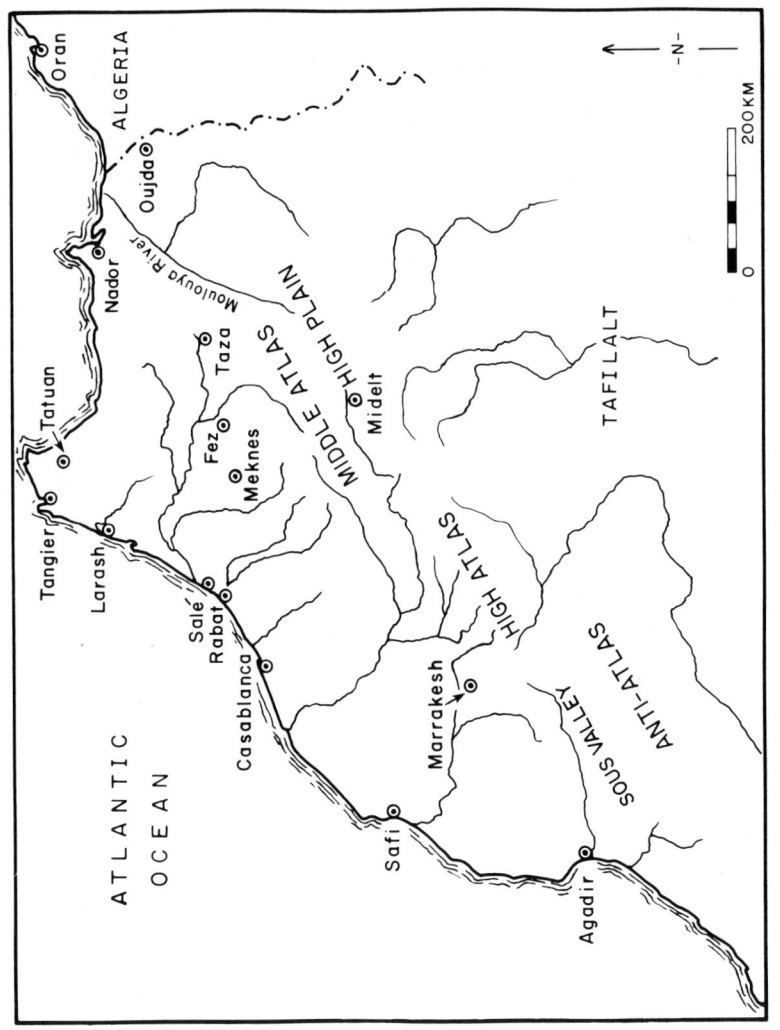

Map 1. Map of Morocco

CHAPTER ONE

The Ethnohistorical Background

This chapter begins with the historical background of tribalism in Morocco (Figure 1) and the relationship of tribes to the central government. The account introduces the key institutions of the *zawiyas* (lodges of religious brotherhoods), and the social segments of the *shurfa* (descendants of the Prophet) and *murabitin* (saintly men) that were crucial in the relationships between tribes, and between the central government and the tribes.

The latter part of the chapter presents a general, synthetic outline of the ethnohistory of the Ait Ayash through the late 19th century, when they had become a sedentary tribe in a region dominated by mobile pastoralists. The account proceeds to detail the interaction with the government and the regional zawiyas that were critical intermediary institutions in the political organization of the Moulouya Plain.

An important facet of the socio-political history of Morocco from the 16th century until the establishment of the French Protectorate in 1912 has been the complex interplay of the *makhzan,* or central government of the Sultanate, with the tribes and other segments of the society, which included the shurfa, murabitin, and, in the urban sectors, the *ulama* (religious scholars), and trade guilds. Tribalism in Morocco, in all but the urban areas, provided the social framework for the distribution of resources, the management of local conflict, and group activity and organization.

The relationship between the central government and the tribes has been conceptualized in the work of French historians, who dominated scholarly study of Morocco, as an opposition of separate political realms. These realms have been referred to as *blad al makhzan* or areas of government, and *blad al siba* or areas of tribal dissidence. However, the formation of this conceptualization tends to obscure the

2   THE AIT AYASH OF THE HIGH MOLOUYA PLAIN

dynamic interplay between the state-organized center and the rural populations, which shared a metaphysical view and formed a single socio-political system that proved flexible and resilient until its transformation in the modern period.

Recent studies have shifted the focus of analysis from opposition between political realms to an examination of processes and accommodations that brought a state-organized center and the peripheral, politically acephalous tribes into one system. (Waterbury 1970; Vinogradov 1974).

The Ait Ayash are one of the Sanhaja tribes of the Central Atlas. The Sanhaja designation derives from an historiographic tradition of following Ibn Khaldoun's classification of Moroccan Berber-speaking peoples into three groups: the Masmouda, the Sanhaja, and the Zenata (1925(1):194-196). The divisions serve at best, for ethnohistorical purposes, in their correspondence to the three separate linguistic blocs of the main Berber dialects of Tashelhit (or commonly Shilha), Tamazight, and Zenatiya (Map 2). The Zenatiya dialect of Morocco is known as Tarifit or Rifian Berber (Abdel-Massih 1971b:X; Martin et al. 1967:45).

The Masmouda, according to Ibn Khaldoun (1925(2):124ff.), were the first of the Berber groups in Morocco. They were predominantly cultivators who settled throughout the western High Atlas and the anti-Atlas, occupied portion of the plains (Berghwata and Dukkala tribes) and reached parts of the Rif chain (Ghomara). The Zenata were the last to arrive into Morocco. Some groups of them crossed the eastern steppes and spread into the lower Moulouya valley and into the Atlantic plains. The Miknassa among them founded the city of Meknes. Other groups settled in Sijilmasa and the Saharan oases of the Tafilalt in the eighth century.

The Sanhaja consisted of three major branches. The Algerian branch furnished the sedentary populations of the country (Kabylia, among them) and contributed to the political life of the country through the dynasty of the Zirids (tenth to twelfth centuries) and that of the Hammadids. The second branch, whose collective clans were known as the *mulaththimin* (the muffled ones, or veil wearers), penetrated into the western and southern reaches of the Sahara where they figured in the history of the Kingdom of Ghana, and later (in the 11th century) provided the politico-military basis for the Almoravid dynasty of Morocco and Spain. The third branch of the Sanhaja are those today identified as Imazighen in southeastern and central Morocco. In Ibn Khaldoun's account (1925(2):121-124), this branch occupied the

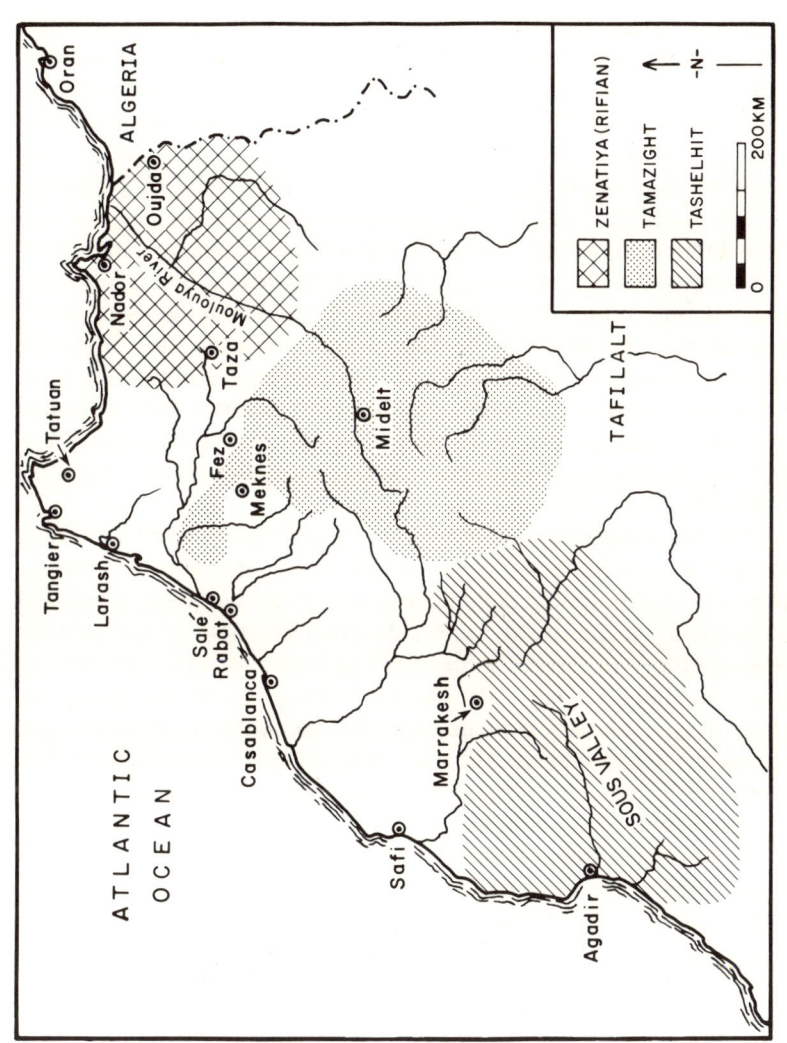

Map 2. Distribution of Berber dialects

4   THE AIT AYASH OF THE HIGH MOLOUYA PLAIN

Saharan oases of Morocco and gained the pastures of the eastern High Atlas as far west as the Oum ar-Rbia river by the fourteenth century.

The regional history for this period (14th to 16th centuries) is totally obscure; for while Ibn Khaldoun locates the Sanhaja of the third branch in the *Fazaz,* which corresponds to the environs of Sefrou and Khenifra of the Middle Atlas, other reports (cf. Leo Africanus 1600(2):557) place the Beni Ahsen of the Arab Maqil in the High Moulouya plain at this time. It may be that the Sanhaja reported in the Middle Atlas were an advance guard of fissioning communities. The massive migrations for which we have evidence from the encounters recorded in the chronicles between the tribes (or confederations) and the central state do not take place until the 17th and 18th centuries.

The migrations of pastoral populations (meaning Sanhaja of the various branches) out of the arid tracts of the Sahara into the more favored regions of the Atlas highlands and the coastal plains represent a major theme in the history of Morocco for almost a thousand years. From the time of the 11th century Almoravid expansion from the western Sahara, a continuous series of movements followed from population pressure, adjustments to droughts, famines and epidemics, as well as to political processes generated by the central state. These guided the formation of socio-political blocs for cooperation and competition in shifting territorial alignments.

The Ait Ayash and the other tribal groups in the High Moulouya plain in the present first appear in the region in the 17th century, organized in ethno-political confederations that interacted in political contests with the central dynasty. The confederations of the Sanhaja groups are those of the Ait Atta, Ait Yafelman, Ait Idrassen, and Ait Oumalou (Map 3). The Ait Atta fall outside of the scope of our regional focus, as they were located on the southern fringes of the Atlas and the pre-Sahara, but are relevant for the reactions they caused in adjacent blocs by their expansionist organization. The outline below follows the confederations of the dominant *tamazight* or Berber-speaking tribes of the period from historical sources; but as Berque (1958a:7) has noted:

> Cette structure, telle qu'elle ressort des sources marocaines, c'est-à-dire bien hypothetiquement, on s'en doute, est, par surcroît, mouvante. Les noms n'y sont point stables. Ils convient des réalités politiques éphémères. Confédérations, ligues, tribus s'amplifient ou se rompent, surgissent ou disparaîssent. En tout ce monde des sommets neigeux et des plateaux boisés de cèdres, s'écoule, dans le sens de la transhumance d'hiver, vers le Nord et le Nord-Ouest.

Central to the Moulouya region and the highland environs were the Ait Idrassen. On their western flank were the Ait Oumalou, and to

THE ETHNOHISTORICAL BACKGROUND

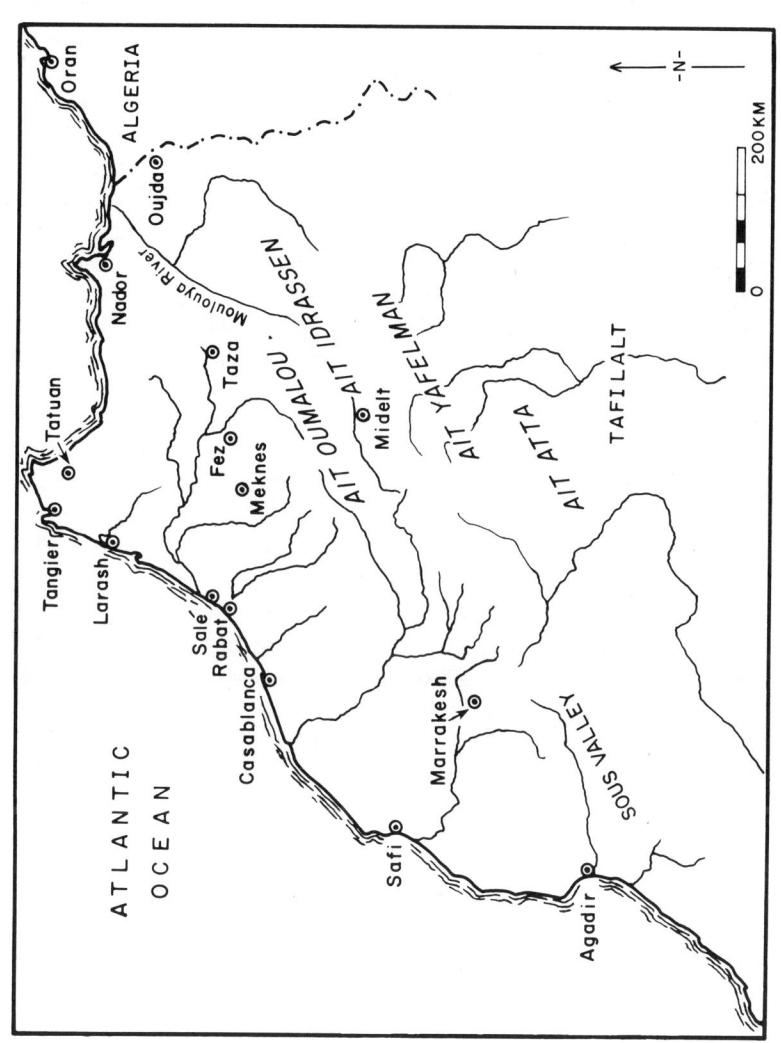

Map 3. Location of Sanhaja tribal confederations

the south were the Ait Yafelman. The Ait Oumalou ('those of the shaded side') referred to the bloc of pastoralist Sanhaja tribes who occupied the slopes of the Middle Atlas, as distinct from groups to the south and east. The principal groups (coalescing under the Ait Oumalou) were the Beni Mgild, Ishqirn, Ait Ishaq, Zayan, and Ait Sokhman. Ephemeral but recurrent solidarity was expressed against the thrusts of advancing groups from the southeast contesting pasture rights as well as against the tax collecting expeditions of the sultans.

The Ait Yafelman was the youngest confederation, according to local traditions. The alliance grouped the tribes of the eastern Atlas south of the Moulouya plain: the Ait Yahia, Ait Haddidou, Ait Izdeg, Gerwan, and Ait Morghad. The name Yafelman ('those who have found peace') reflected the coalescence into a defensive league of an earlier ethno-political grouping of the first four tribes—the Ait Midoul—with the southernmost group of the Ait Morghad who had previously been associated with the tribes of the Ait Atta (Guennon 1934:218). The Ait Atta had developed most fully the genealogical argument for cohesion with a segmentary lineage structure. This permitted them a military advantage over smaller tribal entities for predatory expansion. Their formation may date from the 15th century (Dunn 1972:86). From their original home in the Jebel Saghro mass of the eastern Anti-Atlas, Atta clans spread south and north incorporating additional groups into an ever-expanding kinship organization. The massing effect provided them with the organizational means to gain oases settlements and pastoral domains held by numerically weaker tribes. The Ait Yafelman formation which developed towards the middle of the 17th century was a direct response to the Atta expansion northwards. But for the same period the traditions mention droughts that upset the political balance the Yafelman coalition had sought to establish. Thus, southern groups were forced to continue (either by fission or massive migrations) their search for better pastures and new homes.

The Ait Idrassen appears to be among the oldest of the confederations. Its core members were the Ait Ayash, Ait Ihand, Ait Ouafella, Beni Mtir, and Mjatt.[1] The Idrassen had become powerful in the 17th century before the ascendancy of the Alawite dynasty, and had served as the base for the political aspirations of the Dila zawiya. After successful challenges by the forces of the early Alawite princes, the confederation became moribund in the early 19th century, during the

---

[1]Other members probably attached to the confederation at different periods were the Ait Sadden, Ait Wallal, Imelwan, Ait Youssi, Ait Seghrushen n'Sidi Ali and the Ait Yemmour. The record is very confused. In another collected version, the Ait Yemmour had formed the fifth part of the original Ait Midoul, which with the addition of the Ait Morghad became the Ait Yafelman cf. La Chapelle 1931:29–30 and Drague 1951:129–30, *passim*. Pascon (1977(1):218) places the Ait Yemmour and the Ait Ayash among the tribes of the Ait Yafelman confederation at its inception.

reign of Mawlay Sliman. Its tribal units were either broken up by transfers (Ait Ayash, Ait Ihand, Ait Ouafella) or moved from the central arena of their original core area (Mjatt, Beni Mtir). Of all the Atlas federations, the Idrassen was the only one which was completely dissolved by makhzan measures. While local oral tradition retains accounts of the Yafelman and the Oumalou histories, the Idrassen label evokes little more than the name and the participant members. The tribes that remained in the Moulouya plain, such as the Ayash and the Ouafella, subsequently joined or became identified with the Yafelman throughout the 19th century, and it is this dateline which marks the beginning of local history in the oral accounts. Some information on the history of the Idrassen can be culled from the sources of the dynastic chronicles which are summarized in the next section. The lack of any oral history among the Ait Ayash about the Idrassen past stresses discontinuity between their earlier social form and production base and their subsequent economic and social relations as a small, sedentary tribe. The Idrassen past had no particular functional relevance for the Ait Ayash in the new conditions of the 19th century. Still, it remains relevant to the distribution of groups of unequal size over the social landscape and of the gaps between ecological constraints and productive processes for the period preceding the Protectorate. A synchronic account, without historical depth, would not provide an adequate perspective. The role of supra-tribal pacts[2] and, concurrently, the periodic intervention of the state in regional alignments served over the long term as major parameters in the ecological patterns of the blad al siba.

The structures of the supra-tribal groups, usually organized to different degrees in terms of genealogical proximity, shared several organizational features: a) formation of a military alliance between territorially adjacent populations[3] for the defense of, or for access to contested space; b) attempts to reach a polito-economic balance between groups with similar adaptations (Sanhaja), and without centralized authority; and c) ideological support from the shared faith through the established institutions of the zawiya and the shurfa.

[2]One informant, an Ait Hadiddou elder well-versed in tribal lore, spoke of earlier transtribal alliances in the form of named political moieties, the Tahmid and Tamzoult, to which all the groups of the pre-Sahara and the central Atlas were aligned. He provided the names of the groups attached to the two sides. However, no one among the Ait Ayash and the other High Moulouya groups knew anything of such a system, and no one recognized the names of the moieties. The informant, known as Ou Shdish, assured me that if I questioned elders of the south (Ait Atta), they would confirm his statements. Such political moieties (leffs) have not been reported anywhere outside of the western High Atlas region.

[3]The genealogical argument was always present to some degree in these formations, usually based on some version of relations traced back to the proto-ancestor Goliath (Jalout). The appeal to Jalout was likely derived from Ibn Khaldoun's discussion of origin myths—which he dismissed as fanciful tales—and their perpetuation by scribes as guardians of the past (1925:175–185).

One oral version provided by Ou Shidish, the Ait Hadiddou, gave Jalout four sons, one of whom, Baibi, was killed while very young by Arabs. In another version Baibi is killed after giving issue to the Ait Morghad. Variations abound. The other three sons, named Amazigh, Sous, and Rifi were the respective genitors of the three main Berber groups. Amazigh gave descendants who formed the Ait Midoul, Ait Atta, Ait Youssi, Zayan, Ishqirn, Ait Seri, Ait Attab, Imgran, Ait Sokhman and Ait Hamad.

Concerning the first feature, one notes that only among the Ait Atta did a full segmentary lineage structure develop over time for expansion into already occupied domains. The Atta were located amidst one of the most fully exploited environmental niches of the traditional Maghreb. In the circumstances, they had to rely on a more compelling unity: the alliance became a genealogical structure of nested groups. This joined locally autonomous groups (tribes) into a cooperative military bloc based on the relations of putative descendants of the apical genitor, Dadda Atta. The other federations, as far as can be reconstructed, never developed the argument of common descent lines to any appreciable degree. Their solidarity manifested itself on the basis of contractual accords, and remained more in the realm of the expedient. This was evident of the Ait Yafelman, a defensive coalition against the Atta clans pushing northwards with a political formula for finding 'peace'. The named unity of the Ait Oumalou signaled, on the other hand, a locational reality—those on the northern side, the favored slopes, of a pastoral universe. Little is known of the formation of the Ait Idrassen, so it is not possible to speculate on the basis for their cohesion. In different accounts many other groups are added to its membership,[4] which may indicate shifting participation over time. Some landmarks in the role of the confederation on the history of the 17th century will be discussed later.

The relevance of the second point concerns particularly the distribution of groups (in any long term perspective) over the given space, and the development of symbiotic relations. Local imbalances prevailed, usually because of factors exogenous to the regional organization. The goals of the central state generally conflicted with the plans of the provinces. It was not that the political organization of the countryside was ineffective, but that it was continually subverted. In the expressive phrases of Jacques Berque (1958a:8),

> Dès qu'une dynastie s'en croit capable, elle essaie d'isoler le massif, de le percer de voies, de neutraliser ses forces d'agression son insulte permanente á la citè des plaines.
> Ces interventions de l'exterieur troublent les équilibres locaux. Elles dèsorganisent le système autonome auquel concuraient la vitalité des groupes et les suggestions du milieu, aussi bien qu'un genie à la fois juridique et battaileur.

One might add the suggestion that the juridical and martial spirits may have been themselves consequences of the wider sphere of interaction rather than cultural givens that explained anything about social processes.

---

[4]Segonzac (1910:292) attaches to the Ait Idrassen practically all the tribes of the northern Middle Atlas and the Taza region.

THE ETHNOHISTORICAL BACKGROUND

As noted in point "c", all the confederations maintained a relationship with a religious authority: a zawiya or a murabit. This varied from the initial provision of sanctified auspices for legalizing a contract, to that of gaining a basis for consolidating politico-military authority in a challenge to the established center. An example of the latter case in the 17th century is the Dilaiya zawiya—in effect a maraboutic principality—tied to the population base of the Ait Idrassen.

Before presenting the historical events concerning the High Moulouya region from the 17th through the 19th centuries, it is helpful to survey the most frequently evoked causes of the population upheavals and migrations that mark the history of southern and central Morocco in this period.

CAUSES OF POPULATION MOVEMENTS, 17TH–19TH CENTURIES

From the 11th century Sanhaja migrations out of Senegal (to which they gave their name) and Mauritania into Morocco, the most constant factor in population displacements has been the Saharan environment. Population increments in regions of extremely finite resources created pressure which could only be relieved by relocation of portions of the human groups.[5] Moreover, the maximum development of intensive plant production still left pastoralism as the preponderant strategy. The mobility required by a pastoral economy conditioned a repetitive set of social and political reflexes. M. Lesne, who has studied the historical migrations of the Zemmour federation of Imazighen tribes, writes of the proclivities in the herders' dilemma:

> Le pasteur croit toujours trouver dans l'extension de ses zones de parcours la solution aux difficultés qui se présentent à lui. Victime d'un concept d'infinité, la vie pastorale apparaît comme une incessant conquête de l'herbe (Lesne 1967:103).

The Zemmour originated in the pre-Sahara. They reached the plain and settled there between the imperial cities of Rabat and Meknes in the late 19th century. They had formed the forefront of Sanhaja populations, preceding the Idrassen bloc, and traversed the eastern High Atlas and the Middle Atlas to arrive in the alluvial plains after the migrations of the Arabic-speaking Beni Ahsen and Zaer. Their present location on the littoral marks the farthest advance of the Sanhaja groups in the Atlantic plains.

---

[5]The observation would be gratuitous were it not for the fact that there may be evidence to indicate synchronous underpopulation and underutilization of land in the Atlantic plains. See Noin (1970) (1):233–273).

Third, the aridity and overpopulation in the south were accompanied by periods of drought with famines and epidemics. The mountains to the north were far from being marginal spaces of refuge. Rather they were zones of coveted pastures for a steady stream of challengers to the occupants. Population advances took place, sometimes as wars of conquest—as during the reign of Mawlay Ismail (1672–1727), and the period of 1811 to 1820 — and at others by slow shifts managed by contractual pacts between arrivals and occupants. That which remained constant was the direction of the displacements; all the central Atlas tribal traditions speak of ancestral homes in the pre-Sahara. An historical factor of consequence may have been the migrations of Arab tribes into the western Maghreb. The Banu Hillal reached the northeastern steppes of Morocco in the 12th century, where they were halted by the Almoravids from farther advances. Under the Almohads, they were introduced into the Atlantic plains of the Gharb (Sefian, Banu Malik), of Tadla (Bani Amar, Bani Mussa), and of the Haouz. In the 13th century, the Bani Maqil arrived and settled along the pre-Saharan steppes and Tafilalt. While the successive dynasties of the Almohads and Merinids remained strong, the Maqil were contained from entering the Atlas valleys. With the decline of Merinid authority, two of the groups, the Bani Ahsen (or Hasan) and the Zaer, opened a path traversing the High Atlas and the Middle Atlas toward the northwest. The Bani Ahsen had occupied the Moulouya and Ansegmir valleys by the 14th century, were settled from Missour to the Gigou valley in the Middle Atlas by the 16th century, and ultimately reached the low plains in the 17th century. The Zaer traced another path through the Khenifra region to their present location through a similar time sequence. G. Colin (1938) first advanced the thesis that the massive populations movements of the Sanhaja groups through the 19th century followed the migrations of the Bani Ahsen and the Zaer. The Maqil groups had opened a route through the High Moulouya to the valleys of the Oum ar-Rbia and the Sebou, and, after them, the Sanhaja groups gained the highlands, pushing ahead those who had provoked the 'avalanche'.

Lastly, more direct political circumstances led to population shifts, such as forced transfers after a military defeat by the sultan's armies. The policy of the early Alawites exploited the dilatory attitudes of the highland confederacies by securing the support of tribes for rewards in land on the plains. Following the lead of the Merinid dynasty which had used the Khlot and Sofian tribes of the Banu Hillal, and the Saadians who depended on the support of some of the Maqil tribes, Mawlay Ismail won the allegiance of the Ait Yemmour in the center of the highland arena against their neighbors.

Another policy of Mawlay Ismail was to utilize portions of the

THE ETHNOHISTORICAL BACKGROUND

dissident blocs as 'peace-maintenance' contingents. The Ait Youssi were placed in their present locale during his reign as guardians of the Sefrou-Moulouya portion of the Fez-Tafilalt imperial route. His measures in this respect were systematic. Tribes of the south (Ait Hadiddou, Morghad, Atta, Alwan, Bouzid, Mhammid, and others of the Tafilalt) with murabitin acting as intermediaries, placed fractions of their groups in strategic locations for the Sultan's interests in return for tax dispensations (La Chapelle 1931:28-29, 36-42). Thus, some displacements occurred through the tacit cooperation of the center and those in the blad al siba whose temporal interests motivated them to shifting alliances. Other displacements were forced transfers.

POLITICAL ACTIVITY IN THE 17TH CENTURY

The impact of the Sanhaja confederations, particularly the Idrassen, on the political life of the country reached a peak in the mid-17th century. Following the migration routes of the Maqil Beni Ahsen and Zaer, the pastoralist Imazighen had reached the Moulouya and the Middle Atlas from where they entered into a contest with the ascending Alawites through their political base in the Dilaiya zawiya. The Dilaiya lodge had, in effect, served as "the most famous expression of [their] slow displacement towards the north-west" (Brignon et al, 1967:225). The initial struggles of the early Alawites centered in countering the Sanhaja populations in their goals of gaining the plains, of controlling the arterial roads of the state, and ultimately of establishing the Dilaiya chiefs as the central rulers. In fact, between 1640 and 1660, the Dila chiefs appeared successful in their bid to replace the Saadian shurfa as leaders capable of unifying the country. Their bid failed shortly after, in favor of the Alawite shurfa of Tafilalt who established the dynasty still reigning in Morocco.

SAADIAN FAILURE

The death in 1603 of the greatest sultan of the Saadian line, Ahmad al Mansur, led to the end of effective centralized rule. Even though various contenders held on to imperial cities (Fez until 1641 and Marrakesh until 1659), the rival claims of his three sons created internecine struggles which brought in the most protracted succession crisis in Moroccan history. One son (Abu Faris) was assassinated early. By 1613 the country was divided into two parts under Saadian rule:

Marrakesh, controlled by Mawlay Zidan; and Fez, held by a grandson, Abdallah. In 1610, Abdallah's father, Muhammad al Shaikh (al Mamoun) had allied with Spain and ceded the port of Larash in exchange for support.

Al Mamoun's political maneuver exemplified the dialectics of dynastic power in Morocco. His action alienated the community from which he derived his authority. The authority of a coercive center rested on a foundation of religious claims. Its exercise by noble lineages which traced descent from the family of the Prophet, required that its goals serve the defense of the faithful and the glory of Islam. Mamoun's attempts to bolster his power base drove him to sell Larash to Spain. This removed from his person the religious authority which was vested in him, and in theory emanated from the supporting community. In practice, investiture was won by the person commanding the most effective system of coercion and distribution of rewards.

Al Mansur had resolved the contradiction between absolute power and community approval with an acceptable balance. None of his Saadian successors managed to recreate a viable political network for central government. The contenders, heirs to the Muslim theory of succession through community affirmation, diffused the power base. No one managed to consolidate it with the necessary popular support. Until the expiration of the dynasty, any sultan's appointed representatives were no more than spokesmen for regional or tribal interests (Brignon et al. 1967:218). Political reaction throughout the country was expressed in religious protest, regionally phrased as a defense of the faith through the murabitin, and their *sufi* lodges. The bid for national political roles was opened to the maraboutic zawiyas and the regional interest blocs upholding them.

This period of civil disorder, combined with external factors, contributed to marked economic decline. European commercial activity decreased because of the preoccupation with the Thirty Years War (1618–1648) as well as the scarcity of goods previously available in Moroccan markets. The trans-Saharan caravan traffic had contributed a great deal of the country's revenue during the period Al Mansur gained political control of the Sudan (in particular, Timbuktou). With the loss of effective power, the traffic was diverted to other markets. Much of it was rerouted toward the regencies of Algeria and Tunisia; another part reached the Atlantic ports controlled by European merchants. Moreover, the newly arrived Europeans on the West African coasts could divert the commercial wealth through maritime channels and by-pass the traditional inland routes.

Gold production in West Africa remained stable throughout the century, while imports into Morocco diminished drastically both because of the political debility and because of the circumvention of the

THE ETHNOHISTORICAL BACKGROUND

old trade routes. Sugar production in the southern provinces declined rapidly early in the century. By 1610 many of the sugar mills had closed. The operating mills were no longer in Saadian control but in the hands of regional power holders who were political opponents of the central dynasty. The production kept slowing down. By the 18th century Morocco had become a sugar importer.

In the void of the crumbling Saadian political structure and economic enterprise, the maraboutic chiefs appeared as the advocates of unity and the champions of their regional constituents. The multifaceted institution of the zawiya had long been established in Morocco. What appears to reach full expression in the 17th century is the development of temporal ambitions. These varied in scope. Not all aspired to supreme power. Some were content to control the wealth of a regional principality. Their goals and motives were far from uniform.

By the third decade of the 17th century, and before the political emergence of the sharifian family that proved ultimately successful, three zones of influence and centers of opposition to the Saadians divided the country. In order of importance these were the Dilaiya in the central Atlas, the Semlaliya in the Sous, and the coalition of the warrior Al Ayashi in the north. The leaders of all three centers shared the status of murabitin; they were not shurfa.[6] Beyond their shared social status which was characterized by training in the sufist tradition and a reputation for exemplary living, their political roles were shaped by factors of opportunity and geography which created different bases for gaining popular compliance. In the north, the charismatic figure of Al Ayashi remained throughout his career the saintly warrior against foreigners without transforming his persuasion and influence into a political office. In the south, the Semlali chief sought regional autonomy in terms of control of the strategic commercial network. In the central Atlas, the Dilaiya mobilized political capital in an effort to gain supreme temporal power.

THE WARRIOR SAINT

The reaction against the dissolving Saadian rule in the plains of northwest Morocco ushered in the political figure of Abu Abdallah Muhammad ibn Ahmad, known as Al Ayashi (1573–1641).[7] Muham-

---
[6] The difference between them was described by an Ait Ayashi as follows: "The murabitin, there may be one who is a superior person, but then his son is not. Or vice versa. But the shurfa are different; they are like a river. A river never flows backward."

[7] There is no known connection between Al Ayashi and the tribe of the Ait Ayash. He was also called al Zayyani. Castries speculates he must have been of Berber origin, on the basis of his names, but there is no other evidence. He comments: "Le celèbre 'Moudjahid' bien qu'originaire da la tribu des Beni Malek (El-Oufrani, p. 431) devait avoir des descendants berbères comme l'indiquent les deux ethniques accoles à son non: Ez-Zaiani et El-Ayashi". (Castries 1911a:594n). For an account of his career see Castries (1911b).

mad Al Ayashi became the champion of the Faith against the Spanish presence on the coast. His career centered on the holy war against the Christian intruders, and it appears that he never aspired to power; but in effect, he came to represent the political aspirations of the tribes of the Gharb, as well as the interests of the republic of Bu Ragrag which joined him in alliance with the bond between them that of a common adversary.

Al Ayashi came from the Arab tribe of the Banu Malik (Gharb). He had been a disciple of the murabit Abu Muhammad Abdallah ibn Hassun of Salé, associated with the brotherhood of the Jazuliya tradition. Following his studies, he gained a reputation for theological knowledge and sufist devotion, but chose a path of action rather than of contemplation. Preaching the *jihad* (holy war), he gathered followers and attacked the Spanish-held fort of Mazagan. Mawlay Zidan, the sultan of Marrakesh, in commendation for his zeal which expressed both religious piety and nationalist fervor, appointed him *qaid* (tribal chief appointed over a tribe or town) of Azemmour. From this base, his reputation as a 'saint' of the faith gained him a wide circle of adherents. The Spaniards were able to convince Mawlay Zidan that Al Ayashi posed as much a threat to the throne as to the foreign settlements. Zidan sent his army to chase him from Azemmour, which led Al Ayashi to move north with an army of followers to carry on the jihad against the Spaniards at Mamora on the Sibou river.

At this time, Andalusian Moriscos, expelled by Phillip III between 1609 and 1614, had found refuge (among other North African ports) on the sides of the estuary of Bu Ragrag (later Rabat, and Salé). In the form of three settlements, they maintained for a period a self-governing community that became known as the republic of Bu Ragrag. They duplicated the principality of Andalusians in Tetuan by engaging in the lucrative piracy of Atlantic maritime traffic, especially that of Spain.

Al Ayashi drew the Andalusian community into an alliance. His plans against the Spaniards at Mamora, Larash, and Tangier reflected their economic interests as well as their feelings toward Spain.

For over a quarter of a century Al Ayashi kept up attacks against the Spanish forts, without dislodging them. His prestige and authority spread through all the tribes of the Gharb, mustering growing numbers of troops under his command. By the early 1630's, he became virtual master of the entire region and had eliminated Saadian authority in the Sais, Gharb, Fez al Bali, and Salé.

Nevertheless, Al Ayashi failed to consolidate his charismatic influence into a durable authority structure. Mutual distrust between him and the Bu Ragrag community brought his dominance to an end. In

1637, convinced of Andalusian disloyalty to the cause, he attacked Salé. The Andalusians appealed to the chiefs of the zawiya Dila for aid against the now oppressive warrior saint. In 1641 the Dilaiya army met the troops of Al Ayashi and defeated them. Al Ayashi took refuge among the Khlot tribe, where he was assassinated.

To the end Al Ayashi enjoyed veneration as a saintly man and respect as a warrior. Whether by design or misdirection, the political acumen to consolidate his considerable gains escaped him. The alienation of the Andalusians separated him from the source of material supplies and munition. Also, early in his career, Al Ayashi had received the wary approval of different interest groups that he failed to win to his side. The *qadis* (religious judges) had consecrated him the chief of the jihad. The zawiyas of the Shadiliya in Fez, the Nasiriya in Tamgrout, and the Dilaiya—his eventual adversary—had encouraged his activities (Drague 1951:70). Tribal leaders had urged him to take power, and wide support was offered to him for the fighting; the same support was withdrawn when he sought to centralize the maintenance of order and collect taxes. The creation of a governing system eluded him.

AUTHORITY THROUGH ECONOMIC CONTROL: THE SOUTH

The south of Morocco witnessed the appearance of a series of political formations during this period through zawiyas and murabitin that shared the central objective of capturing and dominating the regional keypoints of the trans-Saharan traffic. Their history falls outside the scope of this background summary. What needs to be related is the political appearance of the Alawite family in the context of the regional power centers of the Dila zawiya in the Middle Atlas and the Samlali zawiya under Abu Hassun in the Sus.

Abu Hassun, the successful contender to economic dominance in the south after the death of Al Mansur, was the grandson of a widely respected murabit of the Samlali zawiya of Illigh in the Sus, the extensive, fertile plain between the High Atlas and the Anti-Atlas near the Atlantic coast. His respected lineage coupled with adroit political maneuvering gained him the largest number of followers against his two most dangerous rivals, Abu Mahalli of the Dra valley, and Yahya al-Hahi—a murabit of the Sus in alliance with the Saadian Mawlay Zidan of Marrakesh (d. 1626). By 1630, Abu Hassun had become the undisputed ruler of the south, with Illigh the capital of a principality which had replaced Saadian authority. His dominance rested on the secure control of the caravan routes and the gold trade, and a military force furnished with arms by European traders, especially the Dutch, active in the Sus. He had created an economically viable state within the boundaries of the southern region; he neither attempted nor needed to extend his influence and control in the north of the country. The presence of European commercial activity within the region permitted him to shortcircuit northern ports and markets. His principal concern centered on the elimination of competitors along the pre-Saharan front.

This aim, rather than interest in central unity, brought him into conflict with the Alawites and the Dilaiya. After gaining control of the Dra valley, he ventured into the Tafilalt. The Alawite challenge began at this juncture. From the time of their arrival in the 13th century to the Tafilalt, the Alawite family had lacked defined political status but enjoyed the privileges and consideration due to sharifian lineages. In 1631, when Abu Hassun's forces penetrated into the oasis of Tabuasamt, the religious figures of the Tafilalt vested the Alawite Mawlay al Sharif as their sultan for the defense of the region. This brought into the southern arena the Dilaiya, in what was one of their first territorial forays. The Bani Zubir of Tabuasamt appealed to them for help against both Abu Hassun and Mawlay al Sharif, to whom they refused allegiance. A truce was arranged in 1633 by the Dilaiya, which placed Tabuasamt under the protection of Abu Hassun. Mawlay al Sharif broke the truce, attacked the fort, was defeated and taken prisoner by Abu Hassun. His exile in the Sus ended some years later in exchange for a substantial ransom; his political role passed to his son Muhammad.

Muhammad, in 1641, had himself proclaimed sultan and chased Abu Hassun's officers from Tabuasamt. Control of the southeastern region did not provide the new power contender an economically viable base. Authority over Tafilalt and Tuat, strategic points in the Sudanese commercial routes, required control of entrepots like Fez or the port of Tlemsen to effect the exchange for European goods. Abu Hassun in the southwest had maintained a lively commercial network through control of Sudanese trade arteries and mercantile exchanges in the Sus with Dutch and English traders at the ports of Agadir and Massa. Abu Hassun's Illigh became a prosperous center, which legend has embellished, without the northern provinces. The challenge of the first Alawites was to create such a network with the commerce of the north and Europe. The objectives of the first Alawites Muhammad and Rashid, centered on this goal—securing a north-south commercial axis. Mawlay Rashid achieved this, and the political union of the country. The dissolution of the independent Samlali kingdom of the Sus followed Alawite ascendance in 1670.

THE DILA ZAWIYA OF THE CENTRAL ATLAS

The base for the political aspirations of the Idrassen and the other Sanhaja confederations was the zawiya Dila[8] (Ait Iddila in Tamazight), founded near 1566 in the region between the High Moulouya plain and Khenifra in the Middle Atlas. Abu Bakr (1536–1612), the founder of the lodge, was the first 'saint' in a family which had long been recognized for its moral qualities and religious scholarship (al-Qadiri 1913:242–244). The family originated from the Mejjat tribe of the Idrassen, which had settled in the 15th century in the High Moulouya between Midelt and Tounfit. The Dilaiya (their name came from the site of the zawiya) had moved to the southwest of Khenifra, where they gained reknown as religious teachers and mediators to the tribes.

Preceding the foundation of the religious lodge, the Saadian sultan Muhammad al Shaikh I had granted the family special status for their religious services with exemption from taxes and corvée (1557). The zawiya was founded at the suggestion of Abu Bakr's sufist mentor, Abu Amar al Qastalli of Marrakesh, to serve as a center for dissemination of the Shadili-Jazouli doctrine and as a lodge for social welfare services. The Jazouli elaboration of the Shadili doctrine taught an orthodox form of sufism, which centered on the exaltation of the Prophet Muhammad. The cult of the Prophet had at first been a sign of mystic devotion which over time had become incorporated as a feature of Muslim orthodoxy. The Saadian dynasty had supported the propagation of the Jazouli doctrine, since it was politically useful. As descendants of the Prophet the movement served to consolidate their spiritual claims to political office. The zawiya, which quickly became established as an important seat of learning, also served as a center for economic redistribution of the goods received as offerings, by what de Castries characterized as "le facile miracle, que l'on constate au débuts de toute zaouia, de défrayer libéralement les uns avec ce qu'il récevait copieusement des autres" (Castries 1911:576). Chiefly largesse and scholarly reputation won the lodge wide popularity.

The second chief of the lodge, Muhammad, constructed a second zawiya a short distance from the original one, with hostels and lodgings said to provide daily meals for 7,000 people (Abun Nasr 1971:220). The greatest religious and legal scholars of the day visited for conferences, instruction and study. Throughout the reign of Al Mansur the Dilaiya received the endorsement of the throne, since their activities reinforced the hegemony of the Saadians. With the political infirmity

---

[8]For history of the zawiya Dila see Hajji (1964), Drague (1951:127–139), Castries (1911a). Primary sources are al-Ifrani [Eloufrani] (1889), al-Qadiri [Al-Qadiri] (1913), al-Zayyani [Ezziani] (1886) and al-Nasiri [Ennasiri] (1906).

of Al Mansur's successors, the Dilaiya's influence over the highland populations and their store of moral prestige permitted them new roles. The second chief, Muhammad, never questioned the authority of the Saadians, but assumed wider responsibilities of arbitration in conflicts. In 1630, when the Andalusians of Salé experienced difficulties with Al Ayashi, they turned to the Dila chief for mediation. Under the third chief of the Dilaiya, Muhammad Al Hajj (from 1636), the temporal extension of authority became a conscious goal. The tribes of the Idrassen federation—the Ait Ayash, Ait Ouafella, Mejjat, Imelwan, Ait Yemmour, Ait Ndhir (Beni Mtir), Ait Ouallal, and Ait Sadden—provided a reserve of manpower ready to carry out the plans of their chiefs.

Muhammad Al Hajj proceeded by constructing a fortified settlement near the two zawiyas and organizing a regular army to replace the contingents brought together by the earlier Dilaiya. In reaction, the sultan at Marrakesh sent artisans to build a mausoleum for the late Dila chief, the father of Muhammad Al Hajj, and a qadi with the mission of securing the continued allegiance of the Dilaiya forces to the Saadian dynasty. The response of Muhammad Al Hajj recognized respect for the Saadian shurfa but denied them the right to continued rule because of their inability to offer a secure government. The Saadian Muhammad al Shaikh II acted on this threat by sending his army from Marrakesh against the zawiya. The Dilaiya troops defeated the Saadian forces in a battle by the Ouad al Abid (1638). At this point, the Dila chief did not pursue a total victory over the Saadian, because of his religious status, but turned instead to the task of securing an economic base with a front on the Atlantic. This meant a confrontation for the zone of influence under the *mujahid* Al Ayashi.

The earlier Dila chiefs had maintained correct relations with Al Ayashi. For Muhammad Al Hajj he became a political impediment. In 1640 the Dilaiya army took Meknes. The following year brought the elimination of Al Ayashi, and the control of the port of Salé. Soon after, Fez, the Sais plain, the Gharb and all the towns of northern Morocco came under Dila rule. For a decade the Dilaiya controlled the most active commercial center of Morocco with a policy of allowing autonomy to the Andalusian towns of Salé and Tetuan. The Moriscos were experienced in dealing with Europeans. This permitted the Dila chief to profit from the active trade (and the profitable privateering) and to assure supply of arms without compromising his moral position by direct contacts with Christians. By 1651, the commercial stakes had grown important enough for the Dila to impose direct rule. Muhammad Al Hajj placed a son, Abdullah, as governor of Salé. A treaty was signed with the Dutch in the same year, and the mutually profitable commercial relations continued until 1659. The concentration of activity in this zone suggests that the Dilaiya did not pursue the extension of control in the Tadla region and the north. One reason for their eventual failure to construct a durable basis for government was their neglect of the diverse regional interest groups. The popular base remained narrow. An historian accounts for the Alawite success as follows:

> The Dala'iyya sultanate was a Berber state. Its successes under Muhammad al-Hajj were due to the martial valour of the Berber tribes of the Middle Atlas and their political cohesion under his leadership, at a time when Morocco was divided into principalities fighting one another and divided amongst themselves. But the base of Dala'iyya authority remained militarily and morally too narrow for Muhammad al-Hajj to be able to found durable government. The identification of his authority with the dominance of the Berber tribes of the Middle Atlas left for the major Arabian tribes no place in the Dala'iyya political structure. The moral authority of the Dala'iyya chiefs continued to be recognized in the Middle Atlas. Outside it their educational and social services were recognized, but these were outweighed by the fact that they were not sharifs (Abun Nasr 1971:222).

This last fact shaped all Dila encounters with both the Saadians and the Alawites. Initial Dila successes were followed by tactics that avoided decisive checks against the shurfa.

The geopolitical location of the Dila lodge, in the highland center of the country, left it strategically vulnerable from all directions. The close identification with the Sanhaja population bloc prevented the tribes of the Atlantic plains from sharing in the political base. In the south, the continued Saadian control of the port of Safi, and of European commerce at Mazagan kept vital economic links outside Dila control. From the southeastern base of the Tafilalt, the Alawite Mawlay Rashid had begun to consolidate an alternate economic network which permitted him the means for fighting political competition.

The first loss of the Dilaiya was the northern province, Habt. The Habt tribes rebelled under Ghailan—a follower of Al Ayashi—in 1653 and took over Qsar al Kabir and other northern towns. At an earlier date (1649) the city of Fez had tried to overthrow Dila rule and the notables had invited the Alawite Muhammad ibn Sharif to assume leadership. The revolt was quelled when the Dilaiya army arrived and the Alawite contender was forced to flee. The Alawites were not ready at the moment to challenge the military forces of Dila, though the disenfranchised tribes of the Gharb and the Fez plains were prepared to offer cooperation to newcomers. In 1660 Salé rose against the Dilaiya governor. The English in Tangier considered an alliance with the besieged Dilaiya in order to establish trade relations, but the conciliatory attitude of Ghailan led them to reconsider support of the Dila.

Salé was lost in 1661. By 1662 the Dilaiya chiefs were no longer capable of maintaining order in Fez, after a series of rebellions and counter-rebellions. The possession of the townships of Fez had served through successive dynasties as the political barometer of ascending power. When in 1663 the leaders of old Fez appealed to Muhammad al Hajj to impose direct rule in order to counter the brigandage of various tribes (Huyayna, Duraid), the Dila chief declined the offer and retreated to the highland capital.

At the same period, the death of the Alawite Mawlay al Sharif (1659) had set off a succession struggle between two of his sons, the one designated sultan of the Tafilalt, Muhammad, and Mawlay Rashid. Rashid was forced to leave the home region and spent some time at the Dila lodge. Nothing is known about his stay there. Later he established himself in northeastern Morocco (Angad plain) where he impounded local wealth and secured the allegiance of Maqil tribes and the Berber Bani Isnassen, previously supporters of his brother. In 1664, Muhammad with his forces came to challenge Rashid's hegemony, and was defeated and killed.

Rashid then won the Tafilalt, secured the northern Rif zone and was able to command a north-south commercial axis for supplies of munition from the Mediterranean. By 1666–67 he controlled Fez, the most important political and economic center of Morocco. It remained for him to eliminate serious rivals, a task that he accomplished in less than a decade.

In 1668 he headed an expedition against the Dilaiya and met the Dila army in the Middle Atlas at Batn Arruman. After a military victory he razed the lodges to the ground (al-Ifrani 1889:472); their exact location remains open to question (cf. Henry 1944). The immediate family of Muhammad al Hajj was exiled to Tlemsen of the Algerian regency, while the rest of the Dilaiya notables took refuge in Fez (Levi-Provençal 1922:336–340). The Alawite spared the lives of his erstwhile hosts but assured the complete destruction of their political base and the consolidation of the Idrassen. Rashid then took Marrakesh in the same year from the maternal kinsmen of the last Saadian (Al Abbas)—led by Abu Bakr ben Kerrum—of the Shabana tribe. He then turned to the north and eliminated the threat of Ghailan, who fled to Algeria, and fought the Shawiya in the plain of Umm al Rbbia.

The highlands did not remain secure. The chronicles (al-Zayyani 1886:11; al-Nasiri 1906:52) record another expedition in 1668, this time against the Ait Ayash, 'who are Berbers of the Sanhaja branch'. No other information is provided for this encounter.

Two years later Rashid secured the Sus region from the Samlali heirs of Bu Hassun, shortly before the end of his seven year reign (1666–1672), which was terminated by a fatal accident.

MAWLAY ISMAIL AND THE SANHAJA

The successor of Rashid, his brother Mawlay Ismail (1672–1727), spent considerable time during his reign in countering the challenge of the highland populations to the control of the empire he finally established. The Alawite policy depended, in contrast to that of the previous sharifian dynasty which gained its end by consolidation through the argument of the jihad, on force of arms. There were established precedents to follow; the Merinids had used the Arab tribes of the Khlot and Sofian for dynastic support, and the Saadians had brought into the center Maqil tribes in opposition to Hillalian groups. The Alawites, in their turn, secured the military cooperation of select Arab and Berber clans placed in strategic intersections where they could neutralize regional political blocs.

Ismail's innovation in military policy avoided the exclusive dependence on the unreliable regional and tribal forces by the creation of a pretorian guard free of overriding social allegiances. This army was estimated by the second half of his reign to number 150,000. Its ranks were recruited from descendants of slaves brought to Morocco in Saadian times and from a core of Black soldiers originally given to a murabit of the Sus (possibly Abu Hassun) by the king of Bambara for use against Mawlay Rashid. This permanent force of *Abids* (Blacks) was also known as *Bouakher,* after the oath of allegiance taken on the book the *Traditions* of al Bukhari. Ismail systematically enlisted blacks from previous military registers and provided them with spouses and quarters, assuring the self-perpetuation of the Abid regiments. The male offspring received vocational and technical training from the ages of ten to eighteen, at which time they joined the ranks. The families were garrisoned outside the important towns as well as in a network of fortified outposts throughout the country. Mawlay Ismail constructed over seventy-six qasbas (fort) according to al Zayyani, to house to Abid forces (al Zayyani 1886:31). Their purposes were threefold. Some served as barracks for the permanent army in the vicinity of important cities. Others served to control the security of the main communication routes (Fez to Marrakesh, Taza to Oujda, and Fez to Tafilalt). A third network of forts was intended to watch over the dissident populations of the central Atlas. While the destruction of the Dila zawiya had eliminated the political expression of the highland populations, the driving energy fed by environmental and demographic conditions had not been modified. Ismail's response had been the cordon of forts manned by the new professional army.

The choice of the city of Meknes as the new capital—the nearest urban center to the Middle Atlas—underlined the importance he gave to the control of the Azrou-Midelt zone, which proved to be the most troublesome region of the empire. A series of campaigns are recorded in the chronicles against the dissidence of the Sanhaja of the Middle Atlas and the High Moulouya plain for a period of twenty years. In 1674, the Sanhaja overthrew the agents of the sultan and refused submission of tax payments.[9] In 1677, Ahmad ibn Abdullah, a grandson of Muhammad al Hajj (Dila), returned with the support of the Turkish regime in Algeria and rallied the Idrassen and the other Sanhaja against the tribes of the Tadla which were in alliance with the sultan. Three successive government expeditions were defeated by the reconstituted Dila coalition, until Ismail himself, occupied at the time with revolts in Marrakesh and the Tafilalt, led his troops and overcame the highland forces. The Dilaite contender remained in the region until 1680, when he disappeared mysteriously.

In 1683, Ismail constructed the fort of Azrou which he manned with 1,000 Abid and their families and a second fort at Ain Leuh with a garrison of 500 Abid. The Idrassen of the region retrenched toward Jebel Ayashi, and continued the brigandage of the commercial route, so he spent a season in the Moulouya plain interrupting the agricultural schedule. This forced the tribes to seek *aman* (pardon) from the sultan. Ismail demanded the surrender of all weapons and horses in exchange for which he offered a pastoral contract. He provided the Idrassen with 60,000 sheep to herd on behalf of the court for the wool and butter. The pastoral clients proved refractory to the economic subservience. The following year (1684) another expedition via the Sefrou route, brought the sultan to spend an entire year on the High Moulouya plain. He constructed another series of forts at Outat (the present Midelt), Dar Tma (on the left bank of the Moulouya river), Tamayoust (northeast of Itzer), Qsay Beni Mtir (near Aghbalou n'Serdan), and others in the northern Middle Atlas (Skoura, Tishoukt, Gigou and Alil). Each fort held 400 Abid cavalrymen. Another campaign in 1687–1688 was followed by the final one of 1692–1693 when Mawlay Ismail decisively brought to an end, for the duration of his reign, the recalcitrance of the central Atlas through a carefully organized confrontation with artillery, cavalry and infantry. The sultan's forces were augmented with troops of newly won Sanhaja allies: the Zemmour and the Ait Yemmour of the Idrassen.

The Zemmour confederation had led the forefront of the Sanhaja migrations and was placed at this point in pasturelands of the Middle Atlas vulnerable to attacks from the fortified qasbas which controlled the access routes to the *azaghar* (winter pastures). Prevented from reversing the direction of their movements by the Idrassen population

---

[9]Mouette 1683:78. Neither al-Nasiri nor al-Zayyani mention the 1674 episode.

behind them, the Zemmour under their chief, Bn Ishou al Qabli, threw in their lot with the sultan and gave their allegiance to the defense of the throne (1688).

The Ait Yemmour, a tribe of the Idrassen confederacy, also opted under their *amghar,* Ali ou Barka, to join the sultan. The Yemmour, in the high plateaus of the Midelt-Itzer-Azrou alignment, found themselves in a position coveted by the Ait Yafelman crowding them from the south and the Ait Ou Malou from the west. Ali ou Barka became an agent of Mawlay Ismail and received arms and ammunition with which he could defend his placement, especially against the Ait Ou Malou whose progess towards the plains had been arrested by the Abid garrisons on the *dir.*

In the last expedition of 1693 Ismail attacked from three directions, the Tadla plain, the Moulouya, and Todgha with three columns. The Zemmour under Ali bn Ishou—the son of Al Qabli—formed one column; the Yemmour under Ali ben Barka another; and a third was under the Qaid Msahel with contingents from fractions of the southern valleys of Todgha, Ferkla, Gheris and Sebbah Arabs of the Tafilalt. The artillery of the sultan, manned by European captives, reportedly tipped the battle. The forces met at Ain Shoua (identified as Boumia), and the Sanhaja were totally defeated. The three qaids were said to have gathered after the battle 30,000 firearms and 10,000 horses.

After this, the sultan gave the Zemmouri chief a force of 10,000 cavalrymen to check the Gerwan of the High Ziz and Midelt, brigands of the route to Tafilalt. Ismail's reign was praised in the chronicles for the establishment of internal security for travelers throughout the country (al-Zayyani 1886:52; al-Nasiri 1906:132–133).

HIGHLAND MOVEMENTS IN THE 18TH CENTURY

The decline in central power in the second quarter of the 18th century, after the death of Mawlay Ismail, ushered in another period of population shifts. The push toward the northwest was reinforced by the advances of the Ait Atta in the eastern High Atlas. The shifts followed two principal axes. In the north, the Zemmour and the Gerwan pushed ahead of them the Bani Ahsan to the central plateau; the Gerwan gained the environs of Agourai. The Beni Mgild reached from the Moulouya to Azrou, slowly replacing the Zemmour, who occupied the northern side of the central plateau; at the beginning of the 19th century they, in turn, pushed the Bani Ahsan into the Mamora region. During this period, the Beni Mtir gained the environs south of El Hajeb and forced the Ait Youssi into the Sais (Sefrou). In the south, the second axis was led by the Zaer (Bani Maqil), followed by the Zayan who took the region of Khenifra.

The turbulence in the highlands followed from the anarchy which prevailed in the plains. The imperial guard of the Abid had been the most trusted instrument of Ismail's political authority. Following the dynastic struggle among his sons, the guard came to view itself as the source of authority; no chosen king was capable of meeting their financial demands adequately, so candidates replaced one another in rapid order during the period termed Mawlay Abdullah's reign (1728–1757).

The Idrassen confederation played a major role in the support of Mawlay Abdullah whose authority was challenged five times by fraternal contenders who were proclaimed and renounced by various political blocs. The consolidation of Abdullah's authority was finally achieved by the middle of the century through a balance of interest groups that included the *gish* tribes (tribes whic provided military service in return for land grants) of the Oudaya and the Maqil, the ulama of Fez and important shurfa, as well as the powerful Gerwan, who repeatedly opposed their former confederates to join the militia of the sultan (Caillé 1953:60n).

Under the reigns of Sidi Muhammad (1757–1790) and Mawlay Yazid (1790–1792) the Idrassen bloc figures prominently in the political life of the center. Under their qaid, Muhammad ou Aziz, the Idrassen frequently confront the Abid and the Oudaya; at one point, the sultan reimbursed the Idrassen for military services against the Abid army. But the confederation had shifted both in locus and composition. For this period the name involves those tribes which had advanced to the plateaus of the Middle Atlas and the environs of Meknes. The groups left behind found new affinities consonant with the realignments in space. The Idrassen political coalition receded from its earlier field of action in the High Moulouya plain, and finally dissolved altogether in the 19th century through territorial dispersion, and the divergence of political goals of its constituent members.

THE AIT AYASH AND THE ZAWIYA HAMZAWIYA BEFORE THE 19TH CENTURY

The placement of the Ait Ayash before the 19th century situates them, as is true for all Sanhaja groups, south and southeast of their present location. Confirmation of their localization is corroborated by their association, from its inception, with the Zawiya of Sidi Hamza (zawiya Hamzawiya), known originally as zawiya n'Ait Ayash. The second *shaikh* of the zawiya, the well-known religious scholar of 17th century Morocco—Abu Salim, described the country of the Ait Ayash ("my country") as located between the headwaters of the Wad Guir and those of the Moulouya.[10]

The zawiya was founded in 1634–1635 (1044 H.)[11] and is located south of Jebel Ayashi and Jebel Maoutfoud in the valley of the Wad Sidi Hamza, one of the affluents of the left bank of Wad Ziz, named after the third *shaikh* (chief) of the zawiya. The story of its foundation follows in general outline the legends of most settlements of Idrissid shurfa in the central Atlas. The shurfa of Morocco trace their descent through two lineages: that of the Idrissid dynasty and the later Alawite dynasty. In sum, the legends recall that members of the family of Idriss ibn Abdullah, the father of the founder of Fez, and head of the first sharifian dynasty in Morocco, were forced to flee from Fez after establishment of the Miknassa dynasty of Abi al Afia. Most turned south to seek safety in pre-Saharan oases, from where, through their spiritual leadership and acts of benevolence, they were invited to settle among different groups of Imazighen.

In the Hamzawiya tradition, the family had settled in the oasis of Figuig, where they became religious instructors, *tulba (taleb,* sing.), and enjoyed the high status due to descendants of the Prophet. A quarrel between two brothers over property rights led one of them, Sidi Abdullah, to 'give up' his rights and take up a life of asceticism. He lived by alms and by periodic employment as a taleb in camps and villages. His wanderings took him to Skoura in the Dades valley and then to Taghia n'Imellwan in the High Semgat region, where Abdullah settled, married and sired a son, Muhammad. From Taghia he left one day on a pilgrimage to the tomb of the saint Bou Azza (located in present Zayan territory). On route, he took shelter in the mosque of an Ait Ayash settlement (Ait Yaqoub), where he overheard a dispute between Ayashis concerning a debt. Shocked by the desecration of the house of prayer, he offered the money himself to the creditor to settle the argument. In gratitude the debtor invited him to his home and offered him his daughter in marriage. Abdullah accepted the offer, and after the completion of his pilgrimage, brought his family from Taghia, married the host's daughter, and settled among the Ait Ayash. His son Muhammad took on the functions of *fqih* (leader of prayers) for the *qsar* (nucleated walled settlement; pl. qsour); it was Muhammad (1573–1656), who after a successful career as teacher, established the zawiya in the region as an educational center for study and prayer. The

---

[10] Abu Salim in the *Rihla (Ma al Mawa'id)* speaks of 'my country' and locates it in space without identifying affiliation. In a copy of the manuscript made by Mawlay Ahmad ibn Nasir (a close affiliate) he substituted for 'my country' the word, 'the territory of the Ait Ayash' (Berbrugger 1846:5,15).

[11] The primary source for the history of the zawiya is *Al Ihya wa l'intiyash fi tarajim sadat zawiya Ait Ayash* by Abdullah ibn Umar ibn Abd al Karim al Ayashi (1756) cf. Renaud (1934; 1939). This account is based on Lesur (1920) and oral sources.

second chief of the zawiya was Muhammad's son Abu Salim (1628–1679), best known for his *Rihla*, or book of travels, which has given him wide popularity since his own day. The zawiya was known during his lifetime, as the zawiya Ait Ayash, just as Abu Salim was most widely known as Al Ayashi. Shortly after the destruction of the Dila zawiya and the expedition against the Ait Ayash, Mawlay Rashid 'exiled' the Ayashi shurfa to Fez, fearing their growing popularity and unknown ambitions far from the center. Mawlay Ismail, on his ascent to the throne, reversed the order a year later.

After the death of Abu Salim from the plague in 1679, the zawiya passed to his son, Sidi Hamza, who increased the size of the center's teaching staff.[12] Over a hundred students are said to have been in attendance, coming from the Sus, the Tafilalt, and even Fez. The reknown of the instruction and piety of Sidi Hamza led to the identification of the zawiya with his name. This also meant the gradual dissociation of the Ait Ayash from its identity, as their political fortune waned under the Alawites. The zawiya, it appears, never countered, or saw its interests divergent from those of the dynasty.

The sultan Sidi Muhammad was responsible for the construction of the mausoleum of Sidi Hamza's successor, who had been one of his teachers (plate 1 at back). In the 19th century, one of the Hamzawi murabitin served as arbitrator during one of the revolts of the Atlas against the throne. The zawiya Sidi Hamza never developed regional political significance. From its inception it concentrated on providing educational facilities, legal counsel, and establishing the economic security of the family through the offerings of land and goods. Their land holdings are extensive, and Captain Lesur reported in 1920 that among the most important holdings are those given them in *habous* (land in mortmain held by a religious institution) by the Ait Ayash.

The zawiya under its first chiefs followed the Nasiriya doctrine. Abu Salim had been initiated into sufist studies by Muhammad ibn Nasir at Tamgrout. In the mid-19th century the seventh successor, shaikh Ahmad, introduced the Tijani doctrine. The zawiya became a lodge of the Tijaniya brotherhood at this time, and also maintained subsidiary (and older) lodges of the Qadiriya and Aissawiya brotherhoods. The latter were headed by their own *muqaddamin* (village administrators) under the direction of the Tijani shaikh.

The association of the Ait Ayash with the zawiya remained close in the pre-Protectorate. The Ait Ayash turned to the murabitin for questions of inheritance and personal problems. Wider political ques-

---

[12] A list of the zawiya library holdings was compiled in 1851–1852 and found its way in 1885 to the National Library of Paris, under *"fonds arabe"* no. 4725, labeled as *A Catalog of the books of the Grand Mosque of Fez* (Renaud 1934).

A recent catalog has been compiled by Ibrahim al Kittani of the Rabat National Library. The catalog lists 606 manuscripts and imprinted items.

tions, however, were deflected into the regional network of another religious figure, the chief of a zawiya of the Derkawa brotherhood in the district of Mdaghra of the Ziz valley, north of Tafilalt. The educational function of the zawiya had declined by the 20th century, and its influence depended on the annual visits and pilgrimages to the tombs of the early shaikhs, especially Abu Salim's whose legend in the countryside was kept alive by his popularity among the urban elite.

In 1920, when the French were scouting for support in the region which was still in dissidence, the heir of the elderly shaikh of the zawiya, Sidi Omar, offered cooperation to the new administration, and it was he who negotiated the early submission of the Ait Ayash in Outat (Midelt). He was subsequently appointed as qaid for the district of Rish; this won the zawiya important leverage in local control and lost it its spiritual posture and influence. The association with the administration continued through the Protectorate period. This permitted the leading family to transfer the institutional land holdings into private title.

THE HIGH MOULOUYA PLAIN IN THE 19TH CENTURY

At the beginning of the 19th century, the High Moulouya plain was occupied principally by Idrassen groups (Map 4). Three large tribes controlled territories along north-south axes with complementary zones in the valleys of the High Atlas to the south, the plain in the center, and pastures in the Middle Atlas, to the north; these were the Ait Ihand, Ait Ayash, and Ait Youssi. To the west, the Ait Ihand held the High Atlas terrain from Jebel Masker, through the Moulouya basin to the deep valleys of the wad Serrou. The Ait Ayash territory stretched from the high basin of the wad Ziz, and the Taarart valley—south of Jebel Ayashi, through the valley of the Ansegmir to the plain of Tanfit up to Talialit. Adjacent to their northern holdings were found the Beni Mtir, between the valleys of the Aguersif and Boulajoul and westwards on the Middle Atlas plateaus.

In the valleys west of the Oudghes were settled fractions of the Mejjat, with pasturelands on the foothills of Masker and permanent settlements in the small valleys north, reaching westwards to Alemsid. The Ait Youssi exploited a third domain aligned north to south, from Jebel Tishoukt in the Middle Atlas through the Enjil plain to Outat (Midelt). In the environs of Outat were found some Gerwan, and also the Ait Ouafella holding the gsour and irrigated lands east of the river Outat and the ranges of Jebel Ayashi.

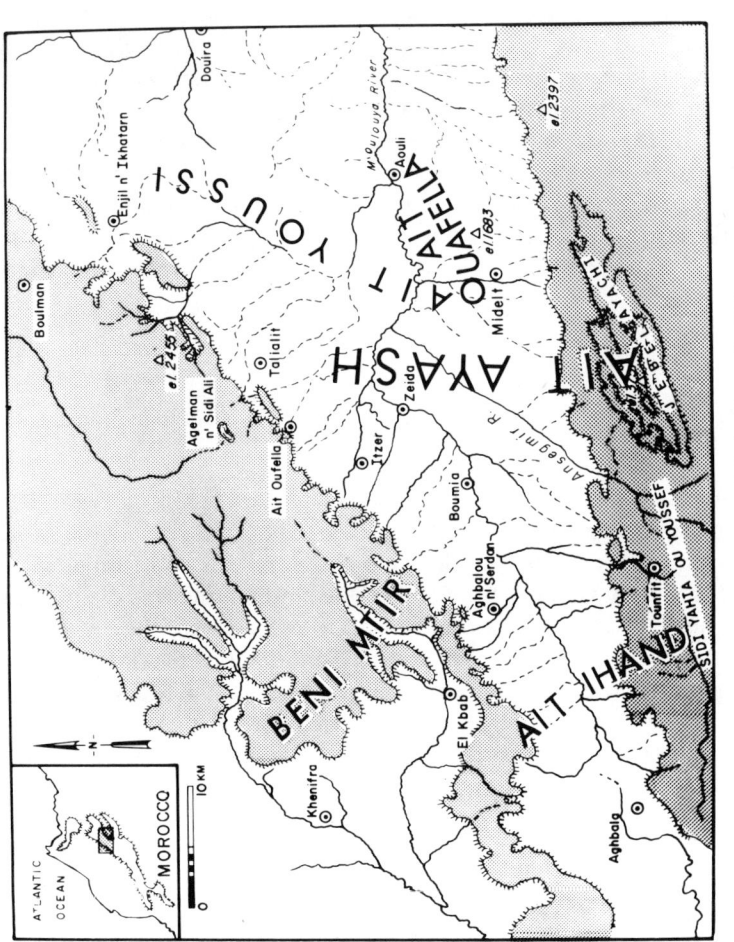

Map 4. Tribes in the High Moulouya Plain in the early 19th century.
Source: (Raynal 1960)

Intruding into the predominant Idrassen bloc were the Beni Mgild of the Ait Oumalou with a wedge of territory near Aghbalou n'Serdan, between the Beni Mtir and the Ait Ihand. The rest of the Oumalou were farther 'ahead' of them in the Middle Atlas, with the Ait Ihand between them. The plateaus of the Middle Atlas which provided seasonal pastures, remained chronically open to access, and subject to contests in which political consolidation provided competitive advantage.

South of the Moulouya plain, the Atlas barrier had served as the frontier for the Ait Yafelman during this period. The Ait Izdeg reached to the High Ziz valley, the Ait Hadiddou ranged between the Ziz and asif Melloul; the Ait Morghad controlled the High Gheris region, while the Ait Yahia were located farther south in the Kerdous. Subsequently, pressure from the expanding Ait Atta as well as forced population transfers under Mawlay Sliman, brought about a resurgence of migrations.

Throughout the periods of population shifts there remained in situ agricultural settlements of shurfa and igourramen (*agourram*, sing. Tamazight for murabit/murabitin, saintly men who did not necessarily claim descent from the Prophet) who survived the displacements and accommodated to new social alignments with new clients, or at worse with new patrons.

THE BREAK-UP OF THE AIT AYASH TRIBE

Up to the 19th century, the Ait Ayash had formed one of the large pastoralist tribes of the Idrassen confederation—as attested by the zawiya associated with its social-territorial identity from the 17th century—with a generalized economy on a fairly diversified resource base. A profound modification of their socio-political structure was realized during the reign of Mawlay Sliman, who, reacting to the insecurity of the commercial road to the Tafilalt and to the power of the Idrassen, headed an expedition against the tribes of the confederation. After winning a military victory, Sliman arranged the dismemberment of the Ait Ayash tribe by a transfer of a portion of its population to the outskirts of Fez, to serve as gish to the Sultan (Guennoun 1939:219).

According to the chronicle of al-Nasiri, the invested qaid to the Idrassen at this time, Muhammad ibn Muhammad ou Aziz, was out of favor with Mawlay Sliman, and in his place the sultan appointed a brother (Bou Azza ibn Muhammad ou Aziz). The Idrassen refused to accept the new qaid, and took as their amghar a cousin of the two brothers (Bou Azza ibn Nassir). In view of the pillaging of the caravan routes and the growing threat of the Idrassen, the sultan was forced to reinstate Muhammad and support him against the dissident Bou Azza. He then attacked the Idrassen with the cooperation of the Ait Oumalou. The combined forces defeated the Idrassen in 1803 at Alil (perhaps Talialit); following this encounter Sliman relocated a section of the Ait Ayash as a way of breaking up the nucleus of the alliance (al-Nasiri 1970:17; al-Zayyani 1886:184).

Profiting from the disequilibrium brought about by the deportation of the Ait Ayash, the Beni Mgild exploited it for territorial expansion. In concert, the Ait Oumalou engaged the Ait Idrassen in a critical battle in 1810, at Dar Eddel (40 km east of Itzer) near Sidi Ayad. The Idrassen, enfeebled by the earlier defeat, suffered further losses. In effect, the date marks the virtual end of the confederation. Subsequently, the Ait Ayash of Talialit ceded their territories to the Mgild and regrouped in the settlements of the Ansegmir valley. One subfraction, the Ait Oufella, stayed in place and became incorporated into the incoming Mgild clan. Other fractions dispersed, or joined at this time the Ait Ayash sent to Fez. Those on the southern flanks of Jebel Ayashi, whether sedentaries or pastoralists, accepted new social ascriptions and incorporation into other tribes, or remained politically isolated—like the village of Taarart of the Ait Ayash, south of Jebel Ayashi. Only the riverine settlements of the Ait Ayash in the Ansegmir valley survived as a land-holding political formation with a corporate social identity (Guennoun 1939:219).

In addition, the Beni Mtir abandoned the Moulouya plain and moved to the Gigou valley and to Azrou, from where they were pushed by the Beni Mgild to their present location around El Hajeb. The various Mgild tribes occupied the ceded territories of Agersif, Boulajoul, Talialit, and also the pastures of the Middle Atlas up to Ain Leuh and Azrou.

During the third or fourth decade of the century, the Ait Yafelman began to figure as the dominant alliance in the High Moulouya plain. The Ait Ouafella of Midelt were warring with their neighbors, the Gerwan, who had been installed in the region after the 1803 defeat of the Idrassen. The Ait Ouafella received the military aid of the Ait Izdeg of the High Ziz and expelled the Gerwan. The Izdeg then took the qsour of the Gerwan and partitioned the land of Midelt with their client allies.

Another group of Yafelman, the Ait Yahia, chased the Ait Ihand from the Tounfit region; the Ihand moved to the high valleys of the Serrou, in a wedge between the confederations of the Beni Mgild and Zayan. Other Yafelman, the Ait Haddidou, slowly infiltrated the qsour and pastures of the high plateaus south of the Ayashi, and the southernmost valleys previously occupied by the Ait Ayash.

THE ETHNOHISTORICAL BACKGROUND 31

Toward 1850, the Ait Ayash organized a counterattack against the Beni Mgild under the chief of the Yafelman, Brahim Isemmour al Izdegi. The Yafelman leader had gained reknown for his successful containment of the Ait Atta, who were considered to have the stronger league, and also, for his protection of shurfa communities in the Tafilalt which had been subject to the pillaging of the expansionist Atta. In the local tradition, the Ait Ayash under Brahim took advantage during the winter transhumance of the Mgild to attack their quarters in the territories they had lost. In retaliation, the entire confederation of the Mgild struck back and pushed the Ayash back to the fortified settlements on the Ansegmir. Brahim was held responsible for the defeat; his followers arranged for his assassination through the second in command[13] (Ibid:220).

In the second half of the century, the new territorial alignments in the Moulouya plain reached a relative stability. On the eastern side, the small tribes of the Ait Ayash, Ait Izdeg and Ait Ouafella stayed close to their irrigated valleys in the qsour overlooking their fields. The Ait Youssi patrolled the Fez-Tafilalt route crossing the plain and maintained links with the makhzan through their quasi-hereditary chiefs. On the western side the various tribes of the Beni Mgild alloted the newly won territories between them for seasonal quarters and pastures and continued their transhumance to the Middle Atlas plateaus and western plains.

Coordinated activity through the para-military confederations diminished in this period. The Idrassen formation dissolved with the final check of the Ait Ayash. The Ait Yafelman confederation was still important in containing the Ait Atta of the south, and all the tribes of the Moulouya, except the Beni Mgild who belonged to the Ait Oumalou bloc, became identified with the confederation.

What remained important were the roles of the zawiyas in providing mediation for conflict resolution that maintained local equilibria and in offering charismatic leaders for coordination of inter-tribal activities, especially in interaction with the makhzan. The dimension of group organization through tribal structures looms large in explanations of rural Moroccan political behavior. The alignment of tribes over space provided the social parameter that organized production processes, but the same alignment did not always provide the viable political units in regional contests. Otherwise the prevalence of groups of unequal size, which is a notable feature of Moroccan tribes, cannot be accounted for satisfactorily. What brought together and directed political energy in alignments larger than those possible with the tribal structures were charismatic religious figures with power that was not

---

[13] The fate of Brahim was not directly the result of the defeat of the Ait Ayash. This is simply the local version of more extensive regional politics (cf. al-Nasiri 1907:193–194).

subsumed in the politics of tribal segmentation. The chief of the Derkawi zawiya of Mdaghra, Sidi Mhand of Arabi, was such a figure in the second half of the 19th century. Before returning to the tribes of the Moulouya plain in the late 19th century, the earlier historical background becomes relevant.

THE 'BERBER REVOLT': RENEWED FAITH AND OLD POLITICS

While the early 19th century campaigns of Mawlay Sliman reduced the political leverage of the High Moulouya tribes, during the same period the Sanhaja groups that had advanced to the northwest participated in a series of encounters that challenged the sultan's authority, and in some interpretations, the Alawite dynasty itself. A sequence of complex and confused events from 1811 to 1822, sometimes referred to as the 'Berber revolt', developed from two sources with the common goal of challenging central power.

One source was the response of the religious brotherhoods to Mawlay Sliman's proscription of the cult of saints. The sultan had endorsed puritan Wahhabite doctrines brought back from Mecca by Moroccan ambassadors, which led him to turn against saint worship. A contemporaneous set of events began with the defensive attack of the recently settled Ait Idrassen in the plain of Meknes against the Ait Oumalou pastoralists who coveted their territories (al-Nasiri 1907: 51–59).

In 1811 the Idrassen tribes of the Zemmour and Ait Yemmour sought the alliance of the Gerwan to attack the Oumalou blocs of the Zayan and Beni Mgild. At the moment of battle the Gerwan switched sides and the Idrassen were defeated. This forced the vanquished Idrassen into the camp of the makhzan. For the next two years Mawlay Sliman fought the Gerwan with alternate victories and defeats, until the Gerwan came to his side as well.

In 1818 a murabit of the Middle Atlas, Boubker Amhaoush, from the zawiya Ait Sidi Ali rallied the Ait Oumalou and the tribes of the Ait Seghroushen n'Sidi Ali and Marmousha of the Middle Atlas in a common front against Mawlay Sliman whose puritan renewal threatened the survival of the rural zawiyas (Drague 1951:141–162). The Idrassen and Gerwan refused to fight against the murabit who embodied their own political aspirations and defected from the imperial army. At the battle of Lenda in the Middle Atlas the sultan was captured and his son Mawlay Brahim was killed. After four days of captivity, during which he was treated with utmost respect as a sharif, a Beni Mgild soldier led him to safety in acknowledgement of his role as spiritual leader of the Moroccan community, even though an immediate political adversary. Amhaoush and his forces then beseiged the city of Meknes and Mawlay Sliman was obliged to negotiate a truce with the mediation of the shaikh of the zawiya Sidi Hamza, Abu Muhammad Abdul ben Hamza.

In 1820, two of the most influential religious brotherhoods, the Derkawiya and the Wazzaniya, joined the revolt of Amhaoush. Both had been close to the court in the initial years of Sliman's rule, but his growing hostility to the brotherhoods culminating in the Interdiction of Moussems in 1815 brought them to act against him. (A moussem is an annual pilgrimage to a saint's tomb and a festival held in his honor). The chiefs of the two orders signed a proclamation raising to the throne a son of the preceding sultan, Mawlay Yazid. The contender to the throne was killed shortly after, and a brother replaced him, but the attempt failed because the Derkawi chief and founder of the order, Mawlay al Arabi (1737–1823), was captured by loyalist Oudaya troops in Fez. Both Amhaoush and the military chief of the Zemmour, Bel Ghazi, were Derkawi adherents, and so long as the revered shaikh remained prisoner they took no action that could endanger his life. Mawlay Sliman kept the Derkawi hostage during the rest of his reign as his most effective lever against Amhaoush and his troops.

The succeeding sultan, Mawlay Abderahman, freed the shaikh, dropped the Wahhabite doctrines, and restablished relations with the brotherhoods, whose energies he directed toward the Turkish-held Algerian territories for the period until 1832, when the French took Oran.

When Sidi Muhammad II (1859–1873) succeeded his father Abderahman, a son of Mawlay Sliman made a bid for the throne. After his unsuccessful attempt, he took refuge with the shaikhs of the zawiya Sidi Hamza which had supported his father during Amhaoush's revolt. He stayed there, according to al-Nasiri's chronicle until "he fell into oblivion" (1907:211).

THE MOULOUYA PLAIN IN THE REIGN OF MAWLAY HASSAN

During the reign of Mawlay Hassan (1873–1894) even the most remote tribes had qaids appointed over them. The distinction between government domain and tribal areas (siba) became effectively blurred because dissidence, more than in other periods, appeared as an episodic response to specific conditions rather than as a permanent refusal of the sultan's authority.

Mawlay Hassan is remembered in oral tradition as an outstanding sultan, and his reign marked a period of wide popularity for the Alawite dynasty, even though it coincided with a grave economic crisis in Morocco following war indemnities imposed by Spain and the wider changes in Mediterranean trade patterns that depressed Morocco's commercial vitality.

One consequence was the makhzan's vigorous pursuit of tax collection from the tribes as a source of state revenue. Mawlay Hassan mounted annual expeditions to the far corners of the country in order to subdue refractory tribes, appoint governors, and collect the taxes.

The earliest local history in the Moulouya plain is attached to the reign of the energetic Mawlay Hassan. His periodic expeditions to the region are used as reference points to date all remembered events. Elders of the Ait Ayash recount vivid and legendary stories about the sultan, while the later period until the establishment of the French Protectorate has faded in memory. The sultan is described in these accounts as a great and just ruler, one whose authority as sharif was never questioned even though his agents were often refused and overthrown. The disagreements with the sultan were over his qaids, who, unlike him, were unjust and tyrannous.

During this period, several large tribes of the eastern and central Atlas were dominated by chiefs from families referred to as 'big tents' who maintained quasi-hereditary positions that subverted the prevalent egalitarian and acephalous organization of the rural social structures. The Ait Morghad in the south, and the Zayan in the Middle Atlas are two examples. Such local power holders were principal candidates as qaids, receiving an official government seal for the power they held on their own account. The many other qaids exhausted easily any tribal support by applying the principle of self-help for recompense, since they received no salaries, and moreover lacked a local power base to maintain their positions. They were tolerated with varying degrees of forbearance.

The British journalist Walter Harris followed in 1893 the expedition of Mawlay Hassan to the Tafilalt and wrote in his account:

> Although there are nominal Kaids and governors over all this portion of trans-Atlas Morocco, it must by no means be thought that they hold any jurisdiction, nor would the above mentioned Kaid [he refers to the qaid of Demnat] have been able to visit Todgha had not the Sultan been approaching. Even in his little town of Demnat, on the other side of the Atlas, his position was never secure, and on the death of the late Sultan last June (1894) his house was razed and he himself murdered. (Harris 1895:314)

In the Moulouya plain a dominant family of the Ait Youssi tribe had provided successive qaids. The ties with the makhzan had been long standing among the Ait Youssi who patrolled the imperial route to the Tafilalt. In the early part of Hassan's reign, the paramount regional figure in the High Moulouya was the qaid Mhand ou Talb ou Youssi. Below him were ranked other qaids, some of whom were known by the lesser title of *khalifa* (deputy) since they served under him. The Ait Ayash were governed by a khalifa, Hmad n'ait Abbi, an Ayashi from the village of Ait Oumghar. A letter from the qaid to his khalifa had been kept by an elder in his village (see plate 2 at the back of the book). Dated 1889, it requests the khalifa to provide one hundred *tallis* (a double sack making a mule load) of wheat for the Sultan and to arrest someone who had taken refuge at the zawiya Hamzawiya. Also the deputy was to notify another qaid to gather provisions of barley, butter and sheep and bring them along with the livestock of the makhzan to the Ansegmir for delivery.

This incorporation into the makhzan through the hierarchy of government agents remained partial. At the same time dissident activity was directed both against the government and its agents. Leadership for such activities was provided by the Derkawi shaikh in the south (Mdaghra), Sidi Mhand al Arabi, who was mentor to all the Yafelman tribes and an implacable enemy of the Alawite dynasty even though he was himself an Alawite sharif. In the oral tradition of the Ait Ayash, Sidi Mhand al Arabi figures as the most important source of their political activities, as well as of the activities of the other groups in the Yafelman confederation. They considered him their guarantor of security because, as they described him, "he was like a king (*ayyelid*) of the south."

Sidi Mhand al Arabi was the heir to the *baraka* (a quality of blessedness or holiness) of the first shaikh of the southern Derkawiya lodge, Sidi Mhand al Bedawi (Zwitten), one of the favored disciples of the order's founder, Sidi Mawlay al Arabi. The chiefly baraka in some brotherhoods was transmitted by testament to spiritual heirs, and not inherited in descent lines. The southern lodge was known as the Derkawi-Bedawi branch. Sidi Mhand came from a shurfa family in Mdaghra where his father had been a qadi, and where he established his zawiya which attracted at one time over five hundred students. His leadership provided a focus for the discontent of all the tribes that came to be identified as Ait Yafelman.

In the expedition of 1888 to the Middle Atlas, Mawlay Hassan won a military victory over the Ait Oumalou bloc which included the Zayan, Beni Mgild and Ait Sokhman. The tribes requested aman and war fines were imposed on them. The Ait Sokhman asked the sultan for a detachment of soldiers to accompany them to their home territory in order to collect the taxes. The sultan dispatched his uncle, Mawlay Serrou, with a contingent of gish troops. On Sokhman territory the soldiers were attacked and the sharif was killed. The ambush was organized by Sidi Ali Amhaoush, a descendant of the murabit who had led the revolt against Mawlay Sliman earlier in the century (al-Nasiri 1907: 368–370). The Amhaoush zawiya subscribed to the Derkawi-Bedawi doctrine and followed the leadership of Sidi Mhand al Arabi who guided the Yafelman. On the advice of Sidi Mhand, the Ait Ayash, Ait Izdeg, and other Moulouya groups participated in the ambush organized by the Amhaoush murabit against the uncle of the sultan.

Two years later, again on the orders of Sidi Mhand al Arabi, the Ait Youssi qaid, Mhand ou Talb, was assassinated in his headquarters by the tribesmen under his command. The pretext for the insurrection were certain acts of impious conduct. Both the chief (khalifa) of the Ait Ayash and the qaid of the Ait Morghad complied with the plot by absenting themselves from the meeting at which the assassination took place. The Ait Ayash said that Hmad n'ait Abbi owed his position more to the approval of the Derkawi shaikh than to makhzan appointment.

Immediately after, a son, Omar ou Youssi, of the assassinated qaid replaced him in his post. Omar maintained a more flexible political attitude than his father. Segonzac, in his comments on the qaids of the Zayan, Mgild and Youssi tribes, observed in 1901:

> Ils tiennent leur pouvoir, non pas du Sultan, mais de leur tribu; le titre de qaid n'est que la consecration officielle de leur autorité. Leur pouvoir est héréditaire: Omar el-Youssi peut citer vingt ancêtres depuis Ioussef ben Idratten l'aieul de la tribu . . . Omar el-Youssi est en pleine révolte pour la troisieme fois (Segonzac 1903:128).

When Mawlay Hassan camped on the Moulouya plain during his last expedition in 1893, some of these accounts were settled. The Ayashi khalifa was brought before the sultan for his complicity in the plots against the qaid and against the sharif Mawlay Serrou. The clear responsibility of the Derkawi Shaikh, the throne's true adversary, was recognized, and the khalifa was pardoned and reinstated as chief of the Ait Ayash, a position he kept until the Protectorate period. The 'saint' Sidi Mhand al Arabi died a short time before the sultan reached the Mdaghra for a confrontation.

The ambivalent attitudes of the tribes toward the government, especially that of a highly esteemed sultan, and the ties to charismatic figures like Sidi Mhand al Arabi, permitted relatively powerless segments like the Ait Ayash to sustain a complex series of responses that placed them in rapid succession into the different nominal categories of a *naiba* (a tax-paying tribe under the authority of the makhzan) tribe and of a *tamazight* (free) tribe, of which the latter ranked in their social universe as the most desirable political status.

CHAPTER TWO

Socio-Political Organization: The Traditional Period

This chapter deals with the socio-political organization of the Ait Ayash before the French Protectorate. In the decades preceding French colonization, the Ait Ayash were a small sedentary tribe of agriculturalists in central Morocco, the localized remnant population of a larger tribe broken up in the early 19th century. They were a rural population in the blad al siba, or the region of dissidence.[1] The tribal framework organized the rural populations which were peripheral to the state-organized center. Moroccan tribes were kin-based territorial groups with segmentary, replicating systems that asserted, in varying degrees, political independence from centralized authority.

Tribalism in the Maghreb, or Muslim North Africa, can be characterized as a political reaction to archaic state formations. It is, in Gellner's definition, "a political and partial rejection of a particular government combined with some acceptance of a wider culture and its ethic" (1969:2). This marginal tribalism that "knows what it rejects" (Ibid.), defines the dissident populations within a political arena that encompasses a state government. At the same time, tribal boundaries between groups served to adjust populations with respect to control and management of localized resources.

The first section of the chapter examines the descent groups and territorial segments nested in the tribe. The following sections outline the political authority system and order-maintenance mechanisms among the Ait Ayash. The chapter concludes with a consideration of the theoretical frameworks which have been applied to Moroccan tribalism.

---
[1]For critical statements on French colonial sociology see Nicolas (1961) and Burke (1972).

THE TAQBILT: POLITICAL UNITY

The Ait Ayash refer to themselves as a taqbilt (tribe, from Arabic qabila) which incorporates the settlements of the Ansegmir valley. They do not claim descent from a common ancestor, nor does the tribal name recall a founding ancestor. Oral traditions about the history of the tribe are minimal. The Ait Ayash suggested I question an elder of the Ait Hadiddou who had a regional reputation as a tribal historian.[2] He told me, "The Ait Ayash were a large and powerful tribe long ago. They controlled the territory south and west of the mountain and gave their name to the mountain" (Jebel Ayashi). When questioned whether this could not have been the other way around he was positive: "Imazighen (Tamazight-speaking Berbers; tribesmen) always call landmarks after their own names. The land had no names without the people. This shows the Ait Ayash were an important tribe far in the past. But all this has been forgotten. Ever since the tribe settled to farm in the valley, it neglected its own past. The Ait Ayash no longer remember they were Ait Idrassen because names change with time, like everything else."

The Ait Ayash, and all Berber tribes, are patrilineal and segmentary. The prefatory 'Ait' in tribal names means 'descendants of', so that even without specific genealogical claims the names connote agnatic descent groups. The Ait Ayash groups which were recognized as distant kin by the shared name, but were territorially removed from the Ansegmir valley, were not included as members of the taqbilt. they were incorporated as segments of other *tiqbilin* (tribes, pl.), or formed their own taqbilt, as did the Ait Ayash who had been transferred to the vicinity of Fez at Ain Afham on the Sais plain in the early 19th century by the sultan Mawlay Sliman.

The taqbilt represents the widest scope of long-term cooperation between the villages, and provided its members with a social identity distinct from that of adjacent populations on the basis of assigning "social meanings to a limited set of acts."[3] The Ait Ayash maintained that their tribe was one of Imazighen, by which they meant that it was neither a gish tribe, tied to the service of the makhzan, nor a naiba tribe, subject to the regular control and taxation of the government. The fact that during Mawlay Hassan's reign they were periodically taxed and under a government appointed chief did not change their evaluation. The important criterion for their tribal status was that they

---

[2]The informant is Ou Shdish who has already been mentioned in earlier notes. My interviews with him were first carried out in the town of Rish after an Ait Ayashi arranged a meeting. Later he visited the Ait Ayash and surprised some Ayashi men with his knowledge of their family histories.

[3]Cf. Blom (1969:74) who deals with a negative case: ethnic homogeneity maintained thoughout an area with a diversity of social forms and behavioral styles.

could defend their territory against other tribes. "Our fathers fought for *tamazirtnun* (our land) and they spilled their blood to keep it. This is what makes of a taqbilt", is how one elder informant explained it.

The taqbilt, in the prevalent organizational model of the Central Atlas region, is the named group identified with a territory. Territory gives a dimension to social identity and stands as the corporate estate of the taqbilt, but is not its validating source. Two principles apply widely to social relations, patrilineal kinship and the explicit contract. A contract, or alliance, specifies mutual rights and obligations in detail, and lasts as long as the parties maintained their spelled out obligations (cf. Rabinow 1975:28–29).

The taqbilt, among Atlas groups, is based on kinship as ties of patrifiliation and on descent as a mechanism for the legal transmission of rights from one generation to the next, along with the separate but complementary notion of alliance blocs as units for the exercise of power in an acephalous political system (Barth 1959:14).

The genealogical argument is variously applied to tribes and tribal segments. Among the expanding and predatory social groupings the organization took on the form of an all-enveloping common descent structure. Politically defensive and numerically smaller groups came to be seen as of mixed descent. Defeated groups and remnant sections lost kinship and tribal status altogether and were called *iqblin* (*aqbli*, sing.). *Qebala* means the south in Tamazight, and iqblin[4] refers to the southern populations, many of sub-Saharan origin, that lacked descent group organization and relied on the protection of tribal patrons. At one end of the social spectrum stood tribal confederations called *khams khumas* (literally five-fifths, or five tribes) whose coalition was treated as a common descent group through a named, putative apical ancestor. At the other end figured the unaffiliated, the iqblin, who 'no longer knew their origins'. In the center stood the majority of Imazighen tribes, each with a distinct identity through maintenance of such cultural boundary markers as their own customary law (*izref*, Berber; *'urf*, Arabic), dialect[5] or lexical variants, style in dress and adornment, and explicit rights and obligations with respect to each other and with respect to the use and control of the territory of the group.

One view of traditional rural Moroccan social organization treats tribes as falling into two general types along an axis of economic strategies (cf. Hart 1967:71). Transhumant groups form segmentary lineage

---

[4]The term *aqbli* is sometimes given a racial meaning for a black person. I think the term indicates group organization and I use it as such. This is how many informants explained it. Some French reports emphasized the derivative racial meaning and resorted to the qualification *iqblin imllalen* (white iqblin) to describe remnant Berber groups which had lost tribal organization (cf. Jacques-Meunié 1958:245–246; Laoust 1934:154–156). There is also a tradition that iqblin came from the Kabylia region of Algeria.

[5]See Abdel-Massih (1971a; 1971b; 1971c) for the dialect of the Ait Ayash.

systems, while sedentary populations form segmentary systems through cohesion of heterogeneous clans. This is generally accurate but leaves out the question of processes in social construction and the deliberate contractual aspects in all the formations. The composition of segmentary kinship systems defines political units, it does not create them. Besides, many pastoralist tribes were 'heterogeneous'. Descent group recruitment had specific political uses not generalized economic ones.[6] J. Berque has written on the social uses of kinship in Moroccan tribes as follows:

> Là ou il y a des legendes genealogiques pour expliquer l'ensemble, deux systèmes coexistent, sans apparement gener le citoyen. Simultanement il professe le rattachement à l'ancêtre general, et l'ascendance different assignée par la tradition à sa famille. Il invoque, selon l'occasion l'une ou l'autre lignée. De fait, la plupart des tribus agregent des elements venus de tous les horizons et en tout cas "d'ailleurs". Cette contradiction entre la personnalité collective et l'origine des cellules qui la composent est veritablement une loi du genre (Berque 1953:264).

The Ait Ayash validated their taqbilt status by their cohesion in defense and by the recollection of ancestral villages to the south held by the tribe before its break-up in the 19th century.

A 19th century manuscript that described the origin of the Atlas tribes (Guennourn 1939:217) states that the Ait Ayash and the Ait Ouafella are peoples of qebala origins, which is to say tribeless. In both cases the qebala attribution reflected the loss of political status during that period. Relative political power was idiomatically perceived in kinship and descent terms. The Ait Ouafella had lost independent tribal status when they appealed to the Ait Izdeg for military aid and were forced to cede territory in return for that aid. The Ait Ayash had suffered a military defeat to the troops of Mawlay Sliman which was followed by the transfer of a part of their population and subsequent territorial losses to the Beni Mgild.

The taqbilt thereafter remained circumscribed by the irrigable surface in the Ansegmir valley which served as the principal basis for the economy. A generous estimate would be a population of 4,500 individuals.[7] Moreover, as a sedentary group in a region dominated by transhumant pastoralists they remained doubly vulnerable in competitive situations. Yet their organization proved viable in maintaining their status as a taqbilt and in resisting incorporation into a larger interest group.

---

[6]For an analysis of permutations of political design and group recruitment, see Sahlins (1965).

[7]Segonzac (1903:166) reported the Ait Ayash could put in the field 1,500 men. A calculation of one-third males over 16 years gives a population of 4,500 persons. A safer estimate would be a ceiling population of 4,000, based on 20 qsour of 40 households each, and average households of five persons.

SOCIO-POLITICAL ORGANIZATION 41

In 1901, E. de Segonzac traveled in disguise through the Atlas mountains on a French intelligence mission, in the cortège of a cooperative religious figure, a sharif of the Wazzani zawiya. He has given rare eyewitness reports of the tribes he visited. His account of the Ait Ayash supports their own views of the past, and also gives a telling sketch of the image they try to project to others.

> Les Aït Aïach méprisent leurs voisins du Nord qu'ils considèrent comme des sauvages. Ils sont riches et peuvent mettre en ligne quinze cents fusils. Ils ne sont pas agressifs, mais les incursions continuelles de leur puissant voisins, les Beni Mgild et les Ait Merrad, ont fait d'eux une tribu très guerriere. La montagne leur offre des réduits imprenables ou l'on cache femmes et troupeaux en temps de guerre. D'ailleurs ils n'ont que peu de troupeaux, toute leur fortune est en cultures, ils sont surtout agriculteurs, sédentaires et cavaliers. . . .
> En résumé ils sont plus civilisés que les Beni Mgild et quand on leur demande la raison, ils répondent: "Nous sommes le coeur du Maghreb." . . .
> Les Ait Aïach passent pour les meilleurs cavaliers du Maroc, leurs ennemis mêmes en conviennent, et leur chevaux font prime. En quoi consiste cette supériorité, je ne saurais le dire. Peut-être ont-ils la main moins dure: leur chevaux paraissent en effet plus souples; mais tout leur art se résume à galoper facilement et à briser les jarrets de leur chevaux dans les fantasias (Segnonzac 1903:166).

The accounts of the tribal elders stressed the warrior posture they maintained as a tribe. The role of the tribe was to defend the territory and strategic resources held as corporate property and to assure the security of its members against other tribes.

HETEROGENEOUS CLANS: IGHSAN

The Ait Ayash taqbilt comprised four descent segments called *ighsan (ighs,* sing., bone). The tribe is conceived as segmentary and the ighsan are treated as equal parts of the same order, but they directly reflect the historical settlement of the villages. The ighsan are putative agnatic descent groups that can be called clans, since the members of each ighs claim descent from the named ancestor but without any attempt to demonstrate links. They serve, in the absence of genealogies, as identity labels. They are heterogeneous in origin and each related two or more villages in a structural segment below the level of the tribe. However this level of segmentation was not involved in any concrete historical instance so far as could be gathered, for structural opposition. The third level of segmentation, of local territorial settlements, served actively for internal alignments.

42 THE AIT AYASH OF THE HIGH MOLOUYA PLAIN

The four clans were the Ait Said on Lahsen, Ait Brahim, Ait Rebaa, and Ait Bougman (Map 5). The Aid Said on Lahsen is considered the only clan of the earlier Ayash formation. The original taqbilt segmented into moieties (*nusf*), one with four clans, the other with five.[8] Two clans of one moiety, the Ait Said on Lahsen and Ait Wifteen, and one clan of the other, the Amr on Ikkou, had settlements on the Ansegmir valley. The others held all the territories ceded from 1810 to 1850. After the breakup of the tribe, only the Ait Said on Lahsen remained in the valley. The emptied villages were eventually occupied by the incoming families that came to form the other three clans. The seven villages of the Ait Said or Lahsen clan were the oldest settlements, and the clan was the only one to claim origin from the earlier tribe. In internal composition, families within the villages recognized separated histories without contradicting the affiliation with the ighs. Political design was not confused with group recruitment.

The Ait Said on Lahsen was held to be the most powerful of the clans because it had provided the *imgharn* (*amghar*, sing.), or chiefs for the tribe. This evaluation reflected the fact that the tribal khalifa, Hmad n'ait Abbi, was of this clan. The clans were not ranked and all had equal access to the collective resources and the available statuses in the society. The prominence of one clan over another was a matter of the personal and family histories within them, not one of structure. The dispositional model of the Ait Ayash organization remained egalitarian.

The ighs of the Ait Brahim included two adjacent settlements, which were described by other Ayashis as families of iqblin, from the southern groups of the Ait Rbba and Beni Mehalli, which had bought fields and had become ritually incorporated as a clan into the tribe. The Ait Brahim themselves simply insisted that their ighs was a part of the tribe and did not dwell on legends of historical incorporation. What others remembered about them was simply irrelevant for tribal ascription. The attribution of separate origins for the ighs may in fact have referred to histories of specific families within the group, which became assimilated as the history of the clan. The legend of origin of a clan does not address itself to its internal composition. What it specified was the relationship between segments of the same level and the connections between the different levels. The assumption of genealogi-

---

[8]The only informant who claimed to know the clan names of the earlier tribal formation was the second qaid of the Protectorate period. He had learned the names from his father, the first qaid. The two top segments were called Ismaililin and Ait Widn. The Ismaililin segmented into four clans: Ait Said ou Lahsen, Ait Illousen, Ait Wifteen, and Ait ou Fellah. The Ait Widn segmented into five clans: Ait Amr ou Ishou, Ait Bou Merhoum, Ait Yaaqoub, Ait Ali ou Boubkir and Ait Rahhou Agoudim.

Families of the Ait ou Fellah remain in the village of the same name now part of one of the Beni Mgild tribes. The Ait Rahhou are still identified among the Ait Yahia at the settlement of Agoudim. The Ait Illousen had a settlement on the right bank of the Moulouya, in the territory occupied by the Ait Mouli of the Beni Mgild, where some remained. During the Protectorate period, a French administrator decided that in view of their heritage they should be reassigned to the Ait Ayash. The Ait Illousen settlement has become the westernmost extension of the Ait Ayash territory.

SOCIO-POLITICAL ORGANIZATION

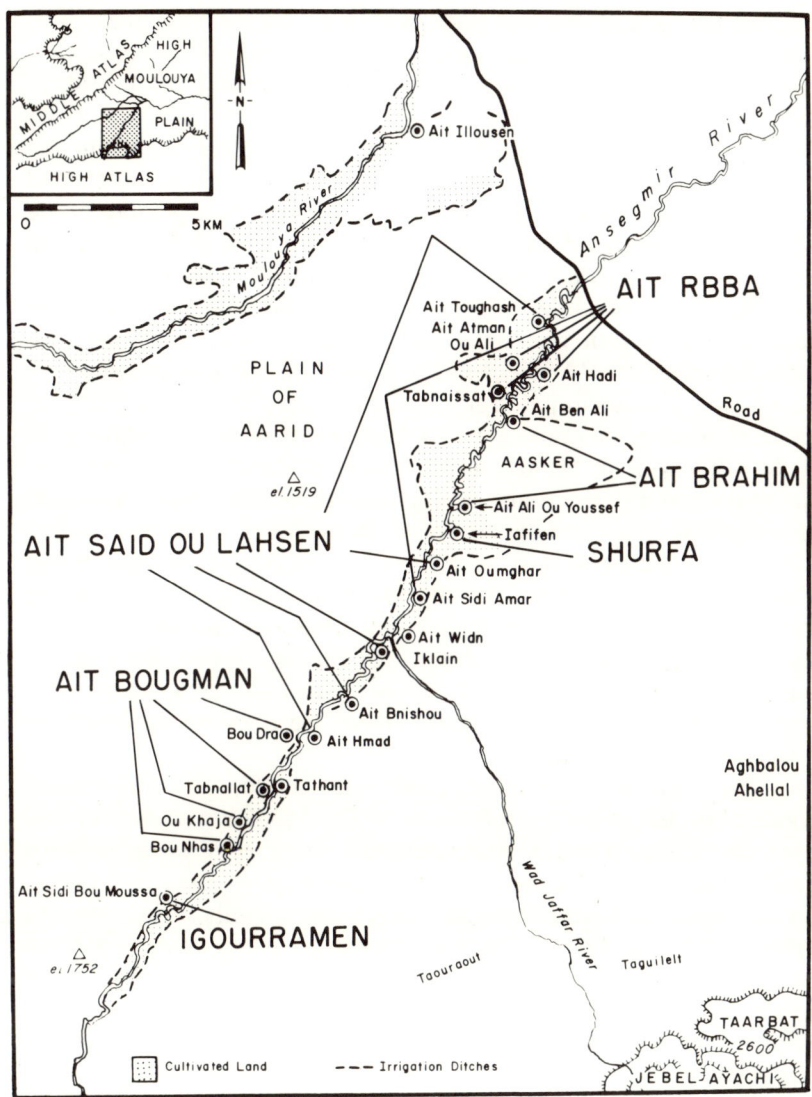

Map 5. The settlements and clans of the Ait Ayash.

cal connections served as the dominant mode of expressing relationships but explicitly cast in a contractual idiom.

The ighs of the Ait Rbba was composed of four non–adjoining settlements. Its history had been forgotten. A core group of the clan, the Ait Sidi Amr ou Hallou, was of reputed sharifian descent. The Ait Sidi Amr occupied a village named after them and were wholly laicized. The shurfa origins were not imputed to the other settlements of the Ait Rbaa, and the Ait Sidi Amr were not exempt from tribal obligations because of their claims. In 1893 when Mawlay Hassan imposed fines on the tribe the Ait Sidi Amr were forced to sell fields to another village to pay their share.

The fourth clan was the last one to be incorporated into the tribe, and its history remains vivid in the oral accounts. It was formed by two minimal descent groups of one of the neighboring tribes of the Beni Mgild confederation. The Beni Mgild comprised two territorial blocs, each of several tribes. One bloc, immediate neighbors of the Ait Ayash, controlled the western portion of the Moulouya Plain won from the Ait Ayash and the other Idrassen tribes. The other bloc ranged through the Middle Atlas plateaus and the edges of the central plains. The socio-political frameword safeguarded their dependence on pastoralism and complex patterns of winter transhumance. Mgild tribal sections located in the valleys of the Tigrigra, Gigou and Moulouya rivers, and other ecologically favorable areas, cultivated winter grains as a subsidiary activity. Dependence on farming varied according to localities. The overall strategy of the confederated tribes required a commitment to mobility for the control and defense of the complementary zones. Year-round sedentism was incompatible with the established system of land use and the socio-political formation that maintained it. Households whose individual circumstances led them to give up a pastoral commitment were forced to leave the political formation.

One tribe of the Moulouya bloc, the Ait Bougman, maintained summer dwellings on the left bank of the Moulouya river and had given up the long distance transhumance to the zone of winter pastures west of the Middle Atlas. They relied instead on shorter seasonal moves within the High Moulouya plain, while the other tribes vacated it for the season. Among the four descent group segments of the Ait Bougman, households in one fraction, the Ait Yahia ou Ahsin, gave up seasonal migrations altogether for a larger commitment to farming. Disputes with the other fractions over rights to fields led to their expulsion.

The expelled group of 55 households sought refuge among the Ait Yahia tribe to the south, who refused them. They turned next to the Ait Ayash. Two settlements on Ansegmir, Taroust and Touftint, remained abandoned at this time since the population shifts of the 1850s. The emigrant group was accepted into the taqbilt through a pact ratified by the saint of the Ait Ayash, the Derkawi chief, Sidi Mhand al Arabi (d. ca. 1892). The Ait Ayash stated that all important decisions they undertook as a taqbilt received the approval of their 'saint'. It was he who urged them to accept the new group by spreading his *taqbut* (cape) on the ground, placing himself on it and saying, "I sit on the land of the Ait Ayash" thereby offering his symbolic protection of the pact between the new 'brothers'.

The Ait Yahia on Ahsin then proceeded to construct a new village near the site of the abandoned Taroust. The other Bougman fractions protested the incorporation of their kinsmen in the neighboring tribe. Sidi Mhand asked the Ait Izdeg to offer support to the Ait Ayash against the attacks of the Ait Bougman, while the expelled section built the village on the Ansegmir that came to be known as Bou Draa (the village built with violence). The objections of the Ait Bougman were expressions in the local lore, of the fraternal rivalry of two closely related fractions, the expelled one and the Ait Said ou Ahsin. Their rivalry reflected the competition for the same land. The second group had also given up long distance transhumance and were opting for a year-round sedentary life. In fact, once the first group was admitted into the community of the sedentary tribe, the second fraction began, what tradition holds to have been, a forcible takeover of other Ansegmir property. They constructed two fortified villages in the vicinity of Bou Draa, whose names stood for the violence that accompanied their beginnings: Ou Khajja (*Khajja,* local name for a rifle newly acquired by the Beni Mgild in this period) and Bou Nhas (*nhas,* copper; for the cartridge shells in current use).

The two sections, once installed, formed the fourth ighs of the Ait Ayash. From this time, Ait Ayash elders said, the tribe became 'strong'. The ritual agnates they gained through the cession of fields added to the security of the taqbilt.

The fortunes of the two sections differed subsequently. The Ait Yahia ou Ahsin, whose tenure was validated by the solemn pact and the protection of Sidi Mhand al Arabi, sponsored a weekly market near Bou Draa. The Thursday market competed with an older market of the Beni Mgild near the town of Boumia.[9]

The Aid Said ou Ahsin families at the settlements of Bou Nhas and Ou Khajja failed to maintain themselves the new circumstances. By the time of the French Protectorate all but three of the original families had sold their fields to outsiders and returned to the Moulouya river settlements. From the viewpoint of other Ait Ayash the failure of the Ait Said ou Ahsin was retribution for their unsanctified tenure in the community, while the success of the Ait Yahia ou Ahsin was the consequence of the baraka of the saint who sponsored the incorporation. The market on the Ansegmir collapsed with the upheaval of the Protectorate military operations, but Ayashi tradition attributes it to internal dissension among the Ait Bougman of the Ansegmir, to the point they could no longer guarantee the safe passage of visitors.

---

[9]The pre-Protectorate Beni Mgild market was northwest of Boumia, at Taddaout n'Souq. The present Boumia market was begun after pacification in the 1930s.

The ighsan were not corporate groups, in that they held no property and had no discernible legal, political or economic functions. They could be called on for structural alignments in intra-tribal conflict management, but more often ephemeral alliances between villages of the same ighs or between villages of different ighsan contained the level of the dispute.

THE QSOUR: TERRITORIAL UNITS

The qsar,[10] or fortified village, was the basic, corporate unit of the Ayash socio-political organization. Each qsar was corporate in maintaining rights over person. Territorial unity and internal kinship alignments provided the crucial division for social order, community policy and decision-making.

There were twenty settlements[11] along the banks of the Ansegmir river at the turn of the century. All but two formed the taqbilt of the Ait Ayash. The two settlements outside of the tribe are discussed later in this chapter. Within each qsar, usually four minimal patrilineal descent segments aligned the households in intra-village interest groups. These were also known as ighsan, or by the diminutive of the term *tighsatin (tighst,* sing., little bone). Each named tighst grouped actual and ritual agnates since open recruitment into the tribe was maintained through ritual incorporation into a tighst.

A stranger and his family were accepted into the taqbilt through the ritual of *tamghrost* (sacrifice). A local sponsor accepted and stood responsible for the newcomer by taking him into his kinship group. Tamghrost entailed the slaughter of a sheep before the residence of the patron. The petitioner and his family were thus accepted into the tighst of the sponsor and became *ou tighsi* (members of the tighst) with the rights and obligations of next-of-kin. By extension, the ou tighsi became a member of the higher level ighs of his sponsor, and of the taqbilt. Ritual collaterality established full tribal status.

Ritual incorporation among the Ait Ayash was arranged through the sponsorship of an individual household rather than of the group. This was a function of the land tenure system. Since the Ait Ayash

---

[10]*Ighrem* is another term for village, but I have consistently used qsar for the particular type of ighrem, the adobe walled settlement found on the Ansegmir valley until the 1940s. Its prototype is the qsar of the Tafilalt region. For description see Laoust (1934:169–177) and Mennesson (1965).

[11]They were in order from the highest point to the south: Ait Sidi Bou Moussa, Bou Nhas, Ou Khajja, Tabnallat, Bou Draa, Ait Hmad, Ait Bn Ishou, Iqqlain, Ait Sidi Amr, Ait Oumghar, Iaffifen (Qsar Shurfa), Ait Ali ou Youssef, Ait Bn Ali, Tabnaissat, Idendel, Ait Hadi, Ait Atman ou Ali, Ait Toughash, Ait Bn Said, and Ait ou Sadden. The names Segonzac gives (1903:294) differ in some respects. He does not give the Ait Bougman villages by name, although local tradition states the Beni Mgild families came during the lifetime of Sidi Mhand al Arabi who died ca. 1892. Some other names are different. The number is the same.

held irrigated fields in individual title and other land in collective title, recruitment into the community was concomitant with purchase of irrigated fields for viable household production. Dry farming on collective land remained a sporadic activity for both ecological and political reasons. The patron who accepted a ritual kinsman stood responsible for his economic integration into the community.

The holding of irrigated land in individual titles did not lead to significant economic differences between the tighsatin, since the contractual aspects of incorporation, the overall segmentary organization, and the corporate nature of the qsour acted as economic levelers.

After the resettlements of the 1850's, the ritual of incorporation was applied for admission of whole groups, in order to bring the tribe's population to a viable size. The qsar of Iaffifen, who were shurfa, had been admitted as a lineage, by offering tamghrost to the qsar of Ait Bn Ishou. Even though the Iaffifen claimed sharifian status, they did not develop economic privileges nor carry out special political roles.

Ritual incorporation through tamghrost remained in practice throughout the Protectorate period until 1956, but the suppression of armed feuding had altered the obligations of kinship. Moreover, families could settle among tribes without incorporation. New settlers during the Protectorate turned to ritual kinship only in cases when they needed to secure co-jurors for the collective oath, a customary jural institution. Thus, differences between incorporated status and status by birth became discernable during this period, especially over questions of rights to collective land.

In the traditional period no differences existed between the two statuses. The principle of the equality of all males and the absence of genealogies on all segmentary levels blurred incipient distinctions between actual and ritual agnates.

Even the minimal segments of the tighsatin were more like clans than like lineages. Patrifiliation rather than descent reckoning was a sufficient condition for ascription. My attempts to elicit genealogies in order to connect the families within a tighst proved fruitless. The Ait Ayash said they never kept genealogies, which is something the shurfa did.

The qsour were the critical and long-standing political segments of the Ansegmir farming population. By virtue of their architecture and placement, each formed a self-managed microcosm except in times of wider disputes. Then the disruption of daily life called for higher level intra-tribal or tribal cohesion. But alternate coalitions of interest groups that crosscut the segmentary descent order and temporarily effaced it were also activiated. The latter were based on alliance pacts that united two families, or minimal agnatic segments, or qsour, or clans within the tribe or between tribes. The pacts, when they endured through more than one critical situation, were known as tada. The Ait Ayash did not recall elaborate rituals for these pacts, other than the tada allies did not intermarry. Generally, they distinguished alliances contracted between fractions, known as *ait tada,* and alliances between two families, known as *ou tada.*[12]

More often, in the anecdotal material of oral accounts, ephemeral pacts based on contingencies united qsour or segments of qsour that stood distant to each other in the segmentary order against those who stood 'structurally' close but situationally opposed in particular competitive encounters.

Two of the Ansegmir settlements were not incorporated into the tribe of the Ait Ayash. One was an independent village of families claiming Idrissid sharifian descent, the Ait Sidi Bou Moussa. They had settled on the Ansegmir, in their account, in the 17th century and had provided a zawiya for the local tribes. Another branch of their lineage had settled in the market town of Itzer further west on the plain. The Ait Sidi Bou Moussa of the Ansegmir had found their fortunes in decline by the end of the 19th century in that they had failed to establish their shaikhs as mediators in tribal politics, the standard service performed by rural zawiyas. They are Tamazight-speakers and the Ait Ayash accept them as *igourramen (agourram,* sing.), as they are still called by local groups. An agourram is a Berber of piety who gains baraka for his scholarship, religious devotion and often miracle-making. The charisma is personal and non-hereditary, unlike the shurfa who inherit the potential for divine benevolence through descent. The Ait Sidi Bou Moussa claimed for themselves the status of shurfa, but were accepted by others as descendants of some distant agourram, whose baraka had lapsed with his person and was no longer evident among his descendents.

As shurfa claimants they maintained a neutral stance in intertribal conflicts and bore no arms. Their village, with a mosque in the center, lacked the high walls and towers of the qsar since their special status provided immunity against attacks. Since their active status as religious specialists had lapsed they were forced to resort to contractual arrangements for security. This was known as *takessa,* from the verb denoting protection. Several versions existed on the specifics of takessa. The version accepted by both Ait Sidi Bou Moussa and Ait Ayash informants specified that a pact was made with a notable *(akhatar)* of the tribe who stood responsible for the conduct of his kin group toward the Ait Sidi Bou Moussa in exchange for an annual fee in kind. The households of the Ait Sidi Bou Moussa contributed a prorated

---

[12]See March (1936) for tada alliances. Also, Bruno and Bousquet (1946), Coursimault (1917) and Vinogradov (1974:74–75). Ou tada relationships still obtain among the Ait Ayash with families of southern groups, facilitating hospitality and travel arrangements.

SOCIO-POLITICAL ORGANIZATION

amount to the payment of the protector. Both the Ait Ayash and other nearby tribes offered takessa to them.

Their economy and production activities were substantially the same as those of the Ait Ayash but they differed in their claims to land rights. The Ait Sidi Bou Moussa held a document, dated 1683, purporting to be a land deed for their irrigated fields and an extensive domain of uncultivated land near the Ansegmir, purchased, according to the document, from the Ait Arfa of the Beni Mgild.[13]

The second settlement outside the tribal formation was a hamlet, called Idendel, composed of agricultural laborers who farmed the estate of the zawiya Sidi Hamza on the Ansegmir valley. Zawiyas received from their client tribes donations in land held in *habous* (pious endowments; gifts given to the zawiya by devotees). The estates of successful zawiyas were widely spread across tribal territories. The zawiya Hamzawiya had received from the Ait Ayash over 500 hectares of land and had imported a labor force from the Ait Rebaa of Gheris in the south to work the land. Overseers from the Sidi Hamza family maintained a residence on the valley to supervise production. Little is known of the organization of Idendel because its population dispersed during the Protectorate period.[14] The political upheaval allowed the majority of the families to escape the domination of the shurfa. Many moved to Midelt when opportunities for labor in the construction of the new town appeared. Since that period the zawiya had found it difficult to maintain its estate, and, in the present, the leading family of the zawiya has sold parcels of it, even though it is habous and in theory inalienable.

SOURCES FOR POLITICAL AUTHORITY: MAKHZAN AND TRIBE

In the three decades preceding the Protectorate period political authority was vested in the tribal chief who held his position as a deputy (khalifa) of the Sultan's regional representative. This position did not follow from the tribal organization but was an imposed one. On the other hand, local assemblies that developed out of the structure of the egalitarian, kin-based segments regulated the internal affairs of the local groups and the nested segments within the tribe.

---

[13] A French translation is kept in the Bureau of the Midelt Circle. The document was initially given to the qaid of the Ait Ayash during boundary settlements with the neighboring Ait Mouli. After the settlement with the Ait Mouli in favor of the Ait Ayash, the Ait Sidi Bou Moussa planned to claim all the land in private title. Their claim was rejected and the appended note added that the authenticity of the document was questioned (Midelt Archives: Translation of land deed of the Ait Sidi Bou Moussa [undated] with note appended).

[14] In the census of 1936, the population of Idendel is given as 263 individuals.

THE JMAA: PATRIARCHAL ASSEMBLY

Each qsar of the Ait Ayash was autonomous in its affairs and was governed by its *jmaa* (assembly, council), composed of the men who were notable by community consensus. In the ideal central Atlas political model, the jmaa comprised the heads of all the households of a permanent settlement or a camping unit, who gathered in public forum for discussion and resolution of community problems with unanimous decisions. The acephalous and diffused authority structure was extended to higher level agnatic segments of the tribe. Selected members from local councils (*ijmaa,* pl.), chosen by the council members themselves, represented their groups on the next level forming a jmaa for the ighs. In turn, elected members from all the ighsan councils formed an assembly for the tribe. On the higher level segments the council elected an amghar with delegated authority over the representative group. In the ideal system, and in some actual cases, the amghar was elected annually with rotation of candidates from the lower segments in order to insure the diffusion of authority. Some Ait Ayash informants gave me this model for their organization, although when pressed for details admitted that it had not worked that way in the remembered past since they had their permanent khalifa appointed over them. The village of the Ait Sidi Bou Moussa practiced this rotation system. They elected an annual headman in turn from the three agnatic segments within the village.

In addition, chiefs were elected for specific purposes such as war (*amghar n'baroud*), irrigation works (*amghar n'tergwa*), pastoralist migrations and communal projects. Their authority lasted for the duration of the project. The system assured impermanence of power. For informants, it represented the way authority ought to have been delegated whether or not it was actually practiced.

In the case of the Ait Ayash the permanent chief with the government seal subverted the tribal authority system on the highest level. Only the local assemblies remained functional.

The formation of the assembly of any qsar called for neither elections nor appointment of its members. Generally all those deemed worthy to speak for the village formed the council. The number of members was not predetermined. Each tighst (minimal descent group) had at least one representative. A council member held tenure as long as he enjoyed the respect or deference of the community. Meetings took place as the occasions demanded in the public chamber within the village main gate or in open forum. Regular concerns were the containment of conflicts, the enforcement of the tribal code and the schedules of communal tasks. The council also supervised inheritance settlements and arranged the collective oaths for jural settlements.

Production tasks were periodically delegated to one man, known as the *muqaddam n'tergwa* (supervisor of irrigation). Muqaddam was a lesser title than amghar n'tergwa who was responsible for the whole tribe. The muqaddam n'tergwa supervised the order of water allocation, the rotation schedules for the daily communal herding of the cattle and draft animals, and the turns for duty as night guardian of the qsar gate. Village gates were locked and guarded during the night hours. The muqaddam also organized the work parties for repair of the irrigation ditches and collected the fines (*izmazz*) on behalf of the jmaa for infractions, destruction of fields by grazing animals, and omission of duties.

The Ait Ayash elders recall the assembly for the tribe with less assurance, since, they say, it met only rarely because its duties were pre-empted by the appointed tribal khalifa. Moreover, inter-village feuds frequently effaced social cohesion. The occasions that called the tribal council together were the times of intertribal conflict when an amghar n'baroud was chosen for the battle. That was a role their khalifa, Hmad n'ait Abbi, never assumed.

PARAMOUNT CHIEF: AMBIVALENCE IN SUBMISSION

From the 1880's through the first decade of this century, the Ait Ayash had a paramount chief in Hmad n'ait Abbi who maintained his position through his appointment as khalifa (deputy) to the Ait Youssi qaid. Hmad n'ait Abbi is always referred to, in the many stories that survive about him, as the khalifa and never as amghar to stress that his was an external appointment and not a tribal office.

His career exemplifies the dialectical relations the tribes maintained with the makhzan. His appointment by the sultan nominally incorporated the taqbilt as a taxpaying, *naiba* tribe. One advantage in siding with the makhzan was that qaids received arms from the government which were superior to the weapons available to siba tribes. At the same time, the khalifa acted more often as a loyal agent of the Derkawi shaikh, Sidi Mhand al Arabi, who opposed the sultan, than as a deputy who represented the interests of the makhzan. Many Ait Ayash consistently claimed that the qualification which put him in office was the endorsement of Sidi Mhand al Arabi, who as mentor of the Ait Ayash and all the Ait Yafelman, was their 'true voice'.

Men remembered stories told by their fathers of the last meeting with Mawlay Hassan in 1893. Hmad n'ait Abbi fled at his approach. The Ait Ayash were the first Yafelman tribe by location to be confronted by the sultan after the plots against the Ait Youssi qaid and Mawlay Serrou. Members of Hmad's tighst searched for him and found him in a mountain hideout from where they led him, bound, to face the sultan. The elder of his descent group who related this account added, "The tribe listened to him when he gave orders, and if he had been right he should not fear the sultan. If he had been wrong, the blame was his. This was not time to leave the tribe helpless."

During this last expedition of Mawlay Hassan a French physician, F. Linares, had accompanied the sultan and kept a diary of the journey's events. At the encampment on the Ansegmir, Linares wrote:

> Les griefs de S. M. Cherifienne contre les Aït Aïach sont graves et nombreux. Il faut procéder à un reglement de comptes. Comme membres de la confédération des Ain [sic] Yafelman, les Aït Aïach ont participé au meurtre du Caid Mohamed Ould Taleb. Après la mort de ce dernier, ils ont dépouillé et désarmé les soldats réguliers qui étaient détachés auprès du Caid. De plus, ces mêmes Aït Aïach ont pris part, en 1888, avec les Ait Chokhman, au meurtre de Moulay Serou, oncle du Sultan. Ils ont, à la même date, en encore alliés aux Ait Shokhman, mis en deroute la colonne de Si Mohammed Seghir, Secretaire pour l'armée. Telles sont les fautes. Quels vont être les châtiments? Voici: le Sultan exige la restitution de tous les fusils volés aux soldats en garnison alors dans la Casbah du Maghzen, laquelle se trouve en face de notre campement. Cette restitution opérée, on pourra donner l'aman et nommer des caids pris dans la tribu des Ait Aiach, comme ils le désirent (Linarès 1932:16).

The outcome of the meeting has already been described. Hmad was granted pardon and reinvested as khalifa. The tribe paid fines according to household land holdings. The rationale for the amnesty rested in identifying the source of the dissidence in the figure of Sidi Mhand al Arabi. The sultan Mawlay Hassan explained his lenience in a statement quoted in Linares' diary, when the expedition reached other Yafelman tribes farther south.

> Puisque vous venez au devant de moi faire amende honorable et implorer l'aman, je suis persuadé, ainsi, qu'on me l'assure, que vous avez été poussés dans la voie de la rébellion par Si Mohamed Ben al Arbi Derkaoui, fauteur de désordres et dont Allah vous a enfin délivrés (mort au Décembre 1891). Vos torts sont donc moins graves que si vous avez agi de votre propre mouvement . . . (Linarès 1932:21).

THE LEGAL AND MORAL ORDER

The sum of the traditional methods for upholding social order among the Ait Ayash was known as the *abrid* (path or road) of the tribe. The abrid was embodied in the customary izref. This legal code was unwritten, but from time to time new rules (*qanoun*) were added which were written down by a taleb for accurate transmission. A select group of elders who retained the code in memory were known as *ait al haqq* (men of truth), and served as final arbiters in determining the rules of the code.

Kinship relationships and descent group alignments ordered among the Ait Ayash, and among all Atlas groups, the allocation of responsibility for enforcement of the izref of the tribe. The process has been described for the Kabyle region of the Maghreb as an 'ethos of honour' which stands

> fundamentally opposed to a universal and formal morality which affirms the equality in dignity of all men and consequently the equality of their rights and duties. Not only do the rules imposed upon men differ from those imposed upon women, and the duties toward men differ from those toward women, but also the dictates of honour, directly applied to the individual case and varying according to the situation, are in no way capable of being made universal. It is the same code which lays down opposing modes of conduct according to the social sphere. . . .
>
> Honour, when it concerns kinsmen or those to whom one is allied, imposes a completely different line of conduct, but one that derives from the same principles: 'Help your own kinsmen,' runs the proverb, 'whether they are right or wrong.' The values of honour are part of the atmosphere breathed by the closely-knit group, the clan or village; thus the precepts of the morality of honour are obligatory in all aspects of private and public life (Bourdieu 1966:228).

Two mechanisms were central to the maintenance of this system, *diya* (the blood fine), and *tagella* (the collective oath). Both depend on and were co-extensive with kin-based alignments. The diya for homicide was set in the code of the Ait Ayash at 200 douros or 200 sheep. The transaction specified an agreement by two parties to settle a legal account while maintaining their honor and avoiding a wider social disruption.

The payment of diya predicated the equal status of the actors; it was the code between Imazighen. Blood payment settled loss of life involving families of the same minimal descent group, or families of different descent groups or qsour, or an Ayashi family and that of another tribe.

The payment in a case of closely related families was offered by the responsible individual and his immediate family. With greater kinship distance between the two sides, the fine was assumed by a wider network of kinsmen, up to the *ait ashra* which literally means the ten closest agnates but most often stood as coextensive with the minimal descent group (tighst).

In the case of homicide within a tighst, the five males in line of inheritance (*ait khamsa*) stood as substitutable for the perpetrator and fled the village for safety until the assembly negotiated for a fine settlement. In cases involving different tighsin, the ait ashra were vulnerable to vengeance and took refuge. If the case involved different villages, only the murderer, without family, took flight.

According to the code, the offender in most cases paid half the fine and his ait khamsa or ait ashra, according to the situation, the other half. The distribution of the fine was shared equally, on the other side, by the immediate family of the victim and the appropriate kin group.

The clarity of the rules does not presuppose rigid adherence to them. In actual cases group involvement and compensation took into account the relative community positions of the two sides. As one local sage put it, "The settlement of diyas was up for bargaining, like taking a cow to the *souq* (market) for sale".

The unpredictable flaring of violence prevalent in the tribal areas, easily escalated to blood feuds which could be brought to an end by the diya. This did not apply to the state of war which was a formally planned encounter with site and date agreed upon. The outcome of a battle gave a winning side. Losses were not reckoned on a debit-credit basis. Formal wars were rare. Most of the violence was in the nature of feuds. In the recollections, extended feuds were as frequent as diya settlements.

One Ayashi elder remembered a blood feud which began with a personal dispute over money, and would have been extended in time, he thought, had it not been arrested by the establishment of the French administration and the 'end of siba'. His father's brother had sold two sheep with deferred payment to an Ayashi from another qsar for a marriage feast. When the two met later at the market of Bou Draa his uncle asked for payment and was refused. In anger he fired at the man and paralyzed him in the legs. He was fined the price of a bull by the guardians of the market for disturbing the peace.

After some time, the informant's uncle was shot and killed by the paralyzed man while passing near his village. Subsequently the brother of the victim with other members of the family including the informant set out for vengeance. They found a close kinsman of the brother's assailant working his fields and killed him. This took place at the inception of the Protectorate and this effectively dissipated the feud, which the informant said, would have continued until both sides felt the account was balanced.

Feuding did not necessarily attest to heavy loss of life. Segonzac, in 1901, commented on the furious energy of a close combat he witnessed between two clans of another tribe and the minimal injuries incurred. He explained this in part as a result of the inferior quality gunpowder, although he thought the weapons were effective, and the method of firing, but most importantly as one of intent.

> Il voudrait blesser grievement son adversaire sans le tuer; s'il l'achève c'est que la furer l'aveugle, car la loi de la guerre veut que toute mort soit vengée par une autre mort, celle du meurtrier de préférence à toute autre. Aucune paix n'est possible entre fractions dont le compte n'est pas égal (Segonzac 1903:111).

The diya provided an alternative form for balancing accounts.

A second mechanism for conflict resolution was the collective oath, a legal procedure for establishing guilt or innocence in the absence of witnesses. The oath called for a collective response from a portion of the community with a moral and practical commitment that served to resolve a case.[15]

The procedure required a number of co-jurors (*imgillan*) to testify at a sanctified site that an accused is innocent. It was a method for determining whether an accusation was true or false by invoking supernatural sanctions. If the co-jurors testified according to a prescribed formula then the accused was considered innocent. If the accused could not get the proper number of co-jurors, or if the co-jurors made a mistake in reciting the oath, then he was considered guilty and he was obliged to make the reparation to the injured party that is specified in the customary law.

The oath was invoked for all kinds of accusations. The tribal code established the number of co-jurors required for each case according to the gravity of the allegation. Accusation of murder of a male demanded 40 co-jurors, that of a female 20 co-jurors, accusation of theft fewer numbers. The closest kinsmen stood as the core of the co-jural group of an accused, but any community member could participate when requested with an offering of tamghrost. The request for co-juror was not easily refused, and gathered a coalition who were known as the ait ashra of the accused, actual and ritual agnates who did not stand to inherit, but were held responsible for a part of the reparation in the case the oath failed. As a legal mechanism the collective oath stressed the solidarity of close-kin alliances for containing initiated or potential violence. The procedure reflected the moral universe of the 'ethos of honor' where the central concern is not with abstract justice but with restoration of social equilibrium by the resolution of ambiguous situations. But the solidarity of the co-juring group had to account for transcendental sanctions, so that the oath did not necessarily lead to the dominance of a strong party over a weak one.

---

[15] An exhaustive analysis of the collective oath is offered in Gellner (1969).

The co-jurors for an accused individual need not be centrally concerned with 'what really happened' in forming their individual decisions to offer support against the accusing party. On the other hand, the coalition of close kinsmen was not automatic in every accusation against one of their own. The corporateness of an accused party's group was tried and tested on each occasion according to the perceived merits of the accused. The proverb "Help your own kinsmen whether they are right or wrong" was not an infallible guide to legal opinions. The belief in supernatural retribution for perjury remained, as a general premise, a force in decisions. This is not to say that it explained the system. By definition, the co-jurors were not witnesses to the case. What they offered was an endorsement of the character and overall behavior of the accused. Moreover their decisions remained sensitive to a number of factors that included an assessment of the determination of the opposing party, their own economic responsibility in case of failure, and others, that prevented an automatic coalition on the "Help your own" principle. The odds favored such a coalition, but there were times when an offender became a risk to his group. Then ways were found to forego the oath.

The theory of the participants accounted for the system in terms of supernatural sanctions. The local belief held that God or the saint before whom the oath is given will punish perjurers. This made the procedure a good way to determine truth, because co-jurors would not risk perjury.

But people did swear 'falsely'. A feature of the collective oath was the perception of divine retribution meted out to the wider community rather than the responsible individual. A natural disaster or social disequilibrium became, after the fact, supernatural punishment. Moreover, the coalition of a strong party determined to win every case eventually lost its credibility with others.

Members of the Ait Ayash clans which had accepted the Ait Bougman clan with a pact, attributed the failure of the market of Bou Draa to the false oaths taken by the Ait Yahia on Ahsin after their incorporation. The Ait Yahia on Ahsin had gained a reputation as a strong and cohesive group that offered unquestioned protection to its members, with oaths before the tomb of Sidi Aish, a local saint's monument on the Ansegmir. But some time later, the group fissioned and one subfraction set up the new qsar of Tabnallat. Divisive quarrels followed. By the early years of the Protectorate period many of the original families had dispersed, very likely in refusing submission to the French. In the view of the other Ayashis this was a matter of divine retribution.

An elder of Ait Oumghar said, "They lacked respect for the sanctity of Sidi Aish and would perjure themselves out of every situation. They felt strong enough to do these things, but in the end they began quarreling amongst themselves. When they appealed for allies no other group was willing to help neither one tighst nor the other. This is how God decided to destroy them, by setting them apart from each other with no support. The market was discontinued because of their quarrels and when the French arrived they were still fighting each other."

The segmentary organization favored the efficacy of the collective oath through complementary oppositions. The opposition of unequal segments brought forth ephemeral pacts that tended to restore balance. Ranked segments did not develop. In the absence of institutions with coercive sanctions, the collective oath and the blood fine contained violence and maintained the social order in which positions of status remained generalized and distinctions of rank, apart from the shurfa and the igblin, were lacking.

SUMMARY REMARKS: SEGMENTARITY, CORPORATENESS AND CONTRACT

Before summing up features of the social formation of the Ait Ayash, some remarks are in order on the general theories that have been applied to Atlas tribal organization.

R. Montagne (1930), described the crucial order—maintenance mechanism as a permanent arrangement of two political moieties, *leffs*. Each leff aligned discontinuous segments of the populations of the settled tribes into a region-wide alliance system. Conflict within one tribe or between two tribes could be checked by the mobilization of balanced segments of the political moieties. So long as the alliance system remained operative and in balanced opposition, the autonomous little 'republics' maintained their integrity without an overarching political authority. The contractual alliance system of permanent leffs reported for the western Atlas region has not been found in the eastern High Atlas and the Middle Atlas regions. Alliances and pacts were crucial mechanisms for social alignments but did not involve region-wide participation nor become permanent political affiliations.

The second general theory holds the more familiar principle of social segmentation: the order maintenance inherent in the internal structure of a segmentary society. Gellner (1969) constructs a paradigm of a "remarkably pure, symmetrical and egalitarian segmentary system" (Ibid. 1968) for the organization of the central Atlas.

Segmentary, behavior first of all, can mean a general disposition in political life, and secondly, can be defined in a narrower sense as a feature of unilineal descent group formations. In the first case, segmentarity is a nearly universal feature of social organization, or so widespread as to be virtually so. Such a general disposition cannot explain particular social configurations. In the second sense, segmentarity has been conceptualized as a functional characteristic of a wide number of societies with unilineal descent groups. Segmentary lineage theory in social anthropology has dealt with such systems in subSaharan Africa and the connectedness of the internal components of the systems with detail and precision (Evans Pritchard: 1940; and Middleton and Tait: 1958). Social structural analysis has stressed the relationship between the parts in terms of principles such as segmentarity which lend coherence to the system. While this approach narrows the use of the concept, an alternative view favors limiting the concept of segmentary lineage still further. In this latter view the term is better restricted to a very few societies whose particular organization serves as a "social means of intrusion and competition in an already occupied ecological niche" (Sahlins 1961). The development of such an organization presupposes the existence of unilineal descent groups as an outcome of the repetitive, long-term use of restricted resources.

Kinship examined as a social system has the characteristics, according to general system theory, of an open system; it is contantly dependent on inputs from the environment in which it is located (Bertalanffy 1969: 124–125). The environment of the Atlas tribes, for example, included both the specific adaptations to the resource base, the local economies, and the political pressures of the central state, historical events. The cognized model for social cohesion was remarkably uniform regionwide but subject to both ecological and social factors which kept it open-ended and flexible.

The argument for restricting the term 'segmentary lineage system' to a limited number of ethnographic cases featuring a full complex of characteristics such as lineality, segmentation, segmentary sociability, complementary opposition and structural relativity (Sahlins 1961) has the advantage of shifting attention to adaptive factors in a regional context, and the specific environmental pressures that shaped local formations.

The eastern Atlas societies had the uniformity of a linguistic bloc (Tamazight), the unity of an historical tradition (Sanhaja), and a diversity of social adaptations. The complement of characteristics of a segmentary lineage organization emerged in the case of an expanding population in an already fully exploited niche. A signal case in the eastern Atlas is the Ait Atta confederation of the pre-Saharan oases and the southeastern mountains. Their segmentary organization served as a mechanism for fusion and consolidation on a larger scale than was possible for the occupants of the contested space (cf. Dunn 1972).

This does not argue against the characterization of Atlas tribes as segmentary. Segmentary behavior as such is a tendency to change the scope of alignments in competitive situations. Segmentary behavior as a widespread feature of political activity operated, as in the legal procedure of the collective oath and the collective responsibility for the diya, to restore equilibrium. The full segmentary lineage system as a social means for predatory expansion disturbs the political equilibrium. Segmentation on different levels of interaction held wide currency, but the segmentary lineage system remained a specific adaptation of rare incidence. Segmentary behavior was also expressed in contractual alliances that could crosscut, and temporarily cancel the formal kinship order.

Another modification of the segmentary order of a formal descent group system was effected by the permanent units for productive activities, specifically qsour or pastoral camping units, according to the economic strategy. These organizational units remained corporate, irrespective of the subdivisions within them and the higher level segments between them and the top political sphere.

Gellner, who has presented that most cogent analysis of rural Moroccan segmentary organization based on descent group constructions, does recognize this feature of Atlas tribes, although his analysis is not directly concerned with specific adaptations. He discusses a case of a 'bad', that is to say unjustified, fratricide wherein blood money is owed by the killer to the wider group of which he and the victim are members.

> This possibility shows how this tribal society does not altogether conform to the ideal type of a pure segmentary society, in which groups existed only in opposition to other co-ordinate groups. It shows a group possessing a kind of corporate identity in opposition to its own erring members.
> There are other, analogous respects in which Berber groups of about village size (300 people or so) are not 'purely' segmentary but do have a corporate existence vis-à-vis individuals or sub-groups, (as opposed to the 'pure' segmentary situation in which groups are 'activated' into overt existence only by opposition to other co-ordinate groups at the same level) (Gellner 1969: 116n).

The corporateness of the Ait Ayash qsour over their sub-groups and persons is expressed in a possibly apocryphal account of a 'good' fratricide that took place in one of the qsour.

The events, in outline, begin with the decision of the village, through its jmaa, to rid itself of one of the families which by community consensus had become insupportable. Charges leveled against it were not specifically uniform in different accounts, but they included usury, illegal appropriation of fields, endemic quarrels, and 'enormous wealth'. By decision of the assembly members from all the tighsatin including the family's own, a date was set (a detail recalled with precision) for a dinner to which the family's adult males were invited and then killed. The women with their children were sent back to their natal families, and the property divided among all the participants. The story has a legendary cast in that important aspects of it such as the charges calling for the ultimate sanction are lost to memory. All the versions stressed the independent stance and power of the family. The penultimate sanction of exile, they argued, would have attached them to another group from where they would remain rivalrous. The suggestion they may have willingly moved to a community more congenial to them was unacceptable, since it would have shown their need for protection from strangers, a sign of weakness. "They felt strong enough to give protection to others, and would never have placed themselves in a position of weakness," a member of their tighst explained.

One of their unsociable actions had been to build a separate dwelling outside the qsar as a defiant gesture both to enemies and the community. Later, during a period when the Beni Mgild were raiding Ayashi villages, they were asked by the jmaa to return for the defense of the qsar. They returned, but remained recalcitrant to the order of the qsar.

The story unfolded in time when one of the surviving children reached maturity and came back to seek vengeance; this coincided with the early years of the Protectorate. Pax Gallica failed to recognize the corporate authority of the qsar and on the assumption of permitting the operation of traditional instituations, supported the claimant to the exaction of diya from the seven participant households.

The foregoing account should make evident that the Ait Ayash socio-political organization depended on a diversity of principles for its validation. The local-territorial groups of the qsour stood as self-managed entities, but relations with neighboring populations were carried out, not as a series of farming villages, but as a tribe of the same order as other tribes. The tribe of the Ait Ayash can be defined as a compromise between a descent-phrased segmentary structure and a territorially based formation. The phrasing distorts the actors' own perception of social construction. The taqbilt, more properly refers to a culturally specific category which was used to establish a claim to a common social identity. The basis for this claim derived from several sources.

Territoriality and local contiguity provided the commitment to

SOCIO-POLITICAL ORGANIZATION 61

the shared name, but not the explanation of the political design. The most palpable basis for socio-political cohesion came from genealogical connections and patrilineal descent. The Ait Ayash carried this basis to the level of the ighsan, which formed putative descent groups. Their coherence on the level of the taqbilt relied on the shared name rather than common ancestry.

Nested descent and residential groups, and contractual alliances on all levels, maintained a segmentary structure which contributed to an extremely flexible, open-ended political formation for managing control over resources and ordering antagonistic factions within the taqbilt and outside it.

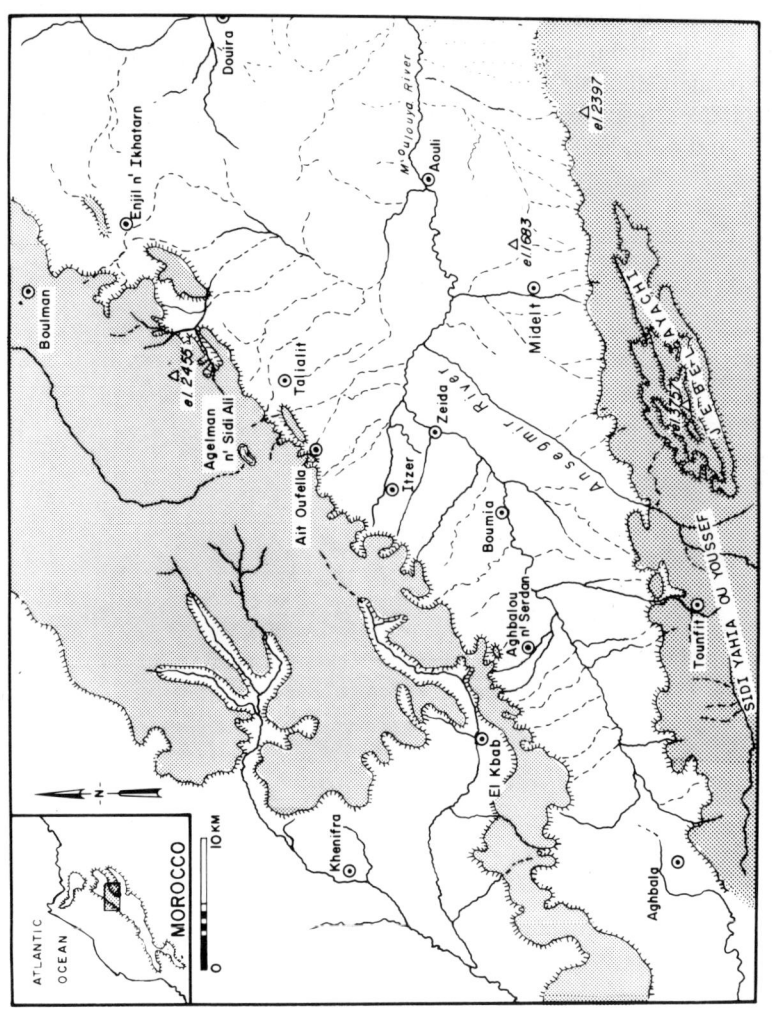

Map 6. The High Moulouya Plain.

CHAPTER THREE

Regional Ecology and Local Groups

This chapter focuses on the regional ecology of the High Moulouya plains and the land tenure system of the Ait Ayash and the other local groups. The traditional economies of the High Moulouya tribes are described, with special reference to the changes that followed the establishment of the Protectorate. A final section deals with the demographic patterns of the region. The principal sources used for this chapter are reports and census data in the Bureau of the Midelt Circle (cited as from the Midelt Archives), and the published studies of Raynal (1960) and Noin (1970). The schematization of the local group economies is drawn from Raynal (1960).

The intermontane plain of the High Moulouya is a region of some 9,200 km² within the angle of divergence of the central Middle Atlas and the eastern High Atlas chains. Situated in the geographical center of Morocco, it comprises the high valley of the Moulouya River and the surrounding slopes of the mountain masses, through which numerous passes, west and south, connect it to other regions (Map 6). As a natural zone it is distinct from contiguous regions: the Middle Atlas to the west with more humid and higher altitudes, the Missour basin of the Middle Moulouya plain (900 m in altitude), the barren high plateaus to the east, and the preSaharan Tafilalt region to the south. The plain, at an average altitude of 1,500 m, belongs, in Emberger's classification, to the Mediterranean arid climatic zone.[1] General characteristics are low rainfall and high evaporation, due to strong winds and elevated temperatures. The

---

[1] Emberger (1930, 1934) uses a formula which takes into account rainfall, the mean minimum temperature of the coldest month and the mean maximum temperature of the hottest month to distinguish, within the broad Mediterranean climatic sequence, the following regions: saharan, arid, semi-arid, sub-humid, humid, high mountain.
See also Martin, Jover, Lecoz, Maurer and Noin (1967) for bioclimatic regions of Morocco.

vegetation is of the so-called steppe type with two different associations. On the better drained soils of the eastern sector the dominant species is *Stipa tenacissima* (*halfa,* arab.), often being the only plant surviving the summer. On the western portion of poorly drained soils *Artemisia herba-alba* (*izri,* tamaz.; *shih,* arab.) is dominant. Both plant communities are very open (Durham University 1956: 53–71; Despois 1964: 73–96).

The most marked climatic characteristic of the High Moulouya is the atmospheric dryness. Humidity rarely reaches 60 percent and most frequently descends to 30 percent in all seasons. This trait contributes to the crusty cover over large stretches of the land, which, in turn, leads to diurnal temperature fluctuations of 20 °C both in the summer and winter seasons. Frost is common during the nights from November until April.

Within the basin and along the higher altitude slopes and the westernmost extension of the steppe zone, internal variations in relief, temperatures and rainfall create a number of microenvironments. The most significant variation for the local economies is the rainfall pattern. The plain is divided by an alignment north-northeast and south-southwest from Itzer to Boumia, along the right bank of the Moulouya and the eastern boundary of the Aarid plateau, and the right bank of the Oudghes to Tounfit. West of this line, annual rainfall exceeds 300 mm and increases considerably at the western headwaters of the Moulouya. To the east of it, in the territory of the Ait Ayash and north of the town of Midelt, rainfall reaches 200 mm at best. The western topography acts as a catchment depriving the eastern plains which are lower by 200 to 300 mm of more regular precipitation.

Three bioclimatic zones can be distinguished within the High Plain (Raynal 1961: 273–74).
1) The plains east of the Itzer-Boumia line where rainfall rests below 250 mm (Midelt: 226 mm). Precipitation is regular during the three months of autumn and spring, with little moisture in December and January. Temperature variations are tied to the topography, with a minimum of 0 °C to −5 °C and a maximum of 40 °C. Snow is rare.
2) The western sector, from Itzer in the north to Aghbala in the southwest. Precipitation varies from 300 mm (Itzer: 372 mm) to 600 mm. Snow lasts several days; at Aghbala the ground remains snow-covered for 30 or more days. Seasonal temperatures are appreciably the same as those of the eastern sector.
3) The mountain border zones of the Middle and High Atlas where similar altitudes receive different amounts of moisture as a function of location and relief. The Middle Atlas border is snow-covered for up to 30 days. The eastern High Atlas side at Tounfit (alt. 1,980 m; rainfall 368 mm) has snow on the ground for a maximum of 20 days. The

spring and autumn rains are lighter than those of the western plains. The annual averages are approximately the same by the added water brought by summer storms on the higher slopes.

A different plant association dominates the cover of each zone. The eastern plains support the steppe cover of esparto grass (halfa) with some white wormwood (shih). The borders of this zone east of the Aouli basin mark the first appearance of pre-Saharan plant associations. The western plains are dominated by several species of Artemisia and other xerophytes with no steppe grasses. The mountain slopes hold remnants of forests in two altitudinal zones. The lower zone, at altitudes of 1,700 to 2,100 m on the Middle Atlas slopes, and 1,700 to 2,200 m on the Higher Atlas, supports the scrub juniper (*Juniperus phoenicia*), highly resistant to dryness, and the holm-oak and thuya. The second zone overlaps at 1,900 to 2,300 m on the Middle Atlas and 2,000 to 2,400 m on the High Atlas with the cedar (*Cedrus atlantica*) and the juniper.

Soils and soil formation are subject to the intensity of heat and cold, the feeble density of the plant cover, sudden scouring downpours, and the high evaporation rate. The Moulouya is naturally a high sediment yield watershed (Carter 1966), a condition which has been accelerated with the agricultural expansion that followed where the transhumant groups of the western sector become sedentary farmers. Good agricultural land is scarce. The limited soil-rich plots give place to pebbly surfaces, or compact rock, or impacted clays that cannot soak up moisture.

In balance against these conditions, the perennial courses of the Moulouya, Ansegmir, Outat and Oudghes rivers and the many mountain springs on the northern slopes of the eastern High Atlas have provided a base for agricultural production.

The High Moulouya lacks, however, a long tradition of permanent settlements. The present populations date their occupation from the 19th century. For the known period since the inception of the Alawite dynasty, it had remained a staging area for the continuous migrations of southern populations toward the lowlands of the northwest. Two major migration routes crossed the plain. The first traversed the eastern high plateaus from Algeria toward the Atlantic coast. The second, and most active historically, is that of the Tamazight-speaking Sanhaja tribes spilling out of the plains and oases of the south in search of pastures. The plain had also formed an important juncture in the trade routes (*triq sultan*) between the imperial cities and the southern entrepot of Tafilalt. This had led to the periodic intervention of the makhzan in reordering regional political alignments with forced population transfers. Ecologically and politically the region formed a transitional zone. In the early years of the 20th century, the various adaptations of Moulouya groups with respect to localized resources consisted of tribes of agriculturalists (Ait Ayash, Ait Izdeg, and Ait Ouafella), pastoralist qsour dwellers (Ait Yahia, Ait Arfa, and Ait Youssi), transhumant pastoralists (the five tribes of the Beni Mgild: Ait Messaoud, Ait Bougman, Ait Mouli, Ait Ougadir, Irklaouen, and the Ait Ihand), and nomadic pastoralists (Oulad Khawa, and Morghbad) (Map 7.)

The predominant economic activity of eastern and central Morocco, the domain of the Tamazight-speaking bloc, was transhumant pastoralism. Within this bloc, two broad ecological zones were distinguished in the complementary expressions of *asamar* and *amalou*. Amalou ('in the shade', i.e., north) connoted the regions of rich pastures in contrast to the dry, southern plateaus and slopes of asamar ('in the sun'). The watershed of the Moulouya belonged, in this repartition of pastoral resources, on the amalou side, a gate to the humid plateaus of the Middle Atlas.

LAND TENURE AND LAND USE

The land tenure system of the Moulouya Plain was that of siba tribes. Land categories and land tenure in pre-colonial Morocco varied according to the political status of the tribes. Tribes in central Morocco were defined in terms of their relationship to the central government as tamazight, naiba and gish. The land rights they held were extensions of their political status. Tamazight tribes won land by right of conquest. Gish and naiba tribes maintained land rights through their specific ties with the makhzan. Since political status fluctuated over time, the tenure system that applied also changed.

Leaving aside the categories of naiba and gish tribes, and the urban centers where Islamic law (*shraa/sharia*) applied, the tamazight tribes used concepts of communal property and collective usufruct.

Collective land is that which a group won by conquest and which all the males of the group exploited in joint usufruct. The members' use shares could not be sold or alienated from the collectivity. The land was property of the whole group and stood as the material manifestation of the solidarity of the group and the equality of its members (Vinogradov 1974: 87–88).

In social settings of material scarcity and political instability, such as the siba zones of Morocco, tribal organization and communal property, or restricted land access through equal use rights of members, provided a tenable solution to land distribution that neither totally unrestricted access nor totally restricted access (private property) could meet. The corporate land holding tribe organized at the same time

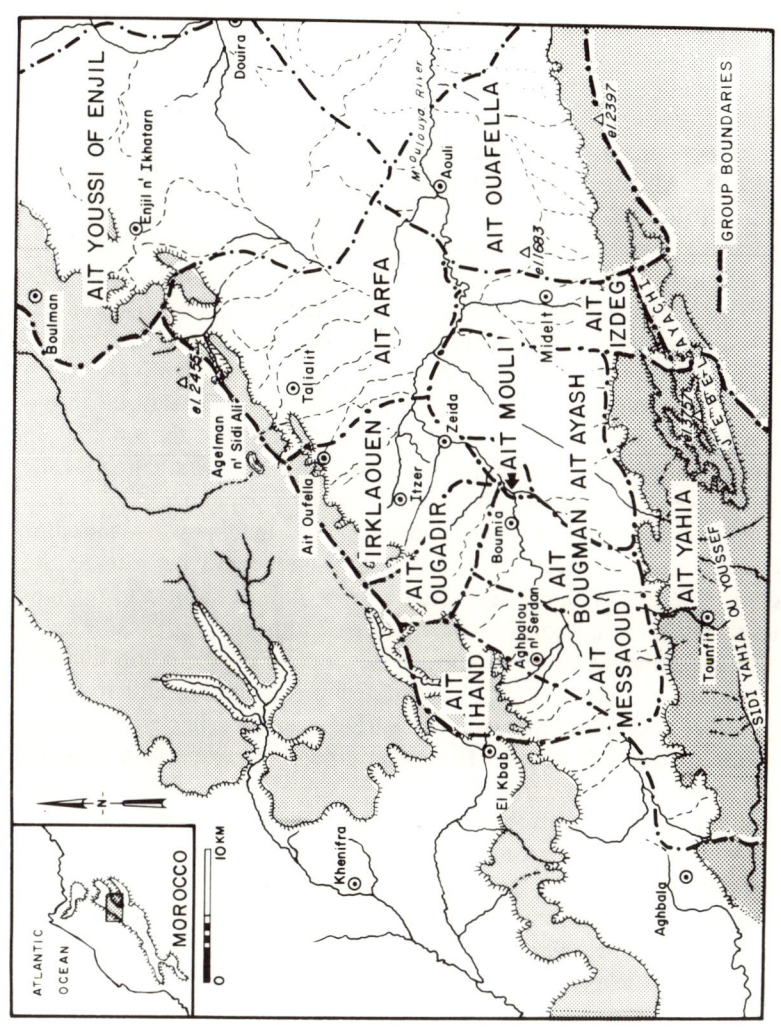

Map 7. Populations of the High Moulouya Plain.

group activity through the agnatic descent structure. The periodic allotment of shares in pastures and farmland to the internal segments and households of the collectivity inhibited economic stratification and maintained the egalitarian disposition of the political formation.

Collective ownership of all productive land has been widely reported for pastoralist and mixed economy tribes among both Berber-speaking and Arabic-speaking populations of pre-Protectorate Morocco. This system was followed in the Moulouya plain with an important modification.

Land tenure in the High Moulouya placed irrigated land (*iyran daw n'tergwa,* tamaz.) in the category of family property held in individual title. All other productive land, whether cultivated or not, was collective (*blad jmaa,* arab.)[2] with use rights to tribal members. The territory of any tribe included four categories: irrigated fields, plowland, pastures, and unexploitable surfaces that formed a 'no man's land' between tribal territories. The holdings that a group defended *bi'l baroud* (with gunpowder, battle) were its communal property.

The concept of individual property in the Moulouya plain met a specific contextual ecological problem faced by the specialized intensive farming communities: the non-extendable limits of the small-scale irrigation systems. Individual property was not a relevant category for the other local economies. Among the groups dependent on animal husbandry and extensive farming, tribal territorial claims expanded or contracted as a function of group size. Land could be won at the expense of weaker neighbors. Boundaries remained subject to realignments through armed contests or alliances and pacts.

In the small-scale communities dependent on irrigation agriculture, a contradiction appears between group recruitment and access to the productive base. The irrigated surface remains fixed while total group size recruited through the agnatic descent segments varies according to demographic fortunes. If collective usufruct rights were applied, then either the number of viable household shares in land would have to be extendable to meet group expansion, or the group would have to be maintained with a ceiling on its size. Since the extension of the irrigated surface remained technically unfeasible, the number of households in the tribe had to be maintained at the carrying capacity of the production base. Berber tribal organization lacked any ranking within its segments to allow privileged access. Membership conferred equal status to all male household heads. Therefore, some other social mechanism had to regulate group size. This mechanism was household property titles which shifted responsibility for acquiring irrigated land

---

[2]Blad jmaa was first used in the Protectorate period by French administrators to apply to collective lands. The Tamazight term for collective holdings in *tamazirt n' taqbilt,* the territory of the tribe; or *tamazirtnun,* our territory.

to the individual householders.³ Tribal membership was a necessary but not sufficient condition for securing this land. It was necessary because security was maintained through the tribal organization.

The Ait Ayash of the Ansegmir exemplify this problem. The irrigation works of the valley could water 1,600 ha of fields which supported some 800 households in an evenly spaced distribution of 20 settlements. This was the surface available to the tribe, although an additional 500 ha was held by the zawiya Sidi Hamza. The allotment of roughly two-hectare shares was met through the individual titles to the fields. Fields were secured through inheritance or through purchase from other members of the tribe; they remained unobtainable to outsiders. The customary law specified inheritance of the father's estate in equal shares by the male offspring. The fragmentation of family land in each generation meant that some had to add to their holdings for viable subsistence production from those who sold their shares and dropped out of the economic community. Since all tribes maintained open recruitment, those who could no longer secure sufficient irrigated land joined other groups.

Individual title to irrigated fields was a qualified form of private property. Private property (*melk*) is recognized by Islamic law but it did not apply as such to siba tribes. Land ownership was tied to tribal membership. Rights of purchase remained exclusive to those defined as Ait Ayash. Priority of claims was granted to close agnates, but the key qualification was tribal membership.

Two sets of changes affected the economic life of the Moulouya region after the pacification program of the French Protectorate. The first was the general policy of discouraging transhumance for security reasons. The second was a wide ranging program of rationalizing agricultural practices, including land rights. The French administration made efforts to create uniform legal land categories and to codify the indigenous land tenure system. The aims of these efforts were contradictory. One central motive was the desire to make indigenous land available for colonization. This carried a sense of urgency because the pressure for colonization in the Atlantic plains was intense and there was a need to find legal mechanisms for land appropriation. Another motive was the felt obligation to protect the traditional life of the peasant. What followed was a confusion in land questions that is far from resolved today, especially in the Moulouya region (Raynal 1960: 301).

These changes transformed the transhumant economies in the plain and brought about new definitions of collective property and of private property. Collective land came to mean, after a series of redefinitions, the unimproved land belonging to a settlement, or a fraction,

---

³For a discussion of private property other than land, see Dowling (1975).

or a tribe with joint usufruct rights. Improved or cultivated land was redefined as joint property which could be divided among the members of the corporate group in shares that conferred private property rights.

The measures were slow in reaching the Moulouya. The crucial problem of administration in eastern Morocco had been security. In the 1930s, after the total submission of the province, the first task was to establish tribal boundaries in order to fix the groups on the ground. The official registration of collective land began in 1949. By this time the economy of the traditional transhumants had been completely transformed. The sedentaries were minimally affected by land conversion and kept all but the irrigated fields as tribal collectives. The sedentarized transhumants of the western sector (Beni Mgild tribes and Ait Ihand) with the need to maximize household agricultural production, and suspicious about eventual disposition of registered collectives, experienced a different perception of land rights. Awareness of the exproporiation of tribal collectives in the plains for colonization led to wholesale conversion of blad jmaa into melk.

> Le simple annonce des delimitations précipite la mise en culture de terres jusqu'alors considérées comme "mortes": tout se passait comme si l'on voulait mettre les autorités devant le fait accompli (Raynal 1960:302).

By 1949, the Ait Messaoud had apportioned all the worthwhile land between the douars and the households so that out of their territory of 34,000 ha they registered only 250 ha as collective land (Ibid.). The registration of titles was haphazard, and written deeds, even today, remain the exception. Surveys of land holdings that were carried out in order to implement a tax on production (*tertib*) collected during the Protectorate were not vigorously pursed in the Moulouya plain. Accurate production figures were less important to the administration than the gesture of submission symbolized by tax collection.

The Ait Ayash and the other traditional sedentaries claimed only the irrigated fields as melk. The ratio of melk to collective land is below ten percent among these groups. The plowing and sowing of collective land does not confer melk rights as it did among the sedentarized tribes of the western sector.

The collective land of the Ait Ayash today represents a kind of security, even without material returns. It provides the basis for whatever limited meaning can be attributed to their group identity. Ironically, the collectives appear to them as of increasing importance because they are not easily lost, like the irrigated fields, through sale.

AGRICULTURAL PRODUCTION

The principal agricultural production of the Moulouya plain is in cereal crops. In some few locations, such as the higher altitudes of the southern piedmont of the Ait Yahia, climatic rigor precludes any other crops. In the others, social precedents as much as ecological factors limit production to grains. Arboriculture has been practiced in a few qsour east of Midelt (Ait Ouafella) and among the Ait Arfa, both recognized in the local traditions as the oldest permanent settlements. Elsewhere the absence of fruit trees and gardens is striking. From the late 1960s outside urban investors have begun to plant apple orchards as commericial ventures.

Two harvests are typical for the region; *amenzou,* the winter cereals, and *amazouz,* the spring planting of the irrigated parcels (Map 8). Amenzou refers to the sowing of both irrigated and dry fields (*bour*), with different cereals on each. The winter grains are hard wheat, barley, soft wheat, and some rye among the Beni Mgild. The preferred subsistence cereal is hard wheat; that of the High Moulouya has renown for its superior quality. There may be some grounds for this claim, in that the rigorous winters control parasitic growths.

A biennial system of crop rotation is maintained on the irrigated fields. The cultivator divides his holdings into two equal sections. Each section is planted one season of the two each year, alternating between amazouz and amenzou. During the annual cycle one-half of the cultivator's holdings is sown in winter wheat and the other half in maize. This allows a fallow period of eight to nine months for each section every two years after the winter harvest. The amenzou on the irrigated strips is planted in October on the section that has been harvested of the maize planted in May. The winter crop on irrigated land is exclusively hard wheat. The spring planting is devoted largely to maize for feed and fodder and also some turnips, carrots, onions and legumes. Occasionally potatoes, first introduced to the region by the French, are also planted. In the qsour close to the town of Midelt a three crop system has been evolving, with vegetables and legumes grown for sale in the local market along with the spring maize and winter wheat.

The unirrigated fields are planted in winter cereals. The most reliable crop is barley, the hardiest of the grains. The second choice is soft wheat. Barley is scorned as food but its yield is more reliable than that of the other cereals. Even in a poor season barley provides an abundance of straw for fodder. The Ait Ayash sell their supplies when they consider their domestic animal needs adequate or more often when the need for petty cash drives them to it.

In newly plowed fields, especially west of Itzer in the higher

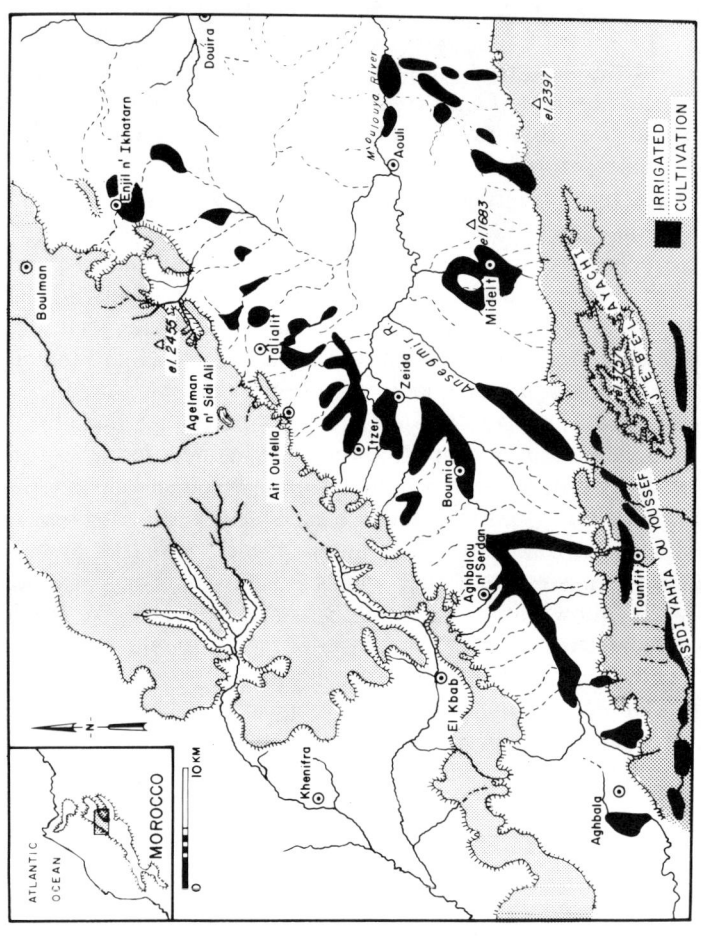

Map 8. Cultivation with irrigation in the High Molouya plain. Dry field cultivation is variable from year to year, and is not shown on the map.

Source: (Raynal 1960)

rainfall zone, hard wheat is sometimes sown the first few seasons, with initially high yields that decline rapidly. Fallow periods on bour vary widely according to location. The most favorable agricultural areas are sown every other year, in the pattern of the Atlantic plains. These areas are limited to the southwestern corner of the region (Ait Ihand and Ait Messaoud). Elsewhere fallow periods of two, three, five and even more years are required. In the eastern zone, fields plowed on the Aarid plain become exhausted after one or two harvests with permanent degradation of the land.

Among the pastoralists who have become sedentary farmers, agricultural land of the western zone is spread extensively across the group territories. The settlements are dispersed near the fields. The extensive farming activity of the western side of the plain has no historical depth. Farming among the Beni Mgild before the Protectorate was not an alternate source of subsistence but a marginal activity that guaranteed provisions in times of conflict and interruptions of the transhumant schedules.

After the suppression of transhumance the Beni Mgild and the Ait Ihand began extensive plowing. In 1936 they cultivated 7,300 ha. By 1950 they had plowed 33,500 ha (Raynal 1960:305).

In the driest zone of the irrigation agriculturalists, bour cultivation is practicable at some distance from the villages on the forest slopes of Jebel Ayashi. During siba it had formed a sporadic activity because of the insecurity. Recently it has been expanded with population pressure and the increasingly inadequate holdings in irrigated land. In 1960, the number of registered proprietors of irrigated land among the three tribes of the Ait Ayash, Ait Ouafella and Ait Izdeg was 2,993 with total holdings of 2,080 ha. Eighty-six percent had property of less than one ha; 13 percent owned from one to five ha; and one percent held more than five ha. For the same groups a total of 200 ha of dry farming was reported by 253 cultivators (Raynal 1960:318–319). This extremely low figure reflects incomplete registrations, a carryover from the Protectorate period when all production was taxed (tertib). More recent figures show a larger total surface with more cultivators, but the individual plots remain small.

Agricultural labor has been minimally affected by mechanization. A government agency, the Centre de Travaux, has a station in Itzer which provides mechanized equipment for rental. This benefits a very low number of cultivators on the western plains with large enough surfaces to merit the expense of tractors and harvesters. New land investments that receive government subsidies and technical aid are planted in fruit trees, specifically apple trees. These investments involve outsiders, urban merchants and government employees. Arboriculture demands a reorientation of techniques that selects out the local farmer who lacks the organizational basis for restructuring land use and labor. The local farmers are well aware of the potential and feasibility of these new cash crops on the land which provides with increasing resistance the traditional subsistence grains.

In 1966 the taxable agricultural household income for the province of Qsar es Souq was set by the Service des Impôts Ruraux at 7,400 DH. (about $1,480). This exempted 93 percent of the households in the province from taxation. The Midelt Cercle reported 27,932 income declarations, out of which 2,852 were subject to taxes (Midelt Archives: Rapport économique et social, 1967).

Crop yields vary widely according to soil grades, quality of management and especially annual rainfall. Reports are altogether inconsistent and information is lacking on the averages over the seven to ten year climatic cycle. The cultivators tend to treat the harvest of the exceptional year as the average. A 1966 report of Midelt Cercle gives average yields of six to 12 quintals per ha in wheat, eight to 14 quintals per hectare in barley, and eight to 15 quintals per hectare in maize. On rainfall plots the harvest of soft wheat gives from two to 12 quintals; on newly plowed fields with heavy rains harvests of 20 to 25 quintals per hectare have been known. The yields of the bour and irrigated fields of the Ait Ayash are generally comparable because of the lack of sufficient fertilizers on the two-crop fields. Chemical fertilizers made available by the *Sociétés cooperatives agricoles* remain economically prohibitive to the subsistence farmers, which is to say all.

The regulation of water rights in the qsour still falls under the care of the informal jmaas. Each jmaa delegates the management of the water division to a muqaddam n'tergwa. The rotation cycle between settlements sharing a channel varies between 15 and 20 days.

Among the Ait Ayash qsour the turn comes every 15 days for four to five days depending on village size. Internal division is prorated according to size of holdings. Where water is the commodity limiting cultivation, the water division is carried out on a 24 hour basis during the turn. Where arable space is the scarcer of the two resources, the division is regulated during daylight hours. Those with additional needs can draw on the supply during the night. The Ait Ayash have, in normal years, an adequate water supply.

The fields of the Ait Ayash are supplied by 11 main channels on both banks, so that political alignments as a function of water diversion never developed.

In another setting, settlements of a fraction of the Ait Youssi located in the contact zone on the Middle Atlas slopes and the plain developed political alliances over litigations concerning water access and the opposition between the higher altitude settlements and the lower settlements.

Matters of water control and its division have been kept out of the new administrative structure of present day villages. Each settlement still pays in kind the muqaddam n'tergwa with contributions from all the water users. During the period of fieldwork, three villages that shared a channel of the right bank organized work parties to clear the ditch which was silted up after spring rains. For the first time they decided to petition the qaid (government agent) for reimbursement, treating the task as labor on behalf of their rural commune (*jmaa l'qarawiya*), the administrative unit which has replaced the tribal structure since Independence. The work was compensated through the program of the Promotion Nationale, a public works relief fund for easing unemployment and underemployment in rural regions. The relief program has from the sixties supplemented the income of both landless and landholding households. The capital investment required for a pair of draft animals harnessed to a wooden plow, seed, and at least half a hectare of land is what separates the independent cultivator from the sharecropper (*akhumas*) who contributes only his labor.

The sowing of one hectare requires 80 to 100 kg (one quintal) of seed in wheat or barley, 50 to 80 kg of maize. In some environs more seed is alloted to dry fields than to irrigated fields of equivalent surface. Among the Ait Ayash bour receives whatever is left after the sowing of the permanent fields. The claim is often repeated that bour gives yields equal to irrigated fields with less seed. The reference is always the exceptional season of heavy rains, as memorable as it is rare.

ANIMAL HUSBANDRY

Most of the High Moulouya plain consists of grazing land defined as "those lands, due to steepness, dryness, thinness of soil, or value as watershed protection have a greater economic value when supporting a natural plant cover useful for livestock and wildlife" (Carter, 1966).

The traditional economy of the transhumants supported this pattern of land use and offered at the same time the most rewarding production activity. In the local formula, the capital investment required for a flock of 100 animals, two-thirds of sheep and one-third of goats, was equivalent to the investment in one hectare of irrigated land. The investment in animals yielded a return of over three times the value of the equivalent investment in grain production.

In 1958 this was estimated to be 160,000 FR against 50,000 FR from the proceeds of a harvest of one hectare under optimal conditions (Raynal, 1960:325). In the present day, state control of grain prices below those of the world market has increased the disparity in returns.

Noin's research on production revenues (1970:1, 213–223) is relevant. On the basis of the 1960 census, and the "Enquête à objectifs multiples" carried out at the same time as the census, and the registers of the Impôt Rural, he asks two questions: What production revenue in the rural regions is necessary to maintain one person? and How much land is needed in the different production activities?

For 1959–1960 the average revenue per rural inhabitant was 392 Dirhams. This was obtained through:

1) 1.8 ha of dry farming
2) 0.6 ha of irrigated farming
3) 0.9 ha of orchards under traditional management
4) 6.8 ha of grazing land in northwest Morocco
5) 80 ha of grazing land in southeast Morocco.

Regional variations in dry cultivation ranged from one to three ha, according to rainfall, soil types, fallow schedules and other factors. Irrigation farming varied from one hectare in the modern sector of Tadla and Doukkala, to 0.5–0.8 ha along the Atlantic littoral, 0.3–0.5 ha in the Rif and the western High Atlas, and 0.1 ha in the pre-Saharan oases of the southeast, which show the most intensive exploitation of land in Morocco. High Moulouya irrigation agriculture (the Ait Ayash and the other qsour dwellers) falls closest to the pattern of the southeastern oases in field sizes, if not in productivity.

Animal herding, similarly, requires different pasture space. In the Rif, three to four ha sustains the per capita production; in the Middle Atlas five to six ha, and in the High Moulouya 12 ha. In the eastern High Plateaus 50 ha is required, while in the Sahara 100 to 200 ha is the minimum.

In 1960, long after transhumance had been minimized, pastoralism still contributed 63 percent of the revenue for the Midelt sector, 77 percent of the Tounfit area, and 68 percent for the Itzer center of the Moulouya plain. The economic contribution of animal stock may be even higher, since the official statistics are generally on the low side. An annual report for the Province of Qsar es Souq in 1967 considered the animal holdings of the Midelt Circle to be ten percent to 40 percent higher than the given figures. The registered figures for that year listed 268,353 sheep, 105,958 goats, 11,285 cattle, 18,550 horses, mules and donkeys, and 909 camels (Midelt Archives: Rapport économique et social, 1967). These figures do not include the stock of the Ait Youssi, who are administered by another circle.

In 1960 the livestock of the region, including that of the Ait Youssi, a population of 5,700 with 12,500 small animals, was 360,000 sheep and 125,000 goats. There were six to seven sheep and two to three goats per inhabitant, three times the number of sheep per inhabitant than in the rest of rural Morocco.

This agrees with Noin's findings (1970:1, 223-229) in which he adapts a standard unit employed by rural economists that permits a discussion of all animal holdings. This is termed a 'large animal unit' (unité gros bétail: u.g.b.) and corresponds to the value of an adult bovine. Coefficients are established on the basis of annual revenue and commercial value of domestic animals given in the "Enquête à objectifs multiples": a sheep or goat = 0.15 u.g.b., a calf = 0.4 u.g.b., etc.

On the basis of this standard, he calculates the number of inhabitants per 'large animal unit'. The ratio of inhabitants per standard unit is high in zones of demographic pressure. In the pre-Saharan oases there are 3.4 inhabitants per l.a.u. (u.g.b.), in the western Anti-Atlas, 2.2 inhabitants per l.a.u., in the Rif, 2.4 per unit. The ratio is the lowest in central and eastern Morocco. In the High Moulouya it is one inhabitant per l.a.u., and in the Middle Atlas, 0.8 inhabitant per l.a.u. The lowest ratio, or the highest number of animals per capita, is found among the Beni Mgild of the Middle Atlas, with 0.5 inhabitants per l.a.u. Large animal holdings in these cases indicate low population pressure rather than optimal physical conditions.

In 1969 the Circle of Midelt with a population of 81,700 individuals (excluding the Ait Youssi) had a ratio of three sheep per inhabitant. The number of draft animals approximates that of other rural regions: one per five individuals. The number of cattle is expectedly lower than that of other regions: one per seven persons, against one per two to three persons elsewhere.

The flocks have access to three categories of grazing space: the tribal collectives of pastures and bour, the clearings in the forest stands and the alfa steppes of the state domain, and the fallow and harvested fields. The second category was part of the first before 1912.

The Midelt Circle includes a territory of 8,080 km^2. In 1967, 244,415 ha were listed as collective land, 311,802 ha as the private and public domains of the State, and 30,276 ha as melk property. 465,700 ha were classified as rangeland, and 10,920 ha were classified as open for grazing. One-fourth of the total surface was described as unexploitable. The declared animal stock for the same year was 374,311 sheep and goats. This total excludes the Ait Youssi stock.

Over a 30-year period, the annual average of the animal stock in the region, even following drought years, has been maintained or reestablished with consistency to the carrying capacity of one head per hectare. This estimate allows for the large animal stock.[4]

---

[4]Raynal (1960:321) estimates it at one head per two ha, but includes the Ait Youssi. My estimate is based on the populations and land in the Midelt Circle only.

Four natural zones of the High Moulouya provide pastures: the grassy *almou* (*ilmouten* pl., meadows), the clearings in the forest zone, the open ranges of shih, and the halfa steppes.

Prairies and forest stands are usually within tribal collective territory and treated as reserved pastures (*agoudal, igoudlan* pl.) closed to access for part of the year. These zones also offer the best bour on the eastern sector.

Prairies are found at altitudes of 2,400 to 2,500 m on the High Atlas side and 1,700 to 1,800 m on the western, Middle Atlas side. The meadows of Jebel Ayashi on the eastern side provide the summer camping sites of the tent dwelling Ait Morghad incorporated among the qsour tribes. Wide stretches of the juniper scrub zone are periodically plowed contributing to sediment runoff and erosion, and the progressive diminution of grazing surfaces. Sections of the state forests have been declared off-limits to pastoralists since Independence, as a conservation measure. The agricultural expansion of recent decades and the needs for firewood have contributed more heavily to the degradation of the region's plant resources than has overgrazing.

The piedmont zones are by far the most valued for pastoralists, but they are also the most limited.

The halfa steppes lack the annual and perennial grasses. The only edible plants they offer to the small animals are some ephemerals. The halfa grass and the associated *Haloxylon scoparium* are grazed only by camels. The lack of permanent water and high summer temperatures limit their exploitation to the winter months.

Throughout the region, agricultural expansion has raised the need for draft animals and their number has increased in recent decades. The draft animals provide transportation to local markets.

During the period of fieldwork, the Ait Ayash perceived their most pressing need to be modern transportation between the villages and the market town of Midelt. They submitted repeated requests through their representative on the rural commune to the local administration for a 'taxi service', an impracticable project.

The preferred draft animal is the mare since the initial investment offers returns in the sale of foals. Yet, it is a risky investment and the hardier mule is more common. Local market prices for mares range between 250 DH and 500 DH while mules bring 300 to 500 DH.

Thirty-five to 40 percent of the households in the region do not own draft animals (Raynal 1960:323–324). This reflects the distribution of agricultural land. The landless as well as the proprietors of plots of less than one-half a hectare find it economically untenable to keep draft animals.

Households with enough land keep one or two milk cows. Their care is arranged through the communal daily herding, *tawala,* maintained by the settlement households for most of the year.

The husbandry of sheep and goats has provided the dominant economic activity for the majority of the region's populations with an exploitation of seasonal bases that maintained a balance between the animal and plant resources. Today, households with flocks of more than 100 sheep and goats comprise between five and 25 percent of the region's total number of households in the different groups (Raynal, 1960:324). With the development of a sedentary lifestyle, the majority have an average flock of 20 head that meets domestic needs for wool, meat, and emergency cash, and is given to the care of a youth in the household.

THE AGRICULTURALIST QSOUR DWELLERS

The eastern sector of the plain is held by the three small tribes of the Ait Ayash, Ait Izdeg and Ait Ouafella. These groups with a total population of 15,500 in 1960, were most fully committed to sedentary irrigation farming. Their adaptation resembled the settlement pattern and resource exploitation of the pre-Saharan oases population, but without the political clientage ties developed in the south, the region from which the Sanhaja populations attribute both their origins and traditions. The similarity is most evident in the physical structure of the qsar which gathers into a social unit those who maintain proximity for resource location and defense. The walled settlements were abandoned in most cases from the 1940s for single constructions built near the old qsour.

The Ait Izdeg are a segment of a larger tribe found to the south of Jebel Ayashi in the environs of Rish. Their settlement in Midelt dates from the 19th century, when they offered military aid to the Ait Ouafella against the Gerwan who were pushed out of the region. The territory of the Ait Izdeg is approximately 30,000 ha, in the center of the Outat river basin. Thirty-three qsour were occupied by two descent segments. The Ait Toulout are installed at the two extremities of the irrigated complex: at the southern limits at Tatouin and near the springs of the headwaters of the river and in the north at Semora, Tashawit, Tajilalit, and Izougaren. The Ait Moumou hold the center of the irrigated valley between Kasba Flilo and Ikhermijioun. In their midst one settlement of Gerwan remains and two Ait Ouafella villages.

The Ait Ouafella are located to the east of the Ait Izdeg in 31 qsour within a territory of 112,000 ha and a population of 4,000. Most of their territory is lower than the Midelt plateau, and drier. The qsour are dispersed along the banks of the Moulouya at Aouli and Tafzout and east by the river Bertat and south on the Ayashi slopes by the mountain springs of Zebzat.

The Ait Ayash qsour occupy a 24 km span of the middle Ansegmir banks from the point the valley fans open after the gorges of the upper Ansegmir. The qsour stood on terraces of consolidated conglomerate that overlooked the irrigated fields of both banks. The population of the Ait Ayash in 1936 was 3,247 in 826 households.[5] In 1960 they numbered 4,050 individuals in 884 households.

The subsistence economies of these three groups were the most specialized of the regional variants, being dependent almost wholly on the circumscribed irrigated land. In recent decades they have expanded bour cultivation with demographic growth and have continued the sale of irrigated fields. The dry fields are at some distance from the settlements.

THE TENT DWELLERS

The only nomadic pastoralists on the High Moulouya are found in and near the territory of the three qsour tribes, which is to say on the borders of the zone long dominated by the fixed agriculturalists. There are two separate groups, small in number but important in the regional economy: The Arabic-speaking Oulad Khawa and the Tamazight-speaking Ait Morghad. Both are detached fractions of larger tribes found outside the region.

The Oulad Khawa, who numbered 190 tent households of 1,050 individuals in the 1960 census, had formed a fraction of the Oulad Khawa of Missour, a tribe of the confederation of the Oulad al Haj. Since the early 19th century, the Oulad al Haj had occupied the steppe plateaus of Douira east of the Middle Moulouya basin. The segment nearest the High Moulouya frequented the eastern edges of the plain. By their own tradition, the Oulad Khawa first arrived in the region to offer support to the Beni Abbou of the Beni Hassan who were being pushed out by the expanding Ait Seghroushen of the southern steppes. When the Beni Hassan moved westward, the Oulad Khawa remained in the area and enjoyed access to the rangelands of the Ait Ouafella at Bou Ayad and Zebzat. They occupied the zone east of the Ait Ouafella qsour with seasonal moves in the pastoral domains of the other sedentary tribes.

---

[5]They were listed in the local census by clans (ighsan) as follows: Ait Said ou Lahsen, 160 households and three tents; Ait Ali ou Youssef, 147 households and 14 tents; Ait Illousen, 62 households and eight tents; Ait Bougman, 104 households and eight tents; Ait Sidi Bou Moussa, 94 households and five tents; Iaffifen, 23 households; Ait Rebaa of Gheris (Idendel), 54 households and two tents; Ait Morghad, 41 tents.

The Arabic-speaking herders and the Imazighen agriculturalists kept social boundaries relevant to their economic commitments but expressed them through ethnic distinctions. Material relations were limited to reciprocal raiding for animals. The Ait Ayash oral tradition is replete with accounts of forays against the Oulad Khawa.

E. de Segonzac, during his visit in 1901, reported the following:

> L'an dernier, à pareille époque, les Oulad Khaoua et les Oulad el-Hadj tentèrent d'enlever les troupeaux des Beni Ouarain, qui paissaient dans la vallée. Les Braber, prévenues à temps devancerent leurs aggresseurs, brulèrent quelques qasbas et "mangerent" quelques douars. Les Ait Aiach arrivés après l'action, ne trouvant plus rien à détruire, enleverent une caravane de soixante et dix chameaux qui fuyait à marches forcées. Depuis lors, entre Arabes et Braber, la frontière est "semée de poudre; un moineau n'y passerait pas" (Segohzac, 1903:185–186).

The frontier Segonzac calls an Arab-Berber frontier was the ecological boundary line between different local economies.

The second group of pastoralists were from the Ait Morghad tribe of the Yafelman confederation. They first appeared in the region early in this century in small camping units. Seasonal ventures for pastures brought them north of the Ayashi crests, where they began longer stays.

In 1930 they concluded arrangements with the colonial administration for a permanent stay. Fifty tents with 300 individuals became incorporated as an appended fraction of the Ait Ouafella. Other tents on Ait Ayash territory secured pasture leases through the qaid of the Ait Ayash. The Ait Ayash had claimed the high pastures of Jebel Ayashi as tribal collectives during this period, when the administration was 'fixing' the tribes in bounded territories. The sedentary Ayash felt that with the pastures unofficially recognized as tribal commons, the presence of outsiders on them could benefit the tribe through the lease fees and would not be particularly threatening to their collective title. The payment of fees established their own prior claims on the land.

The newly established territorial limits of the Ait Ayash, Ait Izdeg and Ait Ouafella included within their boundaries some 45,000 ha of summer pastures, an additional 10,000 ha in the forest zone, and 45,000 ha of winter pastures at lower altitudes. This permitted, according to a 1934 paper on pastoralism in the Midelt archives, the support of all the animal stock of the tribes with short-distance moves within the tribal boundaries. These resources were not fully exploited by the qsour-dwellers themselves who held title to them. The intruding Ait Morghad had filled this narrow resource niche.

The Ait Morghad on the summer pastures of the Ait Ayash were required to purchase irrigated fields in order to be eligible to lease the pastures. In 1956 this was stopped, and they gained full use rights to the collective land.

The Ait Morghad and the Oulad Khawa became by local standards the affluent of the eastern Moulouya sector. For the period of 1946–1956 they comprised less than one-tenth of the population within the Midelt Circle and owned one-third of the animal stock, with an annual average of 31,000 sheep and goats. Those incorporated among the Ait Ouafella constituted less than one-fourth of the tribe and contributed 41 percent of the tax receipts. The Ait Morghad tents formed five percent of the Ouafella population and were responsible for 17 percent of the tax revenues (Raynal, 1960:327).

For the period of Independence after 1956, it is difficult to cull figures of their numbers and holdings because they are treated as integral members of the three rural communes. They continue to dwell in tents year-round but are registered as inhabitants of the villages where they own property. They visit the villages to oversee the management of their fields left in the care of sharecroppers and to use the grain mills. The qsour dwellers resent the pastoralists whom they see as visitors who have overextended their stay. Their resentment recognizes the fact that the pastoralists use the land more fully than the 'rightful' owners of it.

The Oulad Khawa and Ait Morghad tents range during the year from the northern depression of Aouli to the high slopes of Jebel Ayashi. From the first snows until the end of spring, they are found on the halfa steppes. The igoudlan are restricted in the spring, the period of early growth of the winter cereals sown in bour.

The winter quarters require maximum dispersion. Individual households divide the flock into smaller groups given to the care of family members or hired shepherds, and lead the goats to grazing spaces useless to the sheep. The Oulad Khawa cover the easternmost ranges, while the Ait Morghad exploit the territory around Gara Midelt, the landmark after which the French renamed the town of Outat. The two groups are easily distinguished by their tents. The Ait Morghad keep the large, black goat-hair tents of the Imazighen. The Oulad Khawa tents are smaller and striped with yellow bands.

In the summer the Ait Morghad ascend to the ilmouten of the Ait Ayash and the Ait Izdeg on the western slopes of Jebel Ayashi. The Oulad Khawa have access to the high valleys of Bou Agrao of the Ait Ouafella, south of the town of Midelt.

Economic success and large flocks require several adult males in the production unit. Three generation households are frequent among the pastoralists, as they are not among the qsour dwellers. Tent families with depleted stock make contracts to herd the sheep of one or several sedentary proprietors for one-fourth of the lambs.

THE PASTORALIST QSOUR DWELLERS

The adaptation of the pastoralist qsour dwellers supported a mixed economy with a predominance of animal husbandry that minimized the transhumance required by other pastoralists. The tribe of the Ait Yahia on the southern mountain zone and the tribes of the Ait Arfa and Ait Youssi on the northwestern plains of the Moulouya showed variants of this pattern which required extensive land holdings.

The mountain dwelling Ait Yahia occupied a territory of 196,000 ha with a population of 12,000 (1960 census). Their small animal holdings varied annually between 112,000 and 120,000 head. The tribe was a political amalgamation of localized descent segments around a core lineage of murabitin, the Ait Sidi Yahia ou Youssef. The tribal segments are distributed in two parallel tiers.

The Ait Hennini, Ait Sidi Yahia ou Youssef, Ait Ali ou Brahim, Ait Lahsen and Imetchimen are aligned from west to east in the depression between Jebel Amalou and the chain of Jebel Masker and Jebel Ayashi. This tier became known during the Protectorate as the Ait Yahia of the North.

The second tier is localized south of the Jebel Masker crests in the syncline before the barrier of Jebel Maoutfoud and Jebel Akhdar. The groups of this tier, known as the Ait Yahia of the South, are the Ait Amer ou Hammou, Ait Feddouli, Ait Moussa ou Othman, Ait bou Arbi and Ait Sliman.

East of the center market of Tounfit and south of the Masker chain the settlements are of the nucleated qsar type, while west of Tounfit in the Ouirin valley and among the Ait Hennini the Middle Atlas pattern of dispersed dwellings is prevalent. Settlement types were not bounded by any geographical limit. Some eastern fractions like the Imetchimen and the Ait Moussa ou Othman had individual constructions without the walled enclosure. However, all the settlements were permanent and even if animals were moved to distant winter quarters, the moves did not involve the majority of the population, the pattern of the traditional transhumants of the region.

The highland territory of the Ait Yahia provides uneven seasonal pastures. The summer pastures cover 105,000 ha, half in forest, while the winter pastures are limited to 30,000 ha.

Three groups, the Ait Moussa ou Othman, Imetchimen, and Ait Sliman manage to keep their flocks within their group territories year-round. These groups by their location also show a balanced dependence between crop production and small animal husbandry. Their animal flocks are led at the end of winter to the higher pastures following the melting snow, and brought down at the end of summer to graze around the villages. The animals are sheltered in the houses during the winter months. Those with flocks of more than fifty head arrange to move them to lower altitudes for the winter.

A second economic variant obtains with the highest altitude settlements of the Ait bou Arbi, Ait Amr ou Hammou and the Ait Feddouli. The last group is located at an altitude of 2,200 m on the saddle that separates the Moulouya headwaters (Mediterranean drainage) from the Oum er-Rbia headwaters (Atlantic drainage). Cultivation is limited to winter cereals, which ripen in midsummer. Animal husbandry forms the principal productive activity. The groups are required to secure winter quarters for their flocks outside their own territories.

The other tribes with mixed production, permanent settlements, and large flocks are the Ait Youssi and the Ait Arfa who share a similar ecological zone. The two groups have the lowest population densities found in the region: two to three inhabitants per square kilometer. The Ait Youssi average 100 sheep and goats per household and the Ait Arfa 50 per household.

The Ait Youssi of the Moulouya occupy a territory of 200,000 ha that reaches into the fringes of the Middle Atlas. The population focus of this extended, but in large part arid, domain is found on the high plain of Enjil. In the mountain sector the only settlements were hamlets of five to ten dwellings near streams. These were nucleated settlements in the past, which have now been abandoned. On the contact line of mountain and plain true qsour are found.

The Ait Arfa, who were attached to the Beni Mgild confederation, did not share the seasonal migrations of the other Mgild tribes. Located in the most arid portion of the plain, their tribal territory contains only one permanent stream in the mountain zone, and no important spring sources on the contact zone (dir). One fraction, the Rahhou ou Ali, is localized along on Bou L'ajoul, a tributary of the Moulouya. The Ait Bassu are scattered on the Tanfit plain where runoff and seasonal *wadis* (streams) support crop production. The third fraction, the Ait Ben Yakoub, occupy hamlets in the lowest part of the basin, near butte outcroppings. The Ait Ben Yakoub keep walled gardens around the settlements with trees of apricot, plum and other fruit, an economic specialization that reflects long term sedentism[6] as well as the protected location of their terrain.

The territory of the Ait Arfa, which covers 98,000 ha, and that of the Ait Youssi, include complementary zones of permanent pastures

---

[6]According to Beaudet (1969: 7ff.), some Beni Mgild tribes may have reached the Moulouya by Saadian times and advanced to the plateaus of the Middle Atlas by the first half of the 18th century.
 The Ait Sidi Bou Moussa Claim to have purchased their fields on the Ansegmir valley from a Beni Mgild group in the 17th century.

on the Middle Atlas plateaus and large stretches of the plain given to winter grazing.

THE TRADITIONAL TRANSHUMANTS

The fourth economic adaptation of Moulouya populations was transhumant pastoralism, which involved seasonal long-distance migrations of groups and their flocks to winter quarters (azaghar) across the Middle Atlas. The traditional transhumants were five of the Beni Mgild tribes and the Ait Ihand. The transhumant pattern was minimized and then suppressed during the Protectorate period.

The Beni Mgild tribes hold territories of 125,000 ha. Their population in 1960 comprised 20,000 individuals. Traditional land use for these groups had meant intermittent stationings on their pastures in the High Moulouya, intercut with spring and winter moves in a northwestern direction across the high passes of the Middle Atlas. Cultivation remained an expendable subsidiary activity. More recent practices indicate that farming was not precluded by climate. The way of life emphasized seasonal territoriality in complementary zones rather than permanent attachment of a group to a bounded territory. In times of insecurity, the agricultural schedule could be interrupted without disturbing the political integrity of the group.

There were two annual moves, the spring ascent and the winter trek to the azaghar. The spring migration involved a limited number of whole households and shepherds who accompanied the flocks out of the plain to the grassy plateaus of the Middle Atlas. The rest of the households tended the irrigated plots along the river valleys and on the piedmont. Access to the spring and summer pastures was secured through clan links with the northern Beni Mgild. Two of the Beni Mgild tribes (Ait Ougadir and Irklaouen) and the Ait Ihand occupied bases that included sections of the forest zone with sufficient summer pastures, so that the spring ascent remained within their own territories.

The winter migration involved all the households which moved out of the plain after the harvest of the spring crops. Elder household members were left as guardians of the dwellings and stored supplies. The trek was not coordinated on a large scale. Each local fraction chose an amghar for the season who arranged the departure date, itinerary and length of stay with host group. Land rights to the azaghar were negotiable from season to season and fluctuated with factors of demography, size of animal holdings and reorderings of alliances. The claims implied permanent arrangements but remained chronically flexible.

The winter quarters of the Moulouya Beni Mgild and Ait Ihand were located on the plateaus and valleys beyond the western dir of the Middle Atlas at altitudes of 1,400 to 950 m. The Irklaouen wintered with the homonymous northern clan, the Irklaouen of Azrou, and also with the Gerwan at Agourai. The Ait Mouli joined the Ait Mouli who held the dir of Ain Leuh. The Ait Bougman and the Ait Messaoud reached the pastures of the Ait Sgougon at Gertile, between the market center of Mrirt and the northern headwaters of the Bou Regreg. One fraction of the Ait Ougadir, the Ait Qebel Lahram, held claims to the plateau of Ment of the Ait Sgougou. The other fraction, the Ait Ali on Ghanem, found quarters between Ment and the town of Oulmas of the Zayan confederation. The Ait Ihand, a small tribe with a territory of 23,000 ha, were wedged in between the Beni Mgild and Zayan confederations, and were attached to neither formation. They were an isolated remnant of the Ait Idrassen, and were potentially useful to the competing confederations as a buffer zone between them. They continued their custom of descending to the region of Sidi Lamin by the tolerant consent of the Zayan.

The disruption of this pastoral economy from the period of submission of the Beni Mgild and the Ait Ihand in 1930–1931 led to a tenfold increase in cultivation. The official registration of collective lands in the 1940s precipitated a new drive to plow more pastures in order to declare them as private property (melk).

The irrigated land almost tripled in the decade of 1947–1957. In 1947 the Beni Mgild and Ait Ihand had 3,845 ha under irrigation. In 1951 the surface increased to 6,840 ha and in 1956 it covered 9,800 ha (Raynal, 1960:339). The irrigation projects were for the most part hastily planned diversion ditches that watered a limited surface from where runoff led to soil scouring and gully erosion. The extension of dry farming on uneven surfaces also contributed to land degradation by removal of the protective plant cover from the topsoil.

In 1942, their small animals were estimated at 95,000 head. In the decade of 1947–1957 the annual holdings figured at 101,500 sheep and 21,700 goats. This gave an average of 29 animals per household. Present official policy seeks to eliminate pastoral moves between regions with separate administrative centers, but large flocks are still shuttled seasonally, often by trucks. Seasonal displacements in the spring and summer continue today with pasture leases secured by the individual proprietor. Winter transhumance by groups has been abandoned. Pastoral accords that were ratified during the Protectorate are still invoked by wealthy proprietors, usually for lease fees of one per 60 animals. Most of the Beni Mgild keep their flocks on the plain during the winter. The Irklaouen, Ait Ougadir and Ait Ihand lack sufficient territory on the low plains for the critical weeks of snow and are obliged to negotiate it from season to season when pressing need compels it. In all cases now the movements involve the flocks with shepherds, not the households.

The conversion of the mobile pastoral patterns is far from complete. Animal shelters and adequate forage supplies are still lacking.

THE DEMOGRAPHY OF THE HIGH MOULOUYA

The region of the High Moulouya has had a low population growth rate when compared with other Moroccan regions of similar ecological conditions. Other low resource regions have experienced population pressure in recent decades which has been relieved by emigration. This has not happened in the Moulouya plain and the causes of its demographic stability are not clearly determined. The extant demographic studies agree on one fact about the region: the low birth rate. The two relevant works are Raynal (1960) and Noin (1970), the latter based on the national censuses of 1936, 1952 and 1960 and the archives of tertib registrations for the Protectorate taxation on animal and plant production. The tertib records are unreliable for the Moulouya region because the Midelt Circle was one of the centers that was treated in a lenient manner by the administration for the collection of taxes. This meant the reported statistics either exaggerated or minimized household counts according to the situation (Raynal, 1960:297).

The census of 1952 indicated a population of 66,639 for the region, with 9,710 individuals comprising the town sector of Midelt (4,306 inhabitants), Itzer (1,601) and the mining industries of Aouli and Mibladen (3,803). The rural component of 56,829 inhabitants gave a density of 6.2 persons per km^2. Locally, density fell from two to three persons per km^2 among the Ait Youssi and Ait Arfa and rose to 14 per km^2 among the Beni Mgild west of Itzer. The Ait Ayash and the other qsour dwellers had an average of 7.5 persons per km^2.

The first census of 1936 gives a population of 45,811 for the rural sector and 2,858 for the town sector. The annual growth rate over the 16-year period is 1.5 percent, a rate that equaled, if it did not surpass that of Morocco as a whole.[7] The apparent high rate is a function of faulty statistics, especially for the groups that came under colonial administration later than the others in the 1930s. The tribes which had submitted the earliest showed minimal increments. The Ait Youssi of the Moulouya had a population of 5,519 in 1936 and 5,763 in 1952. The Ait Ayash, Ait Izdeg and Ait Ouafella were registered with a total population of 15,198 in 1952, and 14,152 in 1957. In this case the

---

[7]Raynal (1960:299) gives a rate of 0.8 percent for rural Morocco in this period. This appears low; cf. Noin (1970 (2):93–116).

Figure 1a **Pyramids of probable ages in two regions with different characteristics with respect to fertility.**

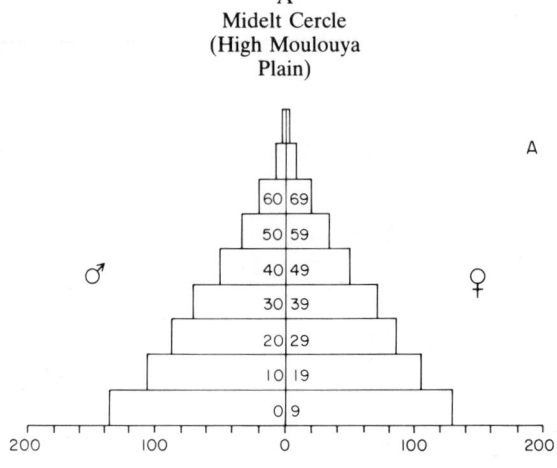

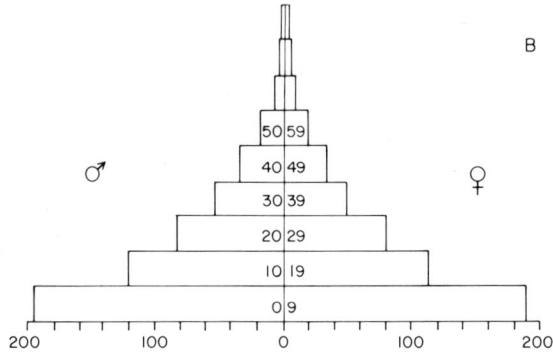

Figure 1b **Comparison of the age structures of the two regions with the population model for Morocco (1960)**

	Morocco (in %)	Midelt Cercle	Louta Cercle
0–19 yrs.	54.5	47.1	61.2
20–64 yrs.	42.2	48.3	36.6
65 yrs. and over	3.3	4.6	2.2

Methode utilisée: données redressées pour tenir compte des déformations intervenant par suite de la mauvaise connaissance de l'âge.

Source: Noin (1970. 2:28–9)

earlier figure may have been inflated, following the exaggerated family declarations that prevailed during the war years in the 1940s when some food stocks (particularly sugar) were rationed.

The stability of the High Moulouya populations can be appreciated through the perspective of the country-wide demographic growth of rural populations over the last half century. In 1914, the Moroccan rural areas are estimated to have had 4.5 million inhabitants, which was 89 percent of the total population of the country. In the first census of 1936, the countryside with 5.5 million comprised 81 percent of the population. In 1952, 6.5 million rural inhabitants made up 76 percent of the total, and in 1960, 8.5 million comprised 73.9 percent of the Moroccan population. In 1969, 10.2 million rural inhabitants comprised 68.5 percent of the population of the country. Despite a continuous and mounting rural exodus in the 1960s, a numerical increase of more than two percent annually is registered for the rural sector (Noin, 1970 (1):42).

The High Moulouya region has been minimally affected by emigration to urban centers. Immigration into the region has been more significant for the population figures than emigration (Raynal, 1960:300; Noin, 1970 (2):261). What is striking about the region in comparison with the rest of Morocco is the low number of children under 14 years of age.

Morocco is one of the 'youngest' nations of the world in terms of age structures of the 1960 population model (Noin, 1970 (2):11–36). A population pyramid for the rural sector in 1962 showed one-third of the population to be under ten years of age. The High Moulouya region, in contrast, has very different proportions of age groups, when compared with the Lower Moulouya region and the nation-wide age structures (Figures 1a and 1b).

Further comparisons can be made in terms of the age bracket of zero to 14 years, which comprises 45.6 percent of the rural population (1960), and regions with lower percentages for this age group. Central Morocco, which includes the High Moulouya, the Middle Atlas, the Middle Moulouya and the Central Plateau, has a population of which 41 to 42 percent fall in the zero to 14 years age bracket. In the Midelt Cercle the same age group comprises 39 percent of the population. Among the Ait Ayash, Ait Izdeg, and Ait Ouafella the age group represents between 41 and 43 percent of the total; among the Ait Arfa and Ait Youssi 38 to 40 percent, and among the Beni Mgild (Boumia) and Ait Yahia (Tounfit) the age group makes up only 35 to 36 percent of the population (Noin 1970 (2):64 hors texte).

The birth rates within the Midelt Cercle are among the lowest recorded for Morocco. Household sizes average 4.3 persons, 19 percent below the rural Moroccan average. The birth rate in 1962 was 38 per thousand, 20 percent lower than the national mean (Noin, 1970 (2):55–56).

The demographic explosion experienced by other Moroccan regions is absent in the Central Atlas generally, and the High Moulouya in particular. This remains relative to the Moroccan case and does not compare with countries of moderate growth rates.

The explanations which have been offered for the demographic patterns of the High Moulouya are neither consistent nor convincing because of the lack of adequate quantitative data. Raynal (1960) counts among the contributing factors high infant mortality rates, which are elevated throughout the country, and high incidence of sterility. He argues in addition for social causes, specifically abortion:

> On dit couramment que les femmes de pays ne veulent pas d'enfant. Les liens de ménage se rompent aisément. L'avortement est chose banale; au demeurant les maladies vénériennes, assez répandues au cours des générations précédentes, détérminant de nombreux cas de stérilité (Raynal, 1960:299).

Leaving aside for the moment the factors of marriage instability and sterility, the practice of abortion is questionable. My own field notes, based on information from the male population and without systematic questioning on this topic, do not support these claims. Noin, in his demographic study of Morocco, reported on his own research of this topic among the Irklaouen of Itzer. He states categorically:

> Tous les avis, de plus autorisés aux plus humbles, ont été concordants à ce sujet. Les moyens abortifs ne sont pas connus dans le villages (ils le sont d'ailleurs très rarement dans les villes de la région). Les moyens contraceptifs sont totalement ignorés des campagnards à l'exception des anciens militaires qui d'ailleurs n'en font pas usage dans leurs foyers. . . . Contrairement à certaines assertions, les femmes de la région veulent beaucoup d'enfants. Les cas de stérilité occupent largement les médecins. Les sanctuaires sont activement fréquentés pour cette raison (Noin, 1970 (2):55).

My own view sides with that of Noin, that abortion has not been practiced among the Moulouya populations even though colonial reports often stated that abortion was a widespread practice among Berber populations.

Other factors that can be eliminated as variables affecting the birth rate and fertility are female age at first marriage and male emigration. The average age at first marriage is 13 to 15 years against the general rural pattern of 15 to 16 years (Noin, 1970 (2):56). This is difficult to substantiate, because the age usually reported is the legal minimum of fifteen. Male emigration is insignificant for the region.

The marital separations during the brief periods of seasonal emigration for harvest labor have no practical significance on the birth rate.

The relevant variables are 1) the instability of marriages and 2) the high incidence of sterility due to venereal diseases. Marriage instability and its causes will be discussed in Chapter 6; suffice it here to give some comparative statistics. There are twice the number of divorced women in the region between the ages of 20 and 29, the period of maximum fertility, than in the rest of rural Morocco where they make up five percent of the total. Four and five marriages are frequent. The number of married women in the 20 to 29 years age bracket is 88 percent, which is below the rural mean. The relative liberty of women among the Tamazight-speaking populations in forming and dissolving conjugal bonds is atypical of other regions. This is estimated to contribute four percent to the deficit of the birth rate from the country-wide mean (Noin, 1970 (2):55–56).

The far more critical variable that accounts for ten to 15 percent of the 20 percent deficit from the mean birthrate is the high incidence of venereal diseases and consequent sterility, especially from gonococcal infections. Twenty percent of the married women over 30 years of age are sterile (Noin, 1970 (2):56). This is a rate two and a half times higher than the national rate. The only hypothesis I can offer to account for this, is that the houses of prostitution originally set up during the Protectorate for the military personnel in the market towns of the region, have subsequently become permanent institutions and are frequented by local men, especially before marriage. The minimal available medical services guarantee rapid diffusion of infections.

Twenty percent of the women in the region bear only one offspring, which is three times higher than the overall rural percentile. The number of women who have borne nine or more children reaches 11 percent, against the average of 26 percent for other regions (Noin, 1970 (2):56).

SUMMARY REMARKS

The High Moulouya region belongs, in geographic terms, to the arid zone of Morocco, which includes the entire Moulouya basin, the eastern High Plateaus, and all the pre-Saharan settled areas. The entire zone covers half the surface area of the country, is the least endowed in natural resources and has the lowest population densities. The entire zone supports a predominantly sedentary population of 900,000 (1960 census) of which only 64,000 can be counted as purely nomadic pastoralists.

The High Moulouya is, at the same time, by location and by the traditions of its population attached to the eastern Atlas zone of extensive land use. As such, it forms a transitional territory in bio-climatic and social characteristics. The local economies, before 1912, varied between patterns of extensive land use with transhumant pastoralism and circumscribed land use with irrigated farming.

Comparison with other Moroccan regions suggests resource exploitation below productive capacity. The western Haouz, with similar rainfall, climatic and soil characteristics, has an intensity of cultivation five times higher and a density of livestock three times more elevated (Noin, 1970 (1):180). Local production processes have been constrained not by the heavy hand of 'cultural tradition' but by an insecure political climate perpetuated by the pre-colonial state, and later, by the colonial administration.

The demography of the region is characterized by a low fertility rate due to both physiological and cultural causes. The tentative conclusion given in this account finds the principal cause to be a pathology which the participants do not control.

CHAPTER FOUR

The Protectorate Period

This chapter describes the early events in the establishment of the Protectorate regime in Morocco, and the replacement of the temporal institutions of the traditional rural organization by a centralized secular political structure deriving its sovereign power from armed conquest. The second part presents a view of the changes in administration and economy perceived by the Ait Ayash, especially in the activities of the two qaids who controlled the tribe from 1917 to 1956.

THE PACIFICATION OF THE HIGH MOULOUYA

The military operations for the pacification of Morocco were initiated officially in 1912 with the establishment of the Protectorate through the Franco-Moroccan Treaty of Fez, and ended in 1933–1934 with the achievement of total control of the countryside. The earliest appearance of French troops in the High Moulouya took place in 1917.[1] At this time, the Ait Ayash, Ait Izdeg, Ait Ouafella and Oulad Khawa submitted without further resistance. The groups had already encountered and opposed the foreign presence in Morocco at an earlier date and at another site.

In 1907, French army troops had entered the northeastern Moroccan confines of Oujda from Algerian territory. The following year other Algerian-based troops occupied the southeastern region of Bou Denib. In response to this encroachment of Moroccan territory, the murabit Sidi Ali Amhaoush of the zawiya Sidi Ali and disciple of the

---

[1] The sequence of events and dates of French military operations in the central Atlas are based on Guillaume (1946). Local accounts are rich in details but poor in temporal sequence.

late Derkawi chief Sidi Mhand al Arabi, rallied the High Moulouya and Middle Atlas tribes to carry out a jihad (holy war) against the foreign presence.

A regional force of tribal groups led by Sidi Ali met the French army in the distant territory of Bou Denib. The Ait Ayash came with their own amghar n'baroud (chief of battle), Sddiq ou Ali from qsar Iqqlayn, who carried the battle banner. The outcome was predictably disastrous. The local accounts of it differ little from the French version given by General A. Guillaume. Weapons and organization decided the odds.

> La même année [1908] notre apparition dans la région de Bou Denib semble, un moment, devoir faire cesser les luttes intestines pour grouper contre nous les tribus de l'Atlas. Sidi Ali croit l'occasion venue de jouer un grand rôle. Il prêche la Guerre Sainte; cavaliers et pietons venus de la Haute Moulouya et de l'oued El Abid répondent à son appel. Nombre des gens sans armes, avides de butin, participent à la croisade. Mais celle-ci se termine lamentablement. Parvenue au Medaghra, sur le Ziz, la harka apprend le succès décisif remporté par nos troupes sur les premiers contingents venus à leur rencontre. Les Berbères rentrent chez eux, épuisés de faim et des fatigues. L'échec de cette enterprise produit une profonde impression sur Sidi Ali. Il l'incite à la plus extrême prudence (Guillaume 1946:57–58).

The submission of the Moulouya tribes in 1917 was conditioned by this earlier experience. But the nature of the resource base of a specific group's economy, whether movable property in animals or agricultural land, also determined the degree of resistance.

The pastoralist Beni Mgild tribes of the Moulouya stayed in dissidence until 1920–1922. The Ait Yahia, southern neighbors of the Ait Ayash, defended their mountain retreats until 1931–1932. The last holdouts were the High Atlas tribes, south of the Moulouya, of the Ait Isha who resisted until 1932, and the Ait Hadiddou and Ait Morghad who submitted to the French in 1933.

Military control of the High Moulouya plain had formed the objective of the second phase of pacification operations. In 1912, according to General A. Guillaume, the French command lacked an overall plan for the control of the Central Atlas. The order of priorities called for military installations in the urban centers to safeguard the sultan and his government. The first objective was securing the Rabat-Meknes-Fez communication network. Early military actions focused on containing the tribes of the dir zones which threatened the urban centers. This led to the reduction of the Beni Mtir in 1913 and the occupation of the key towns of the Tadla region. Khenifra, the economic and political center of the Zayan confederation, was taken the following year in a move that was meant to reduce the coordinated activities of the confederation. The various Zayan tribes did not submit until 1922. For the next two years (1915–1917) military action centered on the Tadla region, where the early occupation of the market towns had not abated the dissidence of the mobile pastoralists.

The second phase was planned by Lyautey (Guillanme 1946:174–175), who became the first Resident General of the Protectorate. His plan called for securing a passage from Azrou in the Middle Atlas to Midelt in the High Moulouya in order to connect the forces in the southeast which had entered from Algeria with the central command in Meknes. A secure corridor through the highlands would break communications between the tribes north and south of it. The offensive was carried out in 1917. French troops from Bou Denib, which had at an earlier date reconnoitered the High Ziz valley up to Midelt, met with the 'groupe mobile' from Meknes on the High Moulouya Plain and secured the submission of the Ait Ayash, Ait Izdeg, Ait Ouafella and Oulad Khawa.

The Beni Mgild of the Moulouya left the territory with their flocks. French intelligence had not counted on this reaction. The encounters with the Mgild tribes on the dir in 1913 had ended with their 'pacification' after a three month struggle. This led to the impression that the other tribes of the confederation would follow suit on contact. The Beni Mgild confederation never had a paramount chief like the Zayan. The Mgild tribes reacted in territorial blocs without overall coordination. In the north, the tribes in the environs of Azrou, the Irklaouen, Ait Arfa of the Gigou valley, and the Ait Abdi, a total of 2,500 households, submitted to General Henrys in 1913. In the center, the tribes in the most inaccessible terrain, the Ait Abdi of Bekrit of 1,000 households, held out after all the rest had surrendered. In the Moulouya Plain, all the Mgild tribes except the Ait Arfa, some 1,500 households, took refuge in the southern mountains until 1920.

At the same time, there was great activity on the western part of the Moulouya from 1913 to 1923 with a continuous influx of refugee groups which fled their own territories as the French approached (Midelt Archives: Correspondence of Rouast, 22 Feb. 1944). After the defeat of Bou Denib, the murabit Sidi Ali had concluded a pact of solidarity between the Ait Yafelman and the Ait Oumalou which provided unrestricted access to all territories for tribes in flight from the foreign army. The external threat lifted borders and guaranteed refuge but did not precipitate large scale political coalescence. The extended duration of the 'pacification' hostilities led in time to the perception of the French presence as another power segment in the local politics of opposition. The fact that the French were Christians invading a Muslim land was never forgotten. Nevertheless, the protracted span of the resistance did not suspend all regional conflicts. As early as 1915 when a detachment from Meknes advanced at the Gigou valley, the Ait Arfa petitioned the French for aid against their neighbors, the Ait Seghroushen n'Sidi Ali. This permitted the construction of a garrison at Timhadit which served as a staging area for the routes to the Moulouya and the high valleys of the Oum al Rabbia. The following year three and one-half batallions, two squadrons, two batteries and one artillery section reached Agelman n'Sidi Ali and subsequently the market town of Ain Leuh. In May 1917 the town of Bekrit was taken. The Bekrit post provided a surveillance point over the zone of the best highland pastures.

The disruption of the pastoralist schedules had built up anticipation of rapid submissions. The 'group mobile' continued southward to the Moulouya plain where a batallion post was set up at Itzer. The southern troops then advanced through Midelt and joined the Meknes troops on the Plain, bissecting the Central Atlas.

This led to increased resistance rather than the demoralization that General Lyautey had predicted.[2] The northern tribes mobilized under a murabit of the Ait Seghroushen, Sidi Raho. The southern tribes of the Mgild and the Zayan held out for another five years. The Ait Bougman settlements on the Ansegmir joined the rest of the Mgild. The qsar of Bou Draa was not occupied until 1919 (Voinot 1939:179). At this time Bou Draa came to serve as an advance post against the unsubmitted tribes to the south.

After the formal surrender of each tribe, the tribesmen were mobilized on the French side as 'partisan' forces against those still unsubmitted. This was the only way to gain back the weapons that were collected on surrender. Motives of old accounts and opportunities to settle them were not missed. An Ait Ayashi elder justified the early submission of his tribe on these terms: "Before the French came the Beni Mgild were constantly attacking us and we were obliged to offer compensations to their *ikhatarn* (notables) in order to stop the raids. When the French came the Ait Ayash welcomed them. The French took the dirt out of the eyes of the Ait Ayash."

This expresses a part of the actual relationship with the French. Sedentaries have fewer tactical options when confronted with threat than transhumants. Their readier submission is predictable. The manipulation of the French as a novel faction in local contests was a political epiphenomenon. In addition, throughout the period of pacification, covert collaboration between the submitted and dissident tribes was prevalent. One form was the planning of raids on French garrisons for weapons. Their success depended on information provided by the Berbers inside, the 'partisans' of the French.

[2]Guillaume (1946:175) quotes Lyautey as saying the northern tribes would be left to 'stew in their own juices'.

All the tribes resisted the French to some degree. Their first reaction to the military infiltration of infidels and the prospect of foreign rule was one of unmitigated opposition. A. Guillaume, one of the chief strategists of the Central Atlas 'pacification', stated that, "No tribe came over to us without first having been defeated by arms" (Guillaume 1946:7). In some cases the odds were so out of balance that a ceremonial battle was arranged, which the French termed a *baroud d'honneur*.

The third stage of the French pacification centered on the occupation of the Wad al Abid region; the town of Aghbala was taken in 1926. The entire territory was brought under military control between 1929 and 1931. The closing phase brought the surrender of the Ait Yahia in their high valleys in 1932 and finally the Ait Isha, and the last holdouts the Ait Haddidou and Ait Morghad in 1933.

The social changes which took place in rural Morocco with the establishment of the Protectorate are outside the scope of this chapter. Two basic and radical permutations were the transformation and westernization of the governmental structure and the entrance of colonists. The latter did not concern the Moulouya Plain directly because it is a region of marginal resources. The former was responsible for 'the secularization of governmental function' (Hoffman 1967:161) and the centralization of authority, a legacy that was further developed after the end of the Protectorate by the independent government.

RURAL ADMINISTRATION

The first task of the colonial forces after pacification was the selection of local notables to serve the new regime. These were called qaids after the traditional agents of the makhzan appointed over tribes. The new class of qaids no longer coincided with the old class in one important aspect. The old qaids under the independent Sultanate could be overthrown; chieftainship was not institutionalized in the tribal organization. A permanent chief acquired dominance over a tribe by subverting the institutional mechanisms that diffused power. He then reinforced his power with the formal appointment by the Sultan. The colonial situation required that even the most remote settlement had to be given a chief responsible to the Protectorate administration.[3]

Lyautey, the first Resident General, envisioned a government of indirect rule in which colonial officers would serve in a supervisory capacity (*contrôle*) to the qaids who would be drawn from the tradi-

[3]There were 350 qaids in French Morocco and an equal number of Officiers des Affaires Indigènes.

tional chiefs of the tribes. While he assumed the existence of traditional local authority structures, he suspected they were lacking. In an early directive he cautioned his officers:

> Discèrner nettement les influences indigènes à utiliser . . . voir surtout ou sont les influences traditionelles ancrées a racines profondes et se mèfier des autorités improvisés à la suite d'une première impression de ceux venus trop complaissement à nous parce qu'ils ont besoin de se faire une situation (quoted in Bidwell 1973:39).

The selection of qaids was problematic because there were no 'traditional' chiefs.

UNITS OF ADMINISTRATION

The new centralized political administration had also to create a regional organization where none had existed. Under the traditional government, Morocco had been divided into towns and tribes, with no larger territorial divisions. The French established the Region as the largest territorial segment of the country. With some eventual modifications, Morocco was divided into three civil regions, of Rabat, Casablanca and Oujda, and four military regions, of Fez, Meknes, Marrakesh and Agadir (Bachir 1969:39).

Over each region was assigned a *chef de region* who served, at the inception of the Protectorate, as a territorial representative of the Residential authority. The lack of any indigenous office on the same level to which the chef was, in theory, to offer supervisory services, converted the office of provincial governor into a key link in the hierarchy of administration (Bachir 1969:40).

The regions were segmented into territories, and territories were partitioned into circles with lower subdivisions of districts (*circonscriptions*), dependencies (*annexes*) and stations (*postes*). The circle formed the basic administrative unit. General Lyautey drew the plans for Morocco on the basis of his experience under Gallieni in Indochina and Madagascar. Gallieni had created the system of circles for the colonial administration of Indochina, wherein the military commander of a delimited area was simultaneously its civil governor. In Algeria, where Lyautey had also served, the colonial army had created the *bureaux arabes,* in which a political officer held charge of civil affairs and an army officer was assigned military jurisdiction in a separate organizational structure. Lyautey chose the circle organization for Morocco, with one officer exercising civil and military control over his command.

The officer was known as the *officier des Affaires Indigènes* (AI), and was responsible to the region's governor for all activity within his zone. The AI officer served in principle as an agent of supervision over his Moroccan opposite, the qaid. Qaids, however, initiated no policies, but only reacted to new opportunities.

The supervisory authorities extended their 'supervision' 'not only over political matters, but also over administrative and judicial questions. Thus the Moroccan tribal administrators actually were in the position of being agents of the French authorities and had no decision making authority of their own. The establishment of the Protectorate regime thus led generally to the preemption by the government of local decision-making power, and to the concentration of this power in the hands of administrators divorced from the realities of peasant life, or from Islamic life in general (Hoffman 1967:162–163).

At the same time the government was not a modern one as the colonial program chose to preserve Berber tribalism when its social and political functions in self-management had come to an end. Tribes were, in the French view, a reflection of a Berber culture that ought to be kept separate from the Arabo-Islamic culture and brought into a modern orbit, which is to say, a French orbit. The role of the AI officer was to be more than that of administrator; he was to be a cultural missionary. Colonel Berriau in a lecture to AI officer trainees outlined the duties they were to carry out:

> En definitive cette premiere tâche d'apprivoisement consiste à faire oublier aux tribus les agréments illusoires de leur independance passée . . . il se présentera moins au conquerant qu'en conseiller, en homme de bien, qui, après avoir imposé sa force, veut séduire les coeurs, en grand frère sérieux et sage, en tuteur bienveillant et ferme, soucieux de masque les inconvénients de sa tutelle et d'en faire ressortir les bienfaits . . . il ne négligera rien, en un mot, pour créer dans son domaine plus de bien-être, plus de richesses, plus d'ordre, plus de sécurité, plus de bonheur. (quoted in Bidwell 1973:158–159)

Many AI officers did identify strongly with the interests of the tribes under their command. The local archives are filled with reports of cases where the AI officer clashed with his colleagues and superiors over the claims of his group, especially in conflicts over land. Local recollections are on the whole favorable to individual AI officers who protected the interests of their tribe. Altruistic motives did nothing to change the systemic relationship between colonizer and colonized. It still remained a case of "an administrative Robinson ruling over man-Fridays". (Berque 1962:124)

THE QAID

The qaid of the pre-Protectorate had been an agent of the sultan in his capacity as head of state. His authority under government seal gave him the duties of collecting taxes, maintaining the security of roads and hostels, and imposing fines and meting out punishment (except the death sentence). He received no salary. Financial rewards depended on the toll fees collected from commercial traffic passing through his command and self-help.

The role of the Protectorate qaid showed similarities to that of the earlier qaid. His duties included the collection of the tertib, administration of the collective land of the tribe, supervision of new technical services, and representation of the tribe to the government. He was held accountable only to the AI officer supervising him. This left him wide opportunities to enhance personal interests. The only official recompense was a six percent rebate on the collected taxes. The qaid could choose assistants as khulafa (deputies), *shioukh* (administrators over tribal sections) and muqaddimin (village administrators) when the size of the group warranted lower level supervision. Assistants were entitled to four percent of the taxes.

In theory, the qaids were selected by the sultan. A list of local candidates was collected by the AI officer and forwarded to the Resident General who submitted it to the makhzan for the sultan's *dahir* (imperial edict; royal proclamation). In practice the whole process was left to the discretion of the AI officer who chose a candidate without higher consultation.

The qaid and his retinue had authorization to carry arms. His power over the tribesmen was contained only by the forbearance of the AI officer but his authority as a makhzan agent was completely circumscribed (Bachir 1969:123). All official correspondence of the qaid was screened by the AI officer and forwarded to the Secretariat General for approval. In the last half of the Protectorate period qaids had to secure permission from the province chef for travel outside the area.

The official tolerance of corrupt qaids was necessary to maintain compliant and loyal agents.

> It was felt that if a caid were a well-trained, well-paid official, dependent on the central makhzen, the whole balance in the bled would be upset. He would be more permanent, more experienced, more in touch with tribal opinion than the officer of AI, whose role would be meaningless. The caid would be indisputably the effective ruler of the tribe and in effect the Protectorate would be at an end. It was not the corrupt, illiterate caid who was a possible danger, but the modern, efficient one (Bidwell 1973:95).

THE AIT AYASH UNDER THE PROTECTORATE

The Ait Ayash came under the control of the Midelt Circle which administered most of the High Moulouya plain. The Midelt Circle with two other circles, Azrou and Khenifra, formed the territory of Meknes. The territory of Meknes together with the territory of Tafilalt comprised the Meknes Region.

The circle was administered from the newly renamed town of Midelt (1917). The Ait Ayash, after their surrender which was arranged by the zawiya Sidi Hamza chief who had opted for collaboration with the French at an early date, were attached to the poste of Boumia. With the submission of the Beni Mgild, whose center was Boumia, the Ait Ayash requested transfer to the Midelt bureau in order to be with the other Yafelman groups.

The impact of the new administration was felt by the Ait Ayash through the person and activities of their qaid. The position stayed in one family from 1917 to 1956, and was passed from father to son. Ait Ayash informants found it difficult to explain to their own satisfaction how this family gained the position, because, they said, it was not a family of ikhatarn, before French arrival.

When the French reached Midelt they inquired among the town merchants and the Jewish community for the names of the prominent men of the local tribes in order to appoint qaids. There were several ikhatarn among the Ait Ayash, but according to informants, they were reluctant to serve under the foreigners. The popular choice was a descendant of the family killed by its own village. He had made a strong impression on the French who helped him collect the diyas from his natal village which they thought were due to him. He was a natural leader, much admired for his courage. Many stories have accumulated around his return to the tribe as a young adult. Known by the honorific Bou Illoughman (father of the camel) he allied himself with another qsar from where he fought his family's village for the diyas. Bou Illoughman was fatally wounded in an expedition against the dissident Mgild. He would have been selected qaid, informants thought, but with his removal, the other qualified candidates hesitated at the opportunity, and they finally had a qaid by default.

Once the qaid was installed he took decisive control of the tribe. He trained his son for the position and after a dozen years turned over the job to him. It is the second qaid, qaid Cherrou who is best remembered for the role he played in their lives for over a quarter of a century. "Qaid Cherrou did some good things for the tribe," said a contemporary who served as his messenger, "because he kept the tribe strong. But good or bad, he did whatever he wanted and no one could argue with him."

The qaid was seen to be responsible for three important tribal matters. He pursued successfully the claims to tribal land; he controlled the entry of new settlers into the tribe; and he discouraged any economic innovations suggested by the AI officer. His efforts in the first matter were granted to be a positive contribution for the tribe although many questioned that anything he carried out could be seen as beneficial for the tribe. The tribe gained title to considerable collective land which was officially registered in 1951. This land came to symbolize the tribe's main stake in a newly found security because the control of its resources promised new income. The collective land may well have been Ayashi land by historical precedent but the insecurity of siba had prevented the Ait Ayash from using it on a regular basis. Now, the opportunity to lease tribal pastures as well as to plow new fields could be realized on the legally established corporate resources. Qaid Cherrou was given all credit for these plans which initially appeared to favor the tribe, although any actual benefits accrued to him personally.

Once the military phase of the Protectorate was completed, the general rule adapted by the French conferred rights to the groups found on the territory at the time of French arrival. The establishment of boundaries between groups depended in great measure on the persuasiveness of the qaids representing the tribes. The transhumant groups which had abandoned their home camps during the years of resistance experienced the largest problems of tenure claims. Some Mgild tribes had suffered heavy population and animal losses and on their return found neighbors encroaching on their land.

The territories of the sedentary groups were easier to establish. The irrigated zones were clearly defined and it was only on the outer boundaries of the surrounding common land that limits became contestable.

The tribal territory of the Ait Ayash comprises two blocs on either side of the valley. On the western side stretches the Aarid plain that separates the Ait Ayash from the nearest Beni Mgild tribes along the Moulouya river. The plain offers extensive but seasonally undependable grazing surfaces. There is a lack of substantive traditions concerning its occupation by any one group. The tribes surrounding it on three sides claimed the sections nearest them with wide spaces left for sporadic seasonal occupants. The Aarid provided a social border between the qsour of the Ansegmir and the Mgild transhumants whose migrations oriented them away from the plain, in the opposite direction.

In the earliest records of land boundaries in 1934, the Ait Ayash registered a claim on two sections of Aarid (Midelt Archives 4141 A1/1

Bordereau 12/3/1934). One was a plot of 900 ha, Aarid al Tahtani, between the qsar Ait Toughash and the Ait Mouli settlements along the Moulouya river. The other was a section of 500 ha known as Tassamart n'Mellouit near the qsar Ait Illoussen. The rest of the Aarid was claimed at this time by the Ait Mouli and Ait Arfa tribes of the Beni Mgild and by the Ait Yahia in the south. Subsequently the qaids of these groups changed their earlier claims and the Ait Ayash through qaid Cherrou won big concessions. In 1935 an accord was signed by the Ait Yahia which recognized the extension of the southern limits of the Ait Ayash collective land. In 1936, and again in 1938, the Ait Mouli and Ait Arfa gave up their claims to Aarid.[4] In 1951 when the Ait Ayash collective holdings were officially registered, the western portion on the Aarid covered 10,500 ha. Within the western limits and the river, large tracts of alfa steppes are registered as holdings in the private domain of the State.[5] so that the territory from the villages to the western limits is much larger (Map 9).

The collective territory on the eastern side of the valley is more varied ecologically and important economically. It covers some 12,000 ha. From the valley the plain of Aasker slopes to the southeast toward the foothills covered with scrub that mark the transition to the *ari*, mountain. The scrub and forest zones provide firewood, prairies, soil-rich plowland and permanent springs. The Ait Ayash had practiced bour cultivation in this zone before the Protectorate. Several locations were apportioned among the clans and the households within them. Their rights were challenged at times and some accounts told of seasons when the qsar dwellers mounted as an armed party with horsemen guarding while others worked the fields.

At higher altitudes above the juniper scrub zone stood some small villages of Ait Yahia which in their isolation were virtually independent of the tribe. One of these is the qsar Taouraout of the Imetchimen. The qsar was built on a steep hillock, inaccessible to surprise attack, beyond a narrow pass that opened up on the meadows and bour of the Ait Ayash. When the qsour tribes of Midelt submitted to the French in 1917, these mountain villages remained uncontacted. They neither declared dissidence nor came forward to the new governors. Their security relied on their marginality.

The account of the ex-qaid, Cherrou Ouzelmad, given to the author, indicated that the qsar of Taouraout was dangerous to the security of the tribe and to the Ayash collective land that was so near the qsar. As a section of the Ait Yahia, the Ait Taouraout could be coopted into supporting those Yahia in dissidence. They could also

---

[4]Accords of November 18, 1935, June 29, 1936 and April 25, 1938 discussed in a letter of Lt Col. Badie, 1949 (Midelt Archives).
[5]According to the Dahir of August 15, 1928.

104 THE AIT AYASH OF THE HIGH MOLOUYA PLAIN

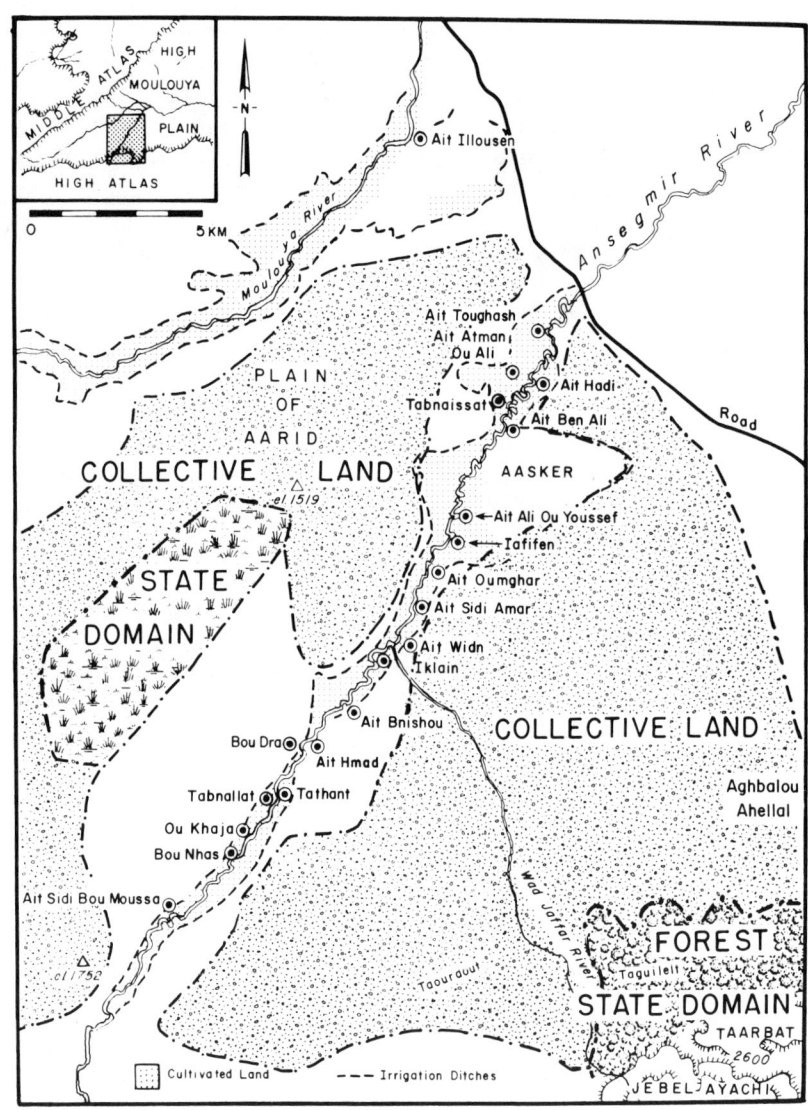

Map 9. Map of the collective land of the Ait Ayash

Source: Midelt Archives, April 1951.

advance counter-claims on the fields of the Ait Ayash. The solution he adapted, at the advice of his son who became the second qaid, was to invite the Ait Taouraout to move to the other side of the pass on the edge of the Ait Ayash boundaries by offering them fields in exchange for sentinel duty on the eastern limits of Ayash territory. The pact was officially recognized and this guaranteed the acceptance of Ayash territorial claims, thereby subverting later claims by others. A new qsar was constructed for the Ait Taouraout near the stream and a channel was built to divert water for the fields surrounding the qsar.

The establishment of the southeastern limits secured 10,000 ha on the Ayashi mountain side. By 1951 this was extended to cover 12,000 ha. The total territory of the Ait Ayash covers 550 km^2 (55,000 ha). This includes state domain, forestland, halfa ranges, and some dry steppes in the north, the latter holding no particular interest to anyone.

The pastures within the territory of the Ait Ayash met all the need of their flocks. In 1936 there were 40 tent households among all the qsour on the Ansegmir. In addition, the Ait Morghad herders, who had filled the pastoral niche on Jebel Ayashi, were attached to the Midelt tribes. Forty-one tents of 221 Ait Morghad were registered for the same year among the Ait Ayash (Midelt Archives: 1936 Census).

The second qaid initiated a policy for regulating the use of the pastures and the entry of 'foreigners' on Ait Ayash territory. A new qanoun was added to the customary code that specified two conditions for access to collective land. First, ownership of irrigated land was required, and secondly, households with more than 50 sheep and more than one cow had to pay rent to the tribe for pasture rights. The first condition was traditional and part of the process of social incorporation along with the establishment of ritual kinship. The new rule was meant for the pastoralists, and kept them from being fully incorporated because the rite of tamghrost was no longer necessary. The pastoralists on tribal land had to buy irrigated fields which created a new situation for the Ait Ayash. The sale of fields to non-Ayashis brought a new scale of values concerning land. Higher prices could be charged to outsiders, and the purchase of land no longer gave any permanent rights on the collective land. This encouraged the alienation of irrigated fields because larger amounts of cash could be demanded, and because greater reliance could be placed on bour cultivation. The newcomers who were not socially incorporated and bought irrigated fields could not plow collective land. Their social connections with the group remained equivocal. The relationship and obligations and rights they established were not with the group, but with the qaid. This is what the

Ait Ayash meant when they credited the qaid with the control of the 'strangers'.

In the same period, the qaid allowed indigent households unable to purchase fields to settle among the Ansegmir qsour. The French administration had initiated many public projects, especially road construction, for which the tribes had to supply corvée labor. The new families provided a source of substitute labor for the tribe and also an agricultural labor force for the growing estate of the qaid. It was a common practice for qaids to obtain forced labor on their private property. Most AI officers chose not to stop the practice because it would be a serious blow to the prestige of the qaids. (Bidwell 1973:82). Not all of them tolerated it. The Ait Ayash tell a popular anecdote about their own and two other qaids. The qaids went to the AI officer called Captain 'Trois' and requested permission to recruit tribesmen as reapers of their fields because they were too occupied to hire men. Captain 'Trois'[6] invited them to his office and gave to each a wooden match. "This will do the work for you," he told them and dismissed them.

The Ayash remember with more bitterness the qaid's refusal to allow any new projects suggested by the French officers. One proposal was to set up an experimental apple orchard on the tribal territory called Aasker. The qaid rejected the plan because it threatened to diffuse his personal control of the tribe. As many pointed out, as soon as he lost his position in 1956 he was the first to sell land and "now Aasker is full of farms planted with trees".

He also rejected a plan to reinstitute a weekly souq on the Ansegmir. The French administration encouraged markets as ready sites for political posts, and many were created where none had existed. During the Protectorate, the economic and information services of markets were supplemented with the services of judges, medical services, and their use as centers for tax collection and for the announcements of projects. In 1936, there were some 550 souqs in the French zone (Fogg 1936:123). Qaid Cherrou's refusal of a new market of the Ansegmir was well understood to reflect his reluctance to introduce activities he could not control. The decision turned out to be crucial for the future of the villages, for it guaranteed that they had missed an opportunity for economic innovations for several more decades. With Independence one of the first projects of the new administration was to construct a market place in qsar Ait Oumghar as a new economic center for the Ansegmir. That market failed. The right moment had been missed for starting a new market. The region had, by this time, all the markets it could support.

---

[6]'Trois' was either Capt. Troyes or Capt. Troin, both of whom served as AI officers in the Midelt Circle.

IRRIGATED HOLDINGS

The irrigable surface, which was the most important resource for the qsour dwellers, remained basically unaltered throughout the Protectorate period. The qaid improved new properties of his own on the piedmont zone (Aghbalou Ahellal) and in the valley (Zahira) but no new diversion projects were carried out or, it appears, were even contemplated. The most reliable figures for the irrigated surfaces for the entire region were gathered in 1952. A Franco-Spanish commission was charged with carrying out a study of the watered perimeter of the Moulouya basin in preparation for the projected dam of Mechra-Kellila in the lower Moulouya valley. The commission presented its findings compiled from aerial photographs and ground surveys in the following categories: (1) surfaces irrigated before and after 1927; (2) irrigable surfaces not cultivated in 1951–52; and (3) surfaces brought under irrigation since 1927. The third category was negligible throughout the region.

The irrigated fields of the Ait Ayash were reported to cover 2,222.2 ha (Midelt Archives: Franco-Spanish Commission Report on irrigated perimeters, 1952). In 1951–1952, 508.8 ha were not cultivated. The fallow land is the property of the zawiya Sidi Hamza. The estate laborers of Idendel had dispersed by this date and the report stated that Omar al Hamzawi was unable to cultivate all of his holdings and practiced a three-year fallow system.

The registers for the tertib of 1952 record for the Ait Ayash cultivation of 1,380 ha out of a total of 1,800 ha. The tax report does not include the zawiya holdings, so that the total irrigated land of the tribe (1,800 ha) is more than that reported by the commission. An amended report of 1953 attached to the commission findings altered the actual cultivation of the Ait Ayash to 1,886 ha and the fallow surface to 336 ha (Midelt Archives: Report of Capt. Jean Baptiste, 1953). Presumably the zawiya estate had been partially cultivated, because in the 1969 tax bureau registers the property of the zawiya Sidi Hamza is still listed as 500 ha (Services des Impôts Agricoles Midelt, personal communication). The most reliable estimate of the permanent agricultural surface of the village households is, on the basis of the 1952 commission report, 1,720 ha.

Assuming a ceiling population of 800 households in the pre-colonial setting, this gave an average of 2.15 ha per household. If this was the situation before the Protectorate, the new conditions changed it drastically. The qaid became, and likely remains, the largest landowner in the valley. This is difficult to document because current land registers are unavailable, or if available closed to access, in the Midelt

Bureau. The economic disparities which began to appear in the new political environment with alienation of land, have continued to grow larger and the margin of security smaller. This forms one of the two topics of the next chapter.

CHAPTER FIVE

The Contemporary Period: Government and The Village Economy

This chapter deals with the contemporary political and economic conditions of the Ait Ayash villages. The first section describes the changes that took place in rural administration with the establishment of the independent government of the Kingdom of Morocco in 1956. The second section offers an account of the economic activities of the Ait Ayash by focusing on data concerning one village with special reference to land distribution, land use, and the subsidiary activities that maintain subsistence.

THE ADMINISTRATION SINCE INDEPENDENCE

While the Protectorate administration had methodically preserved tribal structures and division, the independent national government sought to replace them with modern alternatives. The first experiment, in 1956, attempted to introduce local elections for shioukh of tribal factions. A preliminary trial was carried out in the provinces of Casablanca and Marrakesh. The program was quickly abandoned because it tended to reinforce the descent-ascribed divisions of the pre-Protectorate and resembled too closely the colonial system.

In 1958 the government made the dissolution of tribes an official policy by royal proclamation on May 8 (Bachir 1969:149). The king announced that tribal organization was to be replaced with new administrative units, the rural communes, which would serve as the basic cells in the administration of modern Morocco. The rural commune was to be formed on a territorial basis with some specific economic enterprise, such as a market place, as its center. The new administrative unit[1] was to cover a circumscribed area so that members could be within easy distance to carry out meetings. It was to promote common economic interests that fostered cooperation and generated sufficient income to allow locally planned and executed projects. It was anticipated that each commune would need resources valued at one million francs (10,000 DH) or annual market revenues of half that amount in order to become viable (Ashford 1961a:360)

The vision of the more radical politicians in the early years of Independence saw the commune as the "driving element in the total transformation of the country".[2] These plans were not shared by the political program of the monarchy. The rural communes created smaller local divisions which served more effectively as units of political control in the new administration and which perpetuated and refined the highly centralized system of the French colonial period. The 600 tribes of the French Protectorate and the 100 tribes of the Spanish zone came to be replaced by 800 rural communes.

The administration of each commune calls for an elected council (jmaa l'qarawiya) headed by a president chosen by the council members. The size of the commune determines the number of council members. Communes of up to 7,500 members elect nine councilmen.[3] They are responsible for four regular sessions annually, in February, April, August, and October. Councilmen are not salaried.

The first elections for local councils were held in May, 1960 (Chambergeat 1961; Ashford 1961–6; Zartman 1964, Ashford 1967). The elections brought the national political parties to the countryside and the candidates presented themselves as party affiliates. The growth of political parties during the early years of Independence had introduced a new element in Moroccan politics. The parties offered an opportunity for alternative channels of communication between the cities and the countryside and fostered for the rural citizen the hope that he could participate in political life. Their success remained limited because they all tended to be urban-based and with programs difficult for the rural citizen to identify with or to distinguish from the makhzan.

---

[1]The concept of the rural commune under the independent government had a precedent in efforts begun in 1951 by the Protectorate government to reinstitute the tribal assemblies of the traditional organization. The French administration had planned with the Dahirs of February, 1951 and July 6 1951 to create 2,200 communes. The corruption of the qaids and the failure of the rural administrative system gave impetus to a reorganization plan in order to salvage the colonial enterprise.
  At the same time, a group of intellectuals involved in administration (Jacques Berque, Julien Couleau, Marc Bloch) were promoting agrarian reform. See Ashford (1967:28–32) and Berque (1962:351–353).

[2]Their ideas echoed the reforms envisioned by liberal French officers, one of whom described the reorganized councils in 1953 as the "keystone to the entire system destined to lead the country to internal autonomy on a democratic foundation"—Capt. J. Romieu, quoted in Ashford (1967:29).

[3]Accounts of Moroccan rural administration can be found in Ashford (1961; 1967), Bachir (1969), Cherkaoui (1968) and Nicholas-Mourer (1963).

The first national party, the Istiqlal (Independence), led the country into independence. Its growing strength and popularity countrywide encouraged the king, in 1958, to promote a multi-party system in order to counter the erosion of monarchical control by Istiqlali power. A second party which sought a rural basis, the Haraka Shaabiya (Popular Movement), was formed in 1957. In 1959 a major split in the Istiqlal party led to the formation of the left-wing UNFP (National Union of Popular Forces), whose spokesman Mehdi Ben Barka envisioned 'a synthesis of the three great forces of Morocco, the trade unionists, the peasantry, and the resistance' (Waterbury 1970:217).

In the elections of 1960 the Istiqlal party won countrywide 40 percent of all the seats on the local councils, the Popular Movement won seven percent, and the UNFP 23 percent. But increasingly after May 1960, all political activity became dominated by the king through his control of the Ministry of Interior, Ministry of Justice, the army, the police, the Royal Cabinet, and the press. In March 1961, the king became prime minister, minister of defense, minister of agriculture, and minister of the interior.

From the inception of independence, the rural masses had been waiting for the end to the controls imposed by the colonial regime. After the first year of independent government, they felt the departure of the Europeans had provided them neither material nor political benefits which they expected. Regional uprisings were the result,[4] encouraged by verbal reassurances from the government of mass participation in political life. The uprisings expressed resentment at not being effectively integrated into the new nation. They were protests against the inadequacy of administration and the lack of expected development, both economic and political.

Following the initial three year period of independent government, the king and his makhzan began increasing control over Morocco's political activity. The creation of the rural communes was a response to 'partisan demands for monarchical concessions' (Ashford 1967:46–47) rather than a serious program intended to transform the rural economy.

The regions created by the French were apportioned into smaller units to form 19 Provinces and two independent Prefectures (Rabat and Casablanca). Each province is administered by a governor under the direction of the Minister of Interior. Within each province the circles are headed by *superqaids,* a new title created to fill the slots vacated by the Protectorate's Officers of Indigenous Affairs (AI). Under the superqaid serve the qaids of the circle, each of whom is

---

[4]The tribes of the High Moulouya region and the Tafilalt participated in 1957 in the short-lived uprising led by the governor of Tafilalt province, Addi ou Bihi. For interpretations of the Tafilalt and other rebellions see Gellner (1972) and Ashford (1961).

responsible for two to four rural communes. Qaids are no longer local notables, but middle level administrators appointed by the Ministry of Interior and assigned to provinces other than their own. They are periodically reassigned to posts in different provinces to assure that they do not develop a local power base. A 'qaidal' academy has been established to train rural administrators.

Under the qaids, local men are appointed as representatives of territorial segments of a rural commune, with the title of shaikh. Over each village, or in some cases over several villages, is appointed a muqaddam, the lowest link in the rural administration. These officials are salaried, unlike the communal councilmen.

The local administration hierarchy retains total control of political activity and is virtually the only source of power and wealth. The political parties have failed to provide alternative sources of political patronage or to serve as avenues to economic opportunities.

The total control of the makhzan over the countryside can be exemplified by its measures to contain the activities of rural communes. After the first elections of 1960, a law was passed (Dahir no. 59–315 of 23 June 1960) which defined the role of the communes as vehicles for local economic and social improvements 'under close supervision from local administration'. The only power given to the communes is strigently limited to discussion of the communal budget. Since most local communities depend almost wholly on subsidies from the central government and are unfamiliar with budget procedures, even this power is more apparent than real. The council has the right to express approval of additional matters that have been cleared for the agenda by superior local authorities. These are limited to minor economic problems and expressly exclude views of a political character or administrative matters. Even local matters not previously approved for the agenda by the qaid or a higher local authority cannot be discussed. The provincial governor also holds power to annul any decision of the council of which he disapproves.

Moreover, as a kind of redundant check, the elections of the councils are carefully monitored by the local authorities. Rarely are any candidates allowed to register who are not hand-picked by the administration. The manipulation of electoral lists, the refusal to register candidates on various grounds, the promises of future rewards for supporting 'official' candidates, are widely applied methods for neutralizing local political activity outside the control of the makhzan hierarchy. The methods select candidates who remain uncommitted to political parties and who appreciate that loyalty to the makhzan is the only avenue for advancement. The lesson has been quickly learned in the countryside that political activity that does not connect the individual to the network of the administration is counterproductive.

The fact that council seats create a link to the makhzan makes them desirable positions for advancement, even though communal councils are ineffective in promoting local activity. It is well perceived that any meaningful economic transformation has to proceed from a larger plan that remains beyond local vision. Favret's comments on Algerian peasants seem apt: "The peasants don't mind the State's being in charge of all economic activity; they resent its failure to be the driving force of the local economy. To them there is only one calling, that of fonctionnaire—a title with which all government employees adorn themselves—all else being mere eyewash and pretence" (Favret 1972:315).

THE RURAL COMMUNE OF THE AIT AYASH

The Ait Ayash form under the Independent government a rural commune which coincides with the population of the tribe and the village of the Ait Sidi Bou Moussa. The commune is administered by a qaid in Midelt, who is also responsible for the communes of the Ait Izdeg and Ait Ouafella. The qaid remains a distant figure to the villagers. Some business is conducted in his office, after long waits. His visits to the villages are rare. Regular contact is mediated through the local officials, the shioukh appointed over the three territorial segments of the Ait Ayash commune, and the muqaddamin. Each territorial segment, called *mshaikhat*, is composed of seven contiguous villages and hamlets, and forms a unit more important in daily life than the overall integration of the rural commune. Under each shaikh, muqaddamin serve as village headmen.

The muqaddam is only infrequently the leading figure in his community. Serving as the lowest link in the administration, he is little more than a messenger for the shaikh and the qaid, by whom he is handpicked. His duties include the distribution of mail, the circulation of notices from government bureaus, the registration of births and deaths, and other such tasks. He can still manage to hold power over local households by his control of subscriptions to work lists for public relief projects and to distribution of seed, plants, U.S. A.I.D. wheat arranged by government agencies.

Since the muqaddam is tied to administrative tasks, many village problems are still resolved by an informal jmaa composed by elders of the prominent households who authenticate titles to fields, adjudicate land disputes, and manage the purely local affairs, which include the hiring of the village fqih, the appointment of a manager of the mosque property and the selection of the supervisor of the irrigation schedule (muqaddam n'tergwa). The jmaa receives no official recognition.

The shioukh wield considerable local influence as makhzan officials. Just as they themselves gained their posts as clients to some patron within the administration, so too, they offer patronage to the villages by virtue of their recognition from above.

The original appointments of the shioukh were made in the following manner. Each village was asked to select one man as its representative. Of these, three were chosen as shioukh and the others appointed as muqaddamin. A second round of appointments followed the communal elections of 1963. At this time the appointments were made directly by the administration. The appointees shared the characteristic of non-involvement in politics in the first years of Independence, specifically in the uprising of Addi ou Bihi. They remained fairly apolitical, in that different men tagged them with different party affiliations and no one was quite sure of their political beliefs, if indeed they held any, other than their pledged allegiance to the makhzan.

THE COMMUNAL COUNCIL

The communal council of the Ait Ayash has been of minimal relevance to the economic welfare of the villages. The council members gain some prestige and minor rewards, since their successful bids show them to be clients of local administrators.

In the first elections of 1960, the Ait Ayash elected a council of nine members. The candidates had to declare a party affiliation. Four of the elected councilmen were of the Independence (Istiqlal) party and five of the Popular Movement (Haraka Shaabiya). Selection of council president was determined by party ties. Two men with the qualification of literacy were nominated. The Popular Movement nominee received four votes of his party and won over the Independence party nominee who received the three Istiqlali votes. Party preferences seemed to be tied to purely local alignments rather than party programs. This was true in the village I knew best, and according to informants, was the case for all the villages.

The explanation of the alignments went something like this: the qaid of the Protectorate had completely proscribed Istiqlal party activities in the closing years of the colonial period. It was only with Independence that people could openly join the party and attend monthly meetings held in Midelt. At the time of Addi ou Bihi's preparations for the uprising in 1957, the few Istiqlali members were directed by the party to oppose the movement. During the regional mobilization, the Istiqlalis were rounded up in the villages and incarcerated for the period of the short-lived affair. With the formation of the Popular

Movement party in 1957 and its official recognition in 1958, many anti-Istiqlalis joined the new party as a natural choice for opposition in village alignments.

In fact, more than the two parties were actively seeking members but in the informants' own view only the two party labels proved important, and this is how they explained village alignments. One Ait Ayashi who supported the UNFP party explained his affiliation as a way to maintain a neutral posture to the two dominant alignments, which he criticized. "The political parties," he said, "are not useful to the tribe. The makhzan advises us to vote for men who would work best for the group, but people vote only for parties. The parties now are like feuds used to be in the time if siba. You choose your side according to your adversary's position. All the villages are divided between the two parties."

Since the work of the council remains inconsequential, it is not surprising that party affiliations figure at best for local opposition.

The irrelevance of the parties in relation to any meaningful local issues was made clearer in the second round of elections in 1963 (Chambergeat, 1963). The UNFP boycotted this campaign nationwide and directed its candidates to withdraw from the elections. At the last minute the Istiqlal party joined the boycott for its own reasons. The councilmen elected for the Ait Ayash commune were unopposed candidates affiliated, at least by inference, with the Popular Movement party. According to some PM members, most of the elected councilmen had not been expected to win over stronger candidates of other parties and weak candidates had been encouraged to run.

In fact, the candidates elected in 1963 had been those who had pledged support of the newly formed royalist front party called the FDIC (Front for the Defense of Constitutional Institutions). A pledge of allegiance had been extracted by the local authorities before the registration of candidates. Nationwide, the FDIC won 10,000 seats in the rural councils out of the total of 11,200 seats. However, the majority of the elected throughout the country were, or had been, affiliated with the Popular Movement party. The local authorities were, in 1963, virtually unrestrained in their manipulation of the elections to place the royalist-front candidates in office. King Hassan had total control of the Ministry of Interior by mid-1963 with no ministerial representation in the cabinet from opposition political parties to check procedures and results. 'Local level participation in national affairs was no longer a significant issue in Moroccan political life' (Ashford 1967:55).

The party candidacies may have meant more for the Ait Ayash had the councilmen held any useful functions to perform once in office. It was difficult to discern what they actually did and whether they even held meetings. Their contacts were with the qaidal bureau rather than with each other. When I asked about the work of the council, one disgruntled Ayashi said, "Their accomplishments are very visible. Before all this, the president of the council (*raiss n'jmaa l'qarawiya*) rode a donkey into town. Now he rides his motorscooter and leaves a cloud of dust behind for all to see."

Early efforts in setting up the communes had concentrated on the creation of market places in order to provide centers for local development. This was pursued in the commune of the Ansegmir valley, and the site of the central village of Ait Oumghar was selected for a new market. The project was initiated with local enthusiasm and the government subsidized the construction of an arcaded market center with twelve merchants' stalls, a coffee house, an infirmary, a slaughter house, and an enclosure for animals. After the constructions were completed in 1958, the village households defrayed for two months the cost of the visits of a qadi and his secretary (adoul) during the market day in order to furnish the standard services available in local souqs. Some of the itinerant merchants who toured the circuit of the regions' markets showed up the first few weeks, and then stopped coming. The unimproved road leading to the market place was in poor condition (and remained so in 1969). The established markets of Midelt and Boumia, both of which offered in addition to weekly souqs a permanent array of shops and services, as well as the other markets of Itzer, Tounfit, and Kerroushen, provided for the needs of a regional clientele. A new market offered no attraction. The infirmary remained unstaffed, the coffee house was never leased, and the entire market plan was dropped. This left the communal council with nothing to plan or administer.

In 1967, the communal budget listed receipts of 86,089 DH and expenditures of 85,257 DH. The figures incorporated the financial contributions in public relief funds by the Promotion Nationale for an irrigation project on the Ansegmir Valley, which provided the major source of alternative income for the villagers.

The communal organization in its political aspect little of consequence to the daily lives of the villagers. The one-party representation on the council at the second elections has tended to deflect frustrations into internal alignments within each village.

In one village the fqih was dismissed after he refused to prepare for burial the body of a villager who had withheld his contribution for the fqih's upkeep because he was of the 'opposite' party. The fqih reapplied for the position some time later, stating he was no longer interested in politics but only in earning his salary. The village remained divided along party lines and could not agree to his rehiring.

Initial exposure to overt political activity through parties and elections tended to reinforce what was already appreciated, that eco-

THE CONTEMPORARY PERIOD

nomic and social enhancement relied on the patronage of the makhzan. The communal council remained powerless as a source of activity and renewal for the community.

Against this background, the issue of the collective land came to figure as a topic of interest. Collective land did not fall within the jurisdiction of the communal council. Thus it came to be viewed as an alternative source of activity for economic amelioration.

COLLECTIVE LAND

In the years since Independence, population increments among the Ait Ayash, especially through migration, have escalated exploitation of the collective land. The continuing sale of irrigated fields and the growing number of landless households is compounded by the needs of southern pastoralists who are driven north by worse conditions in the south.

The livestock of the commune of the Ait Ayash in 1967 included 16,040 sheep, 6,832 goats, 970 cows, and 70 camels. In 1969 the number had increased to 17,612 sheep, 7,000 lambs, 7,620 goats, 1,730 kids, 1,165 cows, and 111 camels (Annual Report, Midelt Archives). The camels reflect the presence of tent dwelling herders, since villagers never keep camels; the herders require them as burden animals, especially for tent transport.

The tent dwellers are unevenly distributed among the Ait Ayash villages. The northern mshaikhat (Ait Illousen), which uses the collective land on the Aarid between the Ansegmir and Moulouya rivers, has no registered pastoralist households. The villages of the central (Ait Oumghar) and southern (Bou Draa) sections which are closer to the collective holdings on the Jebel Ayashi piedmont contain all the tent dwelling households. The Jebel Ayashi zone of the best pastures is also the zone of plowed surfaces (bour) where herders increasingly trespass on the cultivated space. Depredation of the fields causes recurring complaints from the villagers, just as the restriction of grazing hems in the herders. The crowding is compounded by herders from neighboring communes and from southern territories (Rish, Sidi Bou Yaqoub, Gourrama).

Village opinion held that the council should have looked after these problems. Some argued that the president of the council, who is of the Ait Sidi Bou Moussa and therefore not of the tribe, holds no rights to the collective land and lacks the incentive to safeguard it for those who hold rights to it. In truth, the rural councils were never given any authority over collective lands. The councils are not representative bodies for landholding tribes. Neither are the shioukh heads of tribal fractions. The tribes have no longer any official status even though collective land tenure through descent ascription has not been abrogated. Therefore the supervision for this category of land comes under no existing local authority. The minutes of various councils have shown that requests were frequently submitted for control over collective land in order to exploit it on behalf of the community (Ashford 1967:51).

In 1967 the administration advised the Ait Ayash villages to select representatives who would be charged with supervision of the collective land. These representatives are known as *mumtilin* (*mumtil*, sing.). The original plan called for six mumtilin, following a division of the tribe into six sections during the Protectorate period for organizing corvée teams. This proved unsatisfactory because each village wanted its own representative. A compromise settled on fourteen mumtilin. They are charged with the leasing of pastures, notifying the local bureau of trespassers, and approving of new constructions on collective land. The mumtilin receive no compensation since they perform duties for the tribe. But their assignment has been a failure. Some are reported to have accepted bribes from trespassing pastoralists. One of the mumtilin said, "The plain fact is that from the time we were assigned to guard our land we have been unable to chase any shepherd who did not belong on it nor to rent pastures to anyone."

The local problem of the Ait Ayash does not figure as a problem in the wider regional perspective. The herding households registered in the villagers are the regular taxpayers of the region and their use of the collective territory of the Ait Ayash is not an administrative issue. From the perspective of the Ait Ayash, the territory belongs to them and they should be able to convert their rights into benefits. In the wider view, the land is being appropriated by those most in need of it and able to exploit it fully.

The conflict, as the Ait Ayash view it, began during the Protectorate when their qaid ratified the land claims and then initiated the sale of irrigated fields as commodities stripped of social connections. The preemptory rights of kin (*shafaa*) were no longer enforceable when a field that would sell for 20,000 ryals to another tribesman could bring 50,000 ryals when sold to an 'outsider' herder. The process has accelerated in recent years as urban investors buy land at escalating prices. The cycles of indebtedness to storekeepers grow larger, and the need for cash feeds the drive to alienate more land. A way they see to arrest the process is to gain control over the collective land in order to charge pasture fees or to exploit it by herding the flocks of others with contracts for a portion (usually one quarter) of the lambs. The latter possibility remains remote. Herding is highly esteemed but evaluated as too rigorous for those who have adapted to sedentarism. But the strips of fields in the valleys no longer sustain the majority of households. The distinction between richer and poorer households continues to grow and the gap between them becomes larger. Still, all considered the disposition of the collective land as crucial for their future security.

The mumtilin have to rely on the local qaid to initiate any action or, in some cases, succumb to bribes from trespassing pastoralists for quiescence. Before the latter fact became known when some tent households told of fees they had been paying for their use of the land, the mumtilin in April, 1969 were urged to make a concerted effort to clear the land of 'interlopers'. The Midelt bureau of the qaid provided armed *mokhaznis* (soldiers; guards attached to the office of the qaid) who accompanied them to serve notices to several dozen tents on Ait Ayash territory. In each case the men were absent with the flocks and nothing could be accomplished through the women at home. After consecutive visits for three days the matter was dropped by the administration. The pastoralists pay their dues as taxed producers and as subjects for petty extractions from mumtilin and low level officials. The administration remains indifferent, while the villagers feel helpless and the pastoralists insecure. Two incidents indicate something about the plight of the two sides.

An Ait Ayashi on an inspection of his dry fields on the mountainside found a flock grazing on the cereal plants. The shepherd of the animals called two other herders to his aid and a stone hurling fight followed. The farmer, in his fifties, was wounded on the right arm, disarming him. He also received a serious cut on one eye and a broken nose from one stone. On his return to the village in the evening, I provided him with transportation to the hospital in Midelt. His teen-aged son accompanied us, and went to the police station to register a complaint. The man had recognized two of his assailants, and his son gave their names to the police. This kind of confrontation was recurrent. The herders left the region immediately. Two months later gendarmes came to the village to report on the conclusions of the official investigation. The injuries must have been sustained by a fall from the victim's mule. The alleged assailants could not have caused the injuries, because, according to the testimony of acquaintances, they were not in the vicinity at the time of the incident. The villagers expressed little surprise over the verdict. The farmer, they said, was poor and without influence while the herders were rich and capable of persuading officials. One of the elders of the village jmaa summarized the matter: "The fight was against all of us. We stand helpless and cannot defend our land. But in truth what can we do? The makhzan has the arms now and the interlopers have the money to persuade those who decide these matters. The fight has degraded all of us."

The pastoralists are not only in a precarious position in questions of land use, but in economic transactions as well. Wool clippings, for example, are sold in the local markets both by weight and by the fleece. Usually lack of storage facilities and transportation, combined with a need for ready cash presses them to sell their annual wool production to middlemen who pick it up with trucks after the shearing at a price somewhat below that of local markets.

My contact with the tent dwelling households of the Ait Ayash commune remained very limited, but I did arrange to meet some of them through the village families with which they had agricultural associations. The herders descended to the villages only infrequently, to use the grain mills and to oversee the harvest of their fields worked by others.

One invitation I received was for a visit on the day of the sheep shearing. An interested buyer of the wool was also present. He was an employee of the Forestry Service, manning a ranger's post in the vicinity. Since his government service he had acquired four pick-up trucks which he leased to the administration and also used in his own commercial sidelines. The household's flock of 175 sheep was sheared in the course of the morning by itinerant shearers who received one fleece per 25 sheep clipped. The household was composed of the head (in his sixties), his wife, and a married son and his family. They kept 45 fleeces for domestic needs and were prepared to sell 120 fleeces, approximately 180 kg of wool.[5] Two or three were given away. The buyer offered 14,000 ryals (approximately 140 dollars) for the wool, a fair price. The head of household agreed but his son insisted the sale had to be made on a cash basis. After a series of conferences between the father and son with each other and with the forestry ranger, the younger son prevailed and the deal was closed with a full cash payment. A few days later the tent was served a summons from the same ranger for trespassing on state forest preserve with sheep and camels. The fine was 24,000 ryals (approximately 240 dollars).

The case stimulated extended discussion in the village. Some thought the younger man was at fault with his demand for cash payment which irritated the ranger. Trespass on forest land was a costly offense. Herders took extreme care against infraction or at least against apprehension. Proven cases of trespassing were infrequent. Some opinions held that the ranger would revoke the summons in return for some of the cash he had paid for the wool. Most agreed that what the household lacked was a patron within the administration to provide support and security against expensive miscalculations. The tent finally paid the fine rather than continue to deal with the ranger.

---

[5]The average fleece weighs 1.5 kg. Wool prices in Midelt in June and July 1969 varied from 6 DH (120 ryals) to 5.5 DH (110 ryals) per wool clip, and 4 DH per kg.

ON PROPERTY AND PRODUCTION

In 1968 the villages of the Ait Ayash commune, comprising 1,090 households of 4,969 individuals, were estimated to have 1,136 ha of irrigated fields and 1,088 ha of dry fields under cultivation (Midelt Bureau: Bureau des Impôts; Census Report). Data on land cultivation is difficult to obtain, in part because the tax exemption in the province makes it an issue of low priority for the administration. The registered figures record the reports of the shioukh based on their estimates. In 1967 for example the reported dry farming totaled 1,088.90 ha. Precisely the same figure was entered for the following year. Bour cultivation remains, however, extremely variable from season to season in any household.

The estate of the zawiya Sidi Hamza on the Ansegmir is not included in these figures. The zawiya had, in that year's report, declared holdings of 100 ha of irrigated fields and 200 ha of bour; approximately 360 ha of its estate had been sold in six parcels to non-resident land investors.

The following discussion focuses on the field holdings and annual cultivation in only one village. The information on the fields was gathered by interviews with the heads of households. This was part of a more comprehensive village census discussed later in this chapter and the next.

Land measurements were not kept in the past. Field sizes are evaluated by the amount of seed sown although increasingly, with land sales, measurements are taken. In all the interviews, however, the field sizes are reported in terms of the amount of seed required. In order to arrive at the dimensions of a field, I used the widely recognized regional standard of one hectare to one quintal (100 kg) of seed in wheat. Weight measurements are locally figured in volume units, the standard of which is the *abra*. Six abra of hard wheat weigh one quintal. Other grain measures for one quintal are: soft wheat, six and one-half abras; barley, eight abras; and maize, seven abras.

The village, which I shall call Ait Akhatar (a fictitious name), has 452 inhabitants distributed in 72 households. The old qsar of Ait Akhatar stood on a rock outcrop of the east bank and housed forty families. In the 1940s, the apartments of the qsar were abandoned one by one, as the families began building dwellings outside the walls. Only the mosque, inside the qsar gate, remained in use until 1970. In 1969, during the period of fieldwork, the community built a mosque on the clearing in the center of the new village, the site of the threshing grounds. No overall plan guided the building of new homes. Twelve of the original families built the first houses near gardens just outside the

Figure 2 **Social ascriptions and land property in an Ait Ayash village.**

Social categories	No. of households	Total membership	No. of households with irrigated land	No. of households without land
Clan "A"	7	47	7	0
Clan "B"	9	73	9	0
Clan "C"	7	37	7	0
Clan "D"	2	18	2	0
Incorporated with clan "A"	2	14	2	0
Incorporated with clan "B"	16	86	16	0
Incorporated with clan "D"	1	8	1	0
Shurfa	4	27	1	3
Unincorporated settlers of the Protectorate period	16	106	11	5
Settlers since Independence	8	36	5	3
Total	72	452	61	11

eastern and northern walls of the qsar. Fourteen households moved to the opposite bank of the river near family fields. The rest are dispersed east of the main irrigation channel, around the threshing grounds, in what is called the 'new village'. The most recent constructions are multi-dwelling units housing the families of the latest settlers.

Some social distance is maintained between the old families and the settlers who were not ritually incorporated into the tighsatin of the village and who lack rights in the collective land. Marriages and other ceremonies are celebrated separately, and the old families maintain they do not intermarry with iqblin. This does not hold statistically. The social differences are kept alive by the possibility that heirs to the collective land patrimony may accrue benefits that will exclude the unincorporated. Moreover, the differences have a dimension in the property relations, in that the 11 landless households (Figure 2) fall within the category of the unincorporated. However, the pastoralist families, wealthier than most of the village households, are within the same category, and 66 percent of the recent settlers have bought property since their arrival.

While the plowing of communal land has increased over the years, the irrigated land has not changed in total surface along with its wider distribution to more households. The distribution of irrigated holdings among the households of Ait Akhatar is shown in Figure 3. Four of the 72 households are not included; two are of tent dwellers

Figure 3 **Irrigated field holdings among 68 households of an Ait Ayash village.**

Land in hectares	No. of households	No. of members (Household count)		Land per capita in hectares
20–15.1	2	(1)	19	.89
		(1)	14	1.2
15–10.1	1	(1)	24	.6
10–5.1	2	(1)	9	.89
		(1)	5	1.2
5–4.1	2	(1)	4	1.25
		(1)	3	1.66
4–3.1	8	(1)	16	.25
		(2)	9	.44
		(1)	7	.57
		(1)	6	.66
		(2)	3	1.3
		(1)	2	2.0
3–2.6	3	(1)	8	.37
		(1)	6	.5
		(1)	4	.75
2.5–2.1	1	(1)	14	.17
2–1.6	11	(1)	12	.16
		(1)	10	.2
		(1)	9	.22
		(2)	8	.25
		(1)	7	.28
		(1)	6	.33
		(1)	5	.4
		(1)	4	.5
		(1)	3	.66
		(1)	2	1.0
1.5–1.1	1	(1)	9	.16
1–.6	15	(1)	10	.1
		(1)	8	.12
		(3)	7	.14
		(4)	6	.16
		(2)	5	.2
		(2)	4	.25
		(1)	3	.33
		(1)	2	.5
.5–.1	11	(1)	8	.06
		(1)	6	.08
		(1)	5	.1
		(4)	3	.16
		(4)	1	.5
0	11	(1)	10	—
		(1)	9	—
		(2)	7	—
		(3)	6	—
		(2)	5	—
		(1)	3	—
		(1)	1	—

whose holdings I could not ascertain. Another is that of a nuclear family with separate residence from the extended household of which it is a part in terms of property. The fourth is a household which had lost fields through flooding, and the proprietor claimed he had no fields, which was not wholly accurate.

Figure 4 **Dry cultivation among the households of an Ait Ayash village**

No. of hectares plowed in bour	No. of households
23	1
16	1
13.5	1
8	1
7	2
6.5	1
6	3
5.5	1
5	3
4	6
3.5	4
3	9
2.5	2
2	2
1.5	2
1	2
.5	3
0	19
	63

Four non-resident families have land investments in the village. This land is cultivated by their local kinsmen and affines with annual associations. Property of the mosque in habous adds approximately five ha to the exploitable surface. These fields are leased every four years in 12 lots for annual fees of up to 12,000 ryals. The total irrigated surface owned by the village households covers 165.8 ha. This includes the fields on Taouraout which are regularly watered and held as melk. On the basis of irrigated production along, only 13 households own the 0.6 ha per capita land surface to obtain the rural average income of 392 DH.

The two crop production on the irrigated fields has come to be surpassed in surface by bour cultivation. Figure 4 details the distribution of 200 ha of dry fields among 63 households in 1969. Nine households are not included in this table, but the actual total surface is represented because of a number of farming associations between households. Fifty-two households farmed some dry land. There were 20 associations between two and three households for the year. The extent of dry farming varies from year to year. Rainfall is one of the controlling factors, since plowing commences after the fall rains. The seed available to the household is another factor.

Figure 5 **Total annual cultivation of irrigated fields and bour among the households of an Ait Ayash village**

Cultivated land in hectares	Number of households
31	1
18	2
11	1
9	2
8	3
7	4
6	5
5	3
4	12
3	4
2	3
1	3
.5 or less	7
0	13
	63

Those who supplement the production of the irrigated fields with bour cultivation spread the seasonal risks by plowing both on the Ayashi mountainside and on the Aarid plain of the western side. In 1969 five households had bour exclusively on the Ayashi slopes, and nine had plowed only on the Aarid plain. Figure 5 gives the total annual cultivation of 63 households. In all cases the total production surface covers one-half of the irrigated property and the additional dry land planted in winter cereals.

The only crop grown for sale is the potato. Those with sufficient land devote half of the spring planting to potatoes, or else alternate each season between maize and potatoes. The crop was introduced to the Ait Ayash by the French during the thirties. The villagers were provided with seed for two years, and the French set up 'markets' at two of the villages for the sale of the crop after the harvest. Since then, potatoes are grown for cash because storage for home consumption is considered a problem. The practice has been widely adapted in recent years; Raynal (1960:318) reported in 1960 that the three Midelt tribes of the Ait Ayash, Ait Izdeg and Ait Ouafella planted altogether only fifty ha in potatoes. In the village of Ait Akhatar, 42 households planted potatoes when they could afford the seed and fertilizer required. One quintal of seed on a quarter of a ha yields eight to 11 quintals. Raynal (1960: 18) reports harvests of 12 to 15 quintals per hectare. The determining factor in decisions to grow the cash crop rests on prior arrangements for its sale and transportation. Some households negotiate annual contracts with a Midelt merchant who provides the seed and fertilizer and transportation for one-half the harvest and also buys the farmer's share. In 1968 a merchant for Fez bought the potato harvest of two villages at 22.50 DH. per quintal. The retail price in Midelt was 25–30 DH/kg. Without pre-arrangements, the producers are forced to sell at whatever rate is offered. Some said they had sold at 15 DH per quintal but had bought the seed at 35 and 40 DH per quintal.

Those who have gardens near their homes grow vegetables for home consumption. The gardens are few and belong to the 'old' families. Most households have their fields at a distance where they cannot be overseen, which the villagers say is necessary for gardens. The fruit trees in the old gardens provide a source of cash income for the few who own them. The fruits are sold as futures for cash advances before they ripen. The buyer decides the terms and the villagers feel fortunate for any cash sale since they have no other options for the disposition of the produce. One villager of Ait Akhatar sold the fruit of twelve apple trees for a cash advance of 250 DH to a merchant who transported the produce to Casablanca. Apples in the Midelt market in 1969 sold for three DH per kilogram. The buyer gathered thirty cases of 25 kg each from the trees.

The basic diet is bread, tea with sugar, and various meat and vegetable stews (*tajin*). Sugar, tea, cooking oil, meat, and in many households vegetables have to be bought for cash. Daily consumption of bread averages .5 kg per person. A household of four persons requires 7.3 quintals of wheat annually; this represents the production of one hectare at a yield of seven to one. Half of the households of the village cannot meet this subsistence need through their irrigated holdings. Since the majority of the households do not produce sufficient grain for a surplus to sell in exchange for all the other subsistence needs, the alternate sources of income grow in importance as the land is divided among a larger number of households. The traditional alternatives are seasonal migrant labor as harvesters and annual contracts to work the land of others (akhumas). Presently the most important source is the relief work in public projects provided by the Promotion Nationale since the early 1960s. The cash income it provides maintains subsistence in many households and, moreover, its program feeds the hope that some larger economic transformation is possible.

MIGRANT LABOR

The seasonal migration of laborers during harvest in the Atlantic plains involves a considerable portion of adult males. In 1965, a year of good crops, 174,000 men, approximately 11 percent of the male labor force (those between 20 and 49 years old) of the country, traveled from their homes to seek agricultural labor in the plains. The population of the Moulouya plain contributed 5,400 seasonal migrants for that year representing 15 percent of the male labor force of the region (Noin 1970(2): 157–159). Since the male labor force is calculated to represent one-sixth of the total population, the percentage for the Ait Ayash with a population of 5,000 is somewhat higher, contributing 200 men. From the village of Ait Akhatar, 16 men left for migrant labor in 1969, generally for a period of one month. The daily wage they received varied from 6.50 DH to 7.80 DH.

The country-wide statistics indicate that 65 percent of the households of migrant workers own land and only 35 percent are landless households. The smaller participation of the landless can be explained by the fact that most of them work for land-sufficient households with annual contracts (akhumas) which bind them to year-round service. Degree of economic deprivation is not sufficient to predict participation. In the village of Ait Akhatar, 13 migrants are landowners and three are landless. Participation in itinerant labor also depends on the household type and the size of the labor pool in the family. The highest incidence is among those households which include more than one adult male: extended or joint households and nuclear households in an advanced stage of their developmental cycle. The fact that only 16 men migrated for the harvest labor is related to the prevalence of nuclear households among the Ait Ayash. The social factors that favor this type of household will be discussed in the next chapter. The single adult male in the household is kept from leaving by the irrigation schedule of the spring planting, twice every 15 days.

Of the 16 migrants in Ait Akhatar, five were sons in extended families, one was the younger male of a joint household, and four were adult sons of three nuclear households. Of the rest, three were landless heads of households without the akhumas contract; two of these were shurfa who lived by alms. Of the other three, two came from recently divided joint households, which meant they had close agnates to supervise their fields. The third was a household of a widow with six offspring, of which two were young adult males.[6]

The average of one month of migrant labor has been estimated to provided from 10 percent to 25 percent of the annual revenue of participating households (Noin 1970(2): 167–168). This can be exemplified by an Ait Akhatar household composed of one couple and their

---

[6]This was one of the rare households with land property inherited by the female spouse from her father's estate. Her husband had originally come to the village as an akhumas for another family. Subsequently he joined the army for fifteen years. Her natal family had been land-sufficient in father's generation. His property was divided into five shares, one for each of four sons and one for two daughters. One daughter had married out of the village and her half-share was held by a brother. What had been the production base for one household was supporting five households in the subsequent generation.

seven children, ranging in age from 2 to 21 years. The family fields produced, at a 10:1 ratio, 6.7 quintals (or 40 abras). No bour was plowed because the household lacked drafts animals, owning only one donkey. The family consumption of wheat reached 16.4 quintals annually. Two of the sons, nineteen and seventeen years old, worked as shepherds for village families. Each received an annual salary of 200 DH paid in grain, which in wheat amounts to five quintals. Another son added 200 DH to 250 DH to the family income through migrant labor of thirty days. The only other income came from the sale of *zenbbl* (halfa baskets), woven by the household head and sold by the piece in local markets. But even the grain supply was not sufficient. The household head claimed he had to buy grain between harvests. The problem was a common one with many households. They exchanged quantities of grain at the local shops for other supplies during the year and were obliged to buy the same grains later a higher prices.

IKHUMASN AND IKHADAMN

In the traditional agricultural system of extensive farming in the Moroccan plains, the akhumas (ikhumasn, pl.) is the agricultural laborer who receives 20 percent of the heavest. The 80 percent retained by the landowner is intended to provide equal amounts for the seed, for the draft animals, for harvest labor and taxes, and for his own recompense.[7]

The Ait Ayash employ the term akhumas for the laborer who has an annual contract and receives a fee which is not computed on actual crop returns. The akhumas carries out domestic duties during the slack periods of the agricultural cycle. This distinguishes him from the akhdam, the laborer hired for a specific task and period.

Nine villagers in Ait Akhatar worked the land of others as ikhumasn. Three were sharecroppers in a strict sense, receiving one-half the harvest as tenants of non-resident landowners. Two of the landowners are tent dwelling herders and the third is a sharif residing in Midelt, a descendant of Sidi Mhand al Arabi (see Chapter One, "The Moulouya Plain in the Reign of Mawlay Hassan").

The six others worked for local residents who themselves labored on the fields. These ikhumasn are less sharecroppers and more domestics in the top six households of the village. They are younger members of landless or land-deprived families whose contracted fee amounts to two quintals of wheat, two quintals of barley, two quintals of maize

---

[7]Couleau (1968) offers an analysis of the akhumas system as a leveling mechanism for resource access between landowning and landless peasants in the traditional rural setting of North Africa.

and a sheep (*ta'ayat*) for the holiday of Aid al Kabir. They also are given some clothing. This represents the equivalent of 200 DH, the same fee received by the young shepherds of local families.

Over one-third of the household heads take whatever day labor they can find. This means at best a few days' work at reaping, since most households meet their own labor needs.[8] The most labor consuming task of the agricultural cycle is the harvest, which absorbs from four to eight man-days per hectare. Families that plow more than three ha of bour have begun to rent mechanical harvesters which replace the seasonal day work given to others.

The regional agricultural station (Centre de Travaux, no. 32) provides a few unskilled jobs at four DH per diem. In Ait Akhatar, only one man had worked for the station for a period of one month. Other efforts to supplement income include the weaving of esparto baskets used to transport manure from the stables to the fields. Three heads of households practice this handicraft.

The full-time work at the nearby lead mines of Aouli requires resettlement, since commuting transportation is unavailable. One village worker has secured work as a miner and rents living quarters for his conjugal family in Midelt while maintaining his membership in a joint household of seven brothers with undivided property.

Other than the fqih and the grade school teacher, the only non-agricultural specialists are three shopkeepers (only one of whom makes his living exclusively by retailing dry goods), and a butcher. Both the principal shopkeeper and the butcher are shurfa, and own no land in the village.

PUBLIC RELIEF WORK: CHOMAGE

The most important source of additional income for the villagers is the program intended to relieve underemployment with work on public projects provided by the Promotion Nationale. The project on the Ansegmir valley is a water diversion which will bring under irrigation 1,000 ha of Ait Ayash collective land on the eastern bank. The work, begun in 1963, was far from being completed in 1969. The intention was to distribute cash and grain to the indigent and underemployed of the province, so its pace was leisurely, determined to a degree by a lack of an adequate technical staff. The unskilled labor

---

[8]Collective field labor, twiza, is no longer practiced and has fallen into disrepute because it has become synonymous with corvée imposed by qaids during the Protectorate period and by zawiya chiefs and murabitin. During the period of fieldwork, the current saint of the Ait Ayash, an Alawite sharif of Rissani with land property on the Ansegmir, sent a crier through the village recruiting laborers for his fields. Most men I asked said they would be too busy to help. At other times, they told me, the initial field labor of young men was carried out on the fields of the Hamzawiya shurfa for the baraka inherent in it. There was little enthusiasm for the current opportunity for it.

applicants subscribed through registration with the village muqaddam. Subscription is for two week periods with work cards entitling the laborers to two DH and four kg of U.S. A.I.D. wheat per diem.

Since the majority of community members apply for the 'chomeur's' work, there is a maximum limit of six work cards per person. In Ait Akhatar, 32 participants had worked the twelve-week limit for the year. The number may actually be higher since the muqaddam controls the work list and some manipulation is possible. Forty men in the village had participated in the project, according to the information I gathered from the household census. Competition is keen for continued subscription on the work list.

The distribution of the sacks of wheat to card holders is followed frequently by the immediate sale of the wheat for cash to merchants who gather on the occasion. The 100 lb sacks are sold for 18.50 DH and the money is used to repay accumulated debts at the local shops. Payment and distribution are usually delayed months after the work is completed. In many cases the work cards are 'sold' for credit at the shops. The shopkeeper buys the card by extending credit for thirty-five DH. He then collects the cash and sacks of wheat on distribution. Each card has the value of 45 DH.

The doles of wheat and cash permit an extension of credit from shopkeepers before the cycle of indebtedness forces the sale of another field. "Securing credit," said one villager, "is the profession of the Ait Ayash." Some households meet their daily needs by credit on unripened grains. After the harvest they deliver most of their production to the shopkeepers as payment due.

Completion of the irrigation project transfers the improved land into the state domain. The administrative plan calls for the creation of ten plots, each of 100 ha, to be leased on long term for modern farming. The leaseholders need to own the agricultural machines. Exploitation with rented equipment does not constitute, in the official view, modern farming.

The Ait Ayash know they cannot manage such farms themselves. Their hope is that the future proprietors will offer them wage labor to replace the relief work of the makhzan. In this they see their chance to enter the cash economy which has transformed their needs but not their production.

The increased activity in arboriculture[9] on the High Moulouya

---

[9] In 1960, the High Moulouya region had 35,000 fruit trees of which 12,000 had been newly planted by land investors (Raynal, 1960:318). On the territory of the Ait Ayash in 1968 there were 4,267 taxed trees and 2,015 nontaxed trees (Service des Impôts Agricoles, Midelt personal communication).

In 1969 more than 20,000 apple trees were planted within the Ait Ayash Commune (Communication of the super-qaid, Midelt). The new orchards are investments exclusively of non-residents, especially on the fields sold in Aasker. The Aasker fields have remained uncultivated for several decades because of low productivity and very likely because of water shortage. The ex-quid Cherrou sold a tract for 25,000 DH which is now planted with 8,000 apple trees. Irrigated fields sell for 1,000 to 2,000 DH per hectare. Those sold to the new investors in Aasker sell for 2,000 DH per ha.

plain in recent years leads the villagers to the same conclusion, that as day laborers on these new enterprises they will find more security than they now have as grain farmers. One enterprising villager, who was one of the wealthiest members of the community, decided to cultivate in 1968 an additional three ha of abandoned fields in the section known as Aasker (Plate 2). He sowed four quintals of wheat and yielded 24 quintals. He employed six reapers for four days to harvest the grain at six DH per day per laborer, at a total expense of 150 DH. He had 16 quintals left after subtracting the seed and the labor expenses. At a rate of 39 DH per quintal, he had netted 624 DH. He held other land which he cultivated regularly, owned a small flock of sheep, employed an akhumas, and provided adequately for the extended household he supported. However he glumly compared his efforts with those of a land investor who had bought some of the abandoned Aasker fields on which he had planted 40 fruit trees (apple and apricot). The first crop, before all the trees had matured, had yielded the value of 2,000 DH. It was clear to the villager that grain production had been superceded by new crops and techniques, but he did not know how he himself could make the transition to the new economic and political and ecological conditions. Many shared his perceptions and frustration, even without his careful calculations. The traditional ways were gone but the modern world of new crops and techniques remained inaccessible, tied to agricultural investments and credits beyond the reach of the solitary *fellah* (peasant).

COMMUNITY AND COOPERATION

The administration of the villages in the independent period has been both elaborate and inadequate. Within the village, the ambivalent attitudes toward the low-level administrators and the insecurity generated by real and felt deprivations tend to break down a sense of community. Propinquity no longer means intercommunication.

The promised participation in wider political and economic networks has done little to change the village subsistence economy and the sustained cooperation it requires. The rural council inadequately defined in its role and functions, as well as the village headman who is occupied with administrative tasks, do not serve the village households in maintaining the communal tasks needed for the production and maintenance activities.

It is not surprising that despite elaborate rural administration, the village comes to rely on a local jmaa unrecognized by the government. It is the jmaa that engenders the required cooperation in daily tasks.

Regular concerns are the communal herding of the liverstock, water division, the hire of the fqih and maintenance of the mosque, and support in property disputes prior to and during court setlements. The jmaa in the present is an *ad hoc* committee composed of elders from the first founding families who overcome personal differences to deal with questions of community. There is a core group of four men who are joined on different occasions by a few others; informants most often named six members on the jmaa of Ait Akhatar. One of the members frequently oversees the sale of a field or mediating in a family dispute or accompanying litigants to court session. The intervention of the jmaa in personal cases is initiated by an invitation for all or any of its members to a dinner for discussion of the problem.

The foremost responsibility of the jmaa is the water division and the maintenance of the irrigation ditches. For this task they appoint a muqaddam n'tergwa. In the present the muqaddam n'tergwa is a trusted and reliable co-resident charged with the time consuming tasks of water regulation. Fifty households contribute 25 abras (over four quintals) of wheat and 25 abras of maize for his maintenance. At the time of fieldwork the water manager was a landless household head who also kept the village bull which the cattle owners subsidized for breeding purposes. The 57 households that own one or more cows provide three *gamilas* (.5 dkl) of maize annually.

The water manager recruits the labor for channel repairs; each landowning household contributes one worker, irrespective of size of field holdings. The seasonal repairs work in 1969 was compensated for the first time with funds from the Promotion Nationale project. Thirty men from Ait Akhatar and an adjoining village labored for 26 days to complete the repairs. The previous year, when it had been carried out as an unpaid community project, 60 men from the two villages worked for 12 days clearing and widening the ditches.

The muqaddam n'tergwa also collects the izmazz imposed for animal trespassing and field destruction. The minimum fine is one DH for large animals and 50 FR for sheep, goats, and donkeys. He retains one-third of the collected fines and the rest is turned over to the jmaa. Another of his tasks is assigning the household turns for providing firewood to the fqih's household and to the mosque. Two muleloads are donated monthly by the village families in rotation.

The jmaa stands responsible for the hiring and renewal of the annual contract of the village fqih. His salary derives from the leases of the mosque fields. In addition the households contribute variable amounts of wheat for the fqih's upkeep. In 1969 52 households gave a total of 23 abras.

A daily concern of the village is the communal herding of the livestock (tawala). The tawala for the cattle is maintained year-round.

That for the draft animals is carried out up to the time of the spring planting and resumed after the sowing of the winter wheat. Forty-two households provide an adult male, in this context anyone over 15 years old, in rotation for each tawala.

Until a few years ago women and children also served as herders. However, after the loss of two cows during the turn of a woman, the jmaa decided on the basis of the tribal qanoun that she was responsible for their replacement. Since that time only men serve. If a household sends a woman during its turn then it stands accountable for any loss. Men do not have to replace lost animals.

All the households owning animals are required to take a turn, even if they leave their animals out of the daily schedules.[10] On occasion, the jmaa hires a herder for the cows. The households contribute 50 FR. monthly per animal. In this case the shurfa families have to contribute their share of the cash fee but are exempt from providing evening meals and lodging to the herder, which normally is part of the contract. The hired herder is invariably an outsider, usually a young bachelor from a pastoralist group working for cash before marriage. Village opinion holds that the animals are better cared for under a hired herder. Contracts for a cow herder are given for one period, or multiples, of the rotation cycle so that all households contributes equally toward the food and lodging provided to the herder.

CONCLUDING REMARKS

National independence has brought a clear break with the past to the countryside. The modern period, accompanied by strict governmental control, has offered minimal economic transformation. Traditional ways are replaced not by modernization, but by alienation, extended by the dissolution of kin-based and territorial groups and the perception of unrealized possibilities in politics and production. Modernization has offered the props of rural communes and an elaborate administration, while the fields are worked with the same plows and the same expectations that maintained the traditional world and the symbols consonant to it.

---

[10]The households of Ait Akhatar on the west bank of the river do not participate in the tawala because of the river crossing. Shurfa families can send their animals in the tawala and do not contribute their share of labor. This dispensation is not given to shurfa in all villages of the Ait Ayash.

Participation in the tawala is considered a privilege which the community can withdraw. In 1957, three families active in the uprising of Addi ou Bihi and responsible for locking up the village's Istiqlali members were subsequently banned from participation in the tawala until the qaid's office intervened to reinstate their community rights.

CHAPTER SIX

Domestic Organization: Households, Marriage, and Property

This chapter discusses, with a twofold intent, the social and economic factors which are relevant to the types and composition of households among the Ait Ayash and to the marital unions they contract. First, it presents an analysis of existing household types and conjugal unions through the data collected on a specific village given the fictitious name of Ait Akhatar. Second, it offers a reconstruction of domestic units and marriage patterns of the traditional period as based on the recoverable aspects of the social and economic organization.

Most domestic units today are nuclear households. This argument suggests that nuclear family autonomy under the traditional system of land tenure, inheritance, and rights to irrigated land in individual title, served to maintain the riverine community as a whole by necessitating the emigration of individual members who failed to acquire rights (through inheritance or purchase) to sufficient land for household needs. Nuclear family orientation is viewed as a pattern consonant with the traditional organization of the Ait Ayash, and not the result of modernization.

Marriage and the instability of conjugal unions are analyzed in terms of the relations that tie men and women to agnates and to property rights that support subsistence. The tenor of conjugal relations in the early years of a marriage can be seen as adversary relations. Men and women have strong reasons to maintain opposing agnatic loyalties which weaken the social investment they can bring to a conjugal unit.

ON HOUSEHOLD TYPES OF THE TRADITIONAL PERIOD

The extant literature on the organization of rural Berber-speaking communities stresses the prevalence of the extended family incorporating two generations of married agnates as the domestic unit of production before changes brought by the modern period. B. Hoffman, in his synthesis based on French ethnographic reports, notes that the "patrilineal, patrilocal, patriarchal, and agnatic extended family constitutes a fundamental unit of Berber life; it is the basic domestic, economic, and legal entity" (1967:47). His citations refer principally to pastoralist groups which predominated in the countryside, without specific reference to the sedentary communities. Hoffman, in continuing the above quotation, notes, "The extended family is a very strong social unit. . . . particularly so in the Beraber [Tamazight-speaking] country, where this fact is illustrated by the members forming a single tent group ("tent circle") during the seasonal migrations" (Ibid.)

The oral traditions of the Ait Ayash also emphasize the fact that, in the past, large families were important, although this situation no longer holds true. This view of the past does not contradict, although it is in contrast to local accounts, that most households among the sedentary agriculturalists were composed (as they continue to be) of a married couple and their children. The tradition of large families recalls the political cohesion of agnates and descent groups and not necessarily the composition of the domestic units of production and consumption.

Several factors prevented the prevalence of the extended household among the Ait Ayash, aside from its temporary appearance as a stage in the developmental cycle of the family. The cereal production on the irrigated plots did not require a labor pool within the household larger than that provided by a nuclear family. Secondly, the interests of agnates of different generations diverged without canceling episodic political cooperation between them. The need of adult sons to seek independence from parental authority to develop a full social identity fed intergenerational agnatic fission. The extended household arrangement limited the opportunities for full expression of adult male status for descending generation members. The clearest indication of the fissioning process to nuclear-level households during the traditional period can be found in the rule of the customary law of the Ait Ayash, which specified that married sons could demand their share of the family's land property to establish their conjugal households.[1] Another relevant fac-

---

[1]The explanation offered for the customary practice was that sons who were denied their share on marriage would likely quit the natal settlement to seek a life outside the tribe, and the settlement and tribe could not afford to lose an agnate to another collectivity.

Divisible inheritance during the lifetime of the senior agnate did not cancel the solidarity of the agnatic group but did establish independent units of production in social and residential proximity.

Two informants who were brothers and heads of extended households (discussed in the last section of the

tor was that women did not become fully incorporated into the spouse's lineage but remained attached after marriage to the natal family by property relations (discussed later in the section on marriage).

The majority of families in the past were of the nuclear type. Extended households did not form structured economic units that endured through time. Land shortage would seem to favor larger domestic units of extended or joint households. Social pressures and the diffuse nature of production tasks in the annual cycle discourage their long-term survival as economic units. The large agnatic family that promoted the security of the community and increased the life-chances of its members need not be viewed as identical with the domestic units of production. Nuclear households appear to have been the dominant familial economic and production units of the past and represent the majority of the households in the present. Their predominance calls for less explanation than the occurrence of extended and joint households that offer arrangements which counter the processes of fission that normally prevail.

DOMESTIC UNITS IN AIT AKHATAR

The village of Ait Akhatar comprises 72 households, four of which are units of consumption rather than of agricultural production, of solitary widows or divorced women. Sixty-six percent of the domestic production units are nuclear households, 13 percent joint households, 18 percent extended households and three percent households of widows with unmarried children (Figures 6 and 7). I have separated the two households of widows with children from the nuclear households as women are the acknowledged household heads.

There are nine joint households in Ait Akhatar. A joint household is defined as that formed by two or more married brothers and their spouses and offspring. Other kin may be included, such as widowed mothers, unmarried brothers, divorced sisters and their offspring, and rarely unmarried sisters because of the early marriages of girls. The property remains undivided among the agnates, the classic solution in situations of scarce land resources.

Intuitively, given the *minifundia* of the Ait Ayash, one would expect a larger number of joint households both in the past and present. In the pre-Protectorate period, the land tenure and inheritance patterns permitted the continuous circulation of land rights between

---

chapter) disagreed with this account of the customary law. In their view, sons never inherited property before the death of the father. Others insisted the interpretation of the brothers was simple justification of their authoritarian control over their sons. In consideration of the ecological and political circumstances of the traditional period, the view of the majority makes sense.

Figure 6 Composition of households in Ait Akhatar (72 households of 452 individuals)

Age of head of household	Total membership	Solitary unremarried	Total membership	Widows with unmarried offspring	Total membership	Patrilocal extended families	Total membership	Joint families	Total membership	Nuclear families
60 yrs. or more	10	60	—	—	8	89	—	—	1	1
50–59 yrs.	6	34	1	8	2	15	—	—	2	2
40–49 yrs.	9	57	2	27	1	8	2	14	1	1
30–39 yrs.	13	60	5	43	—	—	—	—	—	—
20–29 yrs	6	22	1	4	1*	6	—	—	1	1
Total of each household type.	44		9		12		2		5	
Total of individuals in each type.		233		82		118		14		5

*Household headed by oldest son, whose mother is married to deceased husband's brother, a retired soldier.

households. The size of a family and events in individual life histories such as the quality of management, fines and debts, redistributed holdings in land within and between families through the outflow of ascribed and the inflow of incorporated personnel. Reliance on the share of the ancestral family land proved clearly insufficient for most, even if pooling of resources was encouraged by the social organization, which was not the case. The inheritance of property from one generation to the next gave unequal chances to different groups according to the number of siblings. Joint utilization of the patrimony, even if economically practicable, was arrested by social processes such as the need for adult males to achieve autonomy as heads of households.

In the present, joint households can exploit new opportunities for alternative economic activities to maintain agnatic cooperation. Their success depends to a large degree on the relations of the co-residents. A critical factor is the tenor of relations between the wives and the mother of the husbands. The tenuous connection that wives maintain with respect to property and the material ties with their natal families exacerbate tension between affines. The dominant position of the mother of the husband, when she is coresident, contributes to the incidence of marital instability and to the chances for dissolution of the joint household. Five of the joint households included the widowed mother of the sons. In three of these households, each of which in-

Figure 7 **Social ascriptions and household types in Ait Akhatar**

Kinship or social group	Total membership	Solitary unremarried	Total membership	Widows with unmarried offspring	Total membership	Extended families	Total membership	Joint families	Total membership	Nuclear families
Ighs "A"	2	9	1	9	2	27	—	—	2	2
Families ritually incorporated in ighs "A"	1	8	—	—	1	6	—	—	—	—
Ighs "B"	3	16	5	56	—	—	—	—	1	1
Families ritually incorporated in ighs "B"	15	77	—	—	1	9	—	—	—	—
Ighs "C"	5	25	—	—	1	11	—	—	1	1
Ighs "D"	—	—	—	—	2	18	—	—	—	—
Families ritually incorporated in ighs "D"	—	—	—	—	1	8	—	—	—	—
Shurfa	4	27	—	—	—	—	—	—	—	—
Settlers during Protectorate without ritual incorporation	6	35	3	17	4	39	2	14	1	1
Settlers since Independence	8	36	—	—	—	—	—	—	—	—
Column totals for household type	44		9		12		2		5	
Column totals for members		233		82		118		14		5

cluded two married brothers, five men, after at least two divorces, remained unremarried. Of the five, only one had offspring from a dissolved marriage so that the direct cause of divorce could be due to the childlessness of the women. But since all these marriages were of very short duration, other social causes may have been responsible. The high incidence of divorce in all household types supports the view that the position of women with respect to property determines the social investment both husbands and wives bring to the conjugal unit (Maher 1974). The membership of joint households simply extended the potential for tension that is inherent in the conjugal bond. In the three joint households with unremarried men, the land had been bought in two cases by the coresident agnates and in the other by the parent of the coresidents. Still, the joint enterprise was sustained as much by the unremarried status of one or more men in each case. The status of a bachelor is an untenable one in the domestic economy. These men could maintain their single status by the presence and domestic services of the widowed mothers in the joint households. Only one other man in the village remained unremarried for a year after divorce. His situation was considered a temporary one.

The impetus to sustain joint and extended households is fostered by division of male labor among specific tasks where a sufficient, undivided patrimony permits assignment of the agricultural labor to one member. The other males invest their time in wage labor, trading, animal herding, or whatever other opportunities can be gleaned from local productive activities. In Algeria, where labor emigration has been more significant for rural populations, the thesis has been stated as follows: "Insecurity diminishes as more men join forces economically; the presence of only one man in a household is a sign of indigence or poverty, whereas three men means the hope of security, that is 'wealth' " (Favret 1972:313). The facts that more joint households are not sustained among the Ait Ayash is a function of the minimal opportunities available for absorbing the surplus manpower. Many of the joint households that divided after a trial period reflect the lack of labor alternatives that could have made cooperation viable. This also suggests that economic cooperation in household and property management is a 'modern' solution to problems of maintenance, the more significant as dependence on the land fails to provide the wherewithal for survival.

The five most successful joint households, in terms of their internal solidarity, formed with the addition of a nuclear household, the second largest land-owning family (tighst) of the village (Figure 8, #5–9). The joint domestic units are clearly intended to safeguard the inherited and acquired estates by avoiding division which would reduce individual holdings to subminimal plots, as in the majority of families.

In one household of three brothers, the eldest stands as head. The priority of the senior member is not an inflexible rule; in two other households the second born acted as head. The household head keeps grains and other goods stored under lock and doles them out daily to the women for meal preparation. The second brother is in charge of the agricultural work and marketing. The third tends the

DOMESTIC ORGANIZATION 141

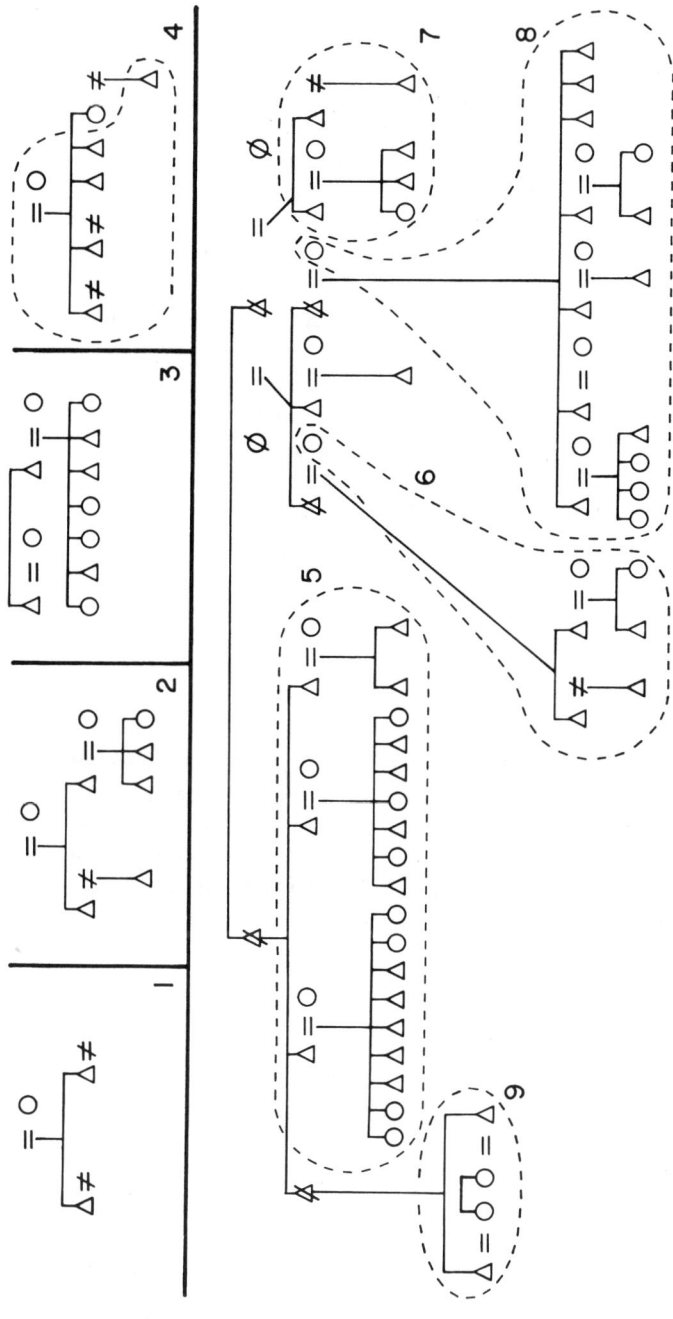

Figure 8 **Joint households in Ait Akhatar**

Note: The diagram are not complete genealogies, but indicate only co-resident members of joint households.

family sheep and also works at any odd job that can add to the family income. The women of the household take turns at the tasks of baking the bread and cooking meals, while the others clean grain, gather firewood, and process wool for weaving into family garments.

In large households like this one, with a total of 18 offspring, ranging in age from 18 years to two months, the women and girls take their meals separately from the men and boys. Sustained harmony in the women's work group is stressed as crucial to the welfare of the household.

Another large household of the same tighst is composed of four married brothers, their spouses and children, three unmarried brothers and their widowed mother. Tasks are permanently assigned to individuals. The oldest operates the village grain mill owned by a resident of Midelt, and also serves as a part-time butcher for the village. The second born directs the household. The third brother is in charge of the fields and agricultural labor. The fourth works as a miner in Aouli and rents a house for his conjugal family in Midelt. An unmarried younger brother who has attended but not completed secondary school is in charge of a small shop next to his brother's rented house in Midelt, selling dry goods (candles, soap, matches). Another unmarried brother has joined the army. The youngest of the seven was sent to secondary school with the intention of completing a degree; he did not prove apt in studies and now tends the family flock.

The household head is married to a classificatory patrilateral parallel cousin (actually FaFaBroSoDa). Their union remains childless. This may have contributed to his selection as head of household, since originally the household was directed by the senior brother who claimed he did not want the responsibility of the position. The senior brother is married to a daughter of the father's brother. At some time before the period of fieldwork, friction between the wives of the household had led the family to demand that the senior brother divorce his wife. He did not counter his agnates' decision openly, and his wife returned to her father's household, the only nuclear household in the lineage, since he had no surviving full brothers. Shortly after, the man joined his ex-wife and demanded economic separation from his brothers who had planned to find for him another spouse compatible with the group of women residing in the household. The family however did not want to lose his services since he was regarded as the most enterprising worker in the household and was popular in the village. Their solution was to let him remarry his ex-wife and to build a separate dwelling for his conjugal family and to continue the economic association, with the real property undivided.

The tighst was regarded by others in the village as one that 'took care of its women" with reference both to female agnates and affines.

The divorce originally proposed from the father's brother's daughter was intended to keep the spouse of the third brother, who was an unrelated affine from another tribe, in the household, while the senior brother's ex-wife would still be looked after since she was a close agnate. She was related to husband's mother as her sister's daughter, the mother's sister having been married to her husband's brother. Nevertheless the proposal had been made to remove the close female agnate as wife in order to maintain the harmony of the women's work group and for the related fact that her material security would not be greatly jeopardized by the suggested divorce.

The other joint households of the tighst are composed of two brothers each. The youngest household is that of brothers, 24 years and 20 years of age, who had married sisters related to them as MoBroDa's and also as classificatory FaBroDa's (actually FaFaBroSoDa's). The matches were seen to offer good prospects for stable unions. The proximity of close agnates and their relationship to the family's material property gave the women a degree of security denied the wives in households where they stood as unrelated affines, which was the case in the majority of Ait Ayash marriages.

MARRIAGE AND THE INSTABILITY OF THE CONJUGAL BOND

Some common features of marriages in Morocco include 1) marriages prearranged for the couple; 2) a material settlement made for the bride by the groom and his family; and 3) a written contract as the legal basis of marriages. The application of these features varies widely in urban and rural settings so that the shared general elements obscure specific individual differences.

A recent study of marriage in rural Morocco argues that "the social importance of the relationship between husband and wife increases or decreases according to the investment which they are able to make in the new domestic unit. The transfer of movable property and, with it, primary allegiance from the couple's families of origin to the new household, is fundamental." (Maher 1974:192) By following this suggestion of relationship between the conjugal bond and property some summary statements can be made about marriage in the Moulouya plain, and more widely in the Central Atlas.

Marriage among Berber-speaking tribes such as the Ait Ayash, Ait Izdeg, Ait Yahia and Ait Hadiddou did not involve any transfer of property from the bride's family into the new domestic unit. Moreover, the material wealth bestowed on the family of the bride by the

Figure 9 **Divorce and number of offspring (103 cases)**

Duration of marriage in years	Number of (surviving) offspring before termination of marriage through divorce				Row totals of dissolved marriages
	0	1	2	3	
Less than 1	45	2	—	—	47
1–less than 2	20	7	—	—	27
2–less than 5	13	8	2	2	25
5–less than 10	—	2	—	—	2
10 or more	1	—	—	1	2
Column totals of dissolved marriages	79	19	2	3	103

groom's family was nominal, if indeed any at all was transferred. The written contract, executed by a qadi, was most often a promissory note specifying the material charges due in the case of divorce. Bridewealth was minimal and appropriated for the expenses of the ceremony. This meant that the new domestic unit was not underwritten by a material investment on the part of the agnatic groups of the couple. One Ayashi explained that, "marriage at that time [referring to the Protectorate period] didn't cost much; just a pair of shoes and a belt for the wife. The divorce cost the shoes and belt that were promised at marriage and not given."

Divorce was (and continues to be for the period of description) common during the early marital careers of men and women. No particular opprobrium is attached to this since short marriages followed by divorces are normal episodes in many life histories. The data on Ait Akhatar (Figure 9) suggest that divorce is rare after a number of children have been produced.

Figure 20 presents a sample of the incidence of divorce in childless and short-term marriages. Seventy-nine per cent of all divorces follow from unions without children. Less than three per cent of the dissolved marriages involved couples with three children. There were no divorces in the village of couples with more than three children. A contrasting pattern prevails among urban proletarian families where the man is apt to seek divorce when the demands of a large number of dependents appear to him insupportable, which is to say, late in the developmental cycle of the domestic unit. (Adam 1968 (2):733-763) In the village sample, 63 per cent of the 103 divorces occurred in the first two years of marriage and with no surviving offspring. Forty-five unions lasted from two weeks to two months.

The incidence of marital instability is a function of the differential ties that men and women have to resources that support subsistence.

Among the agriculturalists, the holdings in irrigated fields are inherited by the males, while female agnates retain usufruct rights which are not transferred on marriage to the new domestic unit. Women maintain both matieral and emotional allegiances to their natal families until, after a series of trial marriages or at an advanced stage of their marital career, the ties to their children take precedence over ties to natal groups. Men transfer allegiance to the interests of the conjugal household over the interests of their agnatic family with comparable delay. The relations that a newly married man maintains with agnates form the surest link to security. His start depends on what he will receive for this share of the paternal estate. Few other economic opportunities are available to him. More recently, urban marriage practices are filtering into the village. Elevated bridewealth price and the transfer of movable property, especially in cash, has become the expectation among the families of the land-sufficient. This is a fairly new phenomenon among the Ait Ayash and is not central to the discussion of marriages and the statistics presented in this chapter.

Marriage among the Ait Ayash does not create a structural alliance in which the affinity tie between two social groups entails a special relationship. Affinal bonds are structurally unimportant. This is a particular instance of processes in kinship systems that aligns them in a continuum by the degree to which they rely on marriage alliances or the descent system to create bonds of cohesion and solidarity. African and Middle Eastern societies emphasize descent rather than marriage as a basis of social solidarity (Irons 1975:132–134). This remains a matter of emphasis placed by different societies on descent and affinal alliance as integrative mechanisms.

Marriage is the initial step for the man to become head of a new household. For the women it is the only avenue to an achieved social status as wife and as mother. Yet, the marital bond is perceived as a difficult state. The dissolution of first marriages is almost expected under 'normal' circumstances. The stability of first marriages from an internal point of view calls for special explanations, while divorces are taken as routine happenstance. Factors associated with patterned marital instability and which are themselves consequences of social relationships in production include differential inheritance and disposition of property among sons and daughters; sexual division of labor and separation of domestic work groups; normative obligations of the spouses in the conjugal relationship; the ratio of material investments given to the new household; maintenance of bonds with the respective families of orientation; and ages at first marriage. The aggregate of these social and economic factors tends to make marriage unstable.

Permanence in marriage is achieved following the wife's evaluation of her new position against her ascribed status in the agnatic household and the husband's weighing of liabilities in the new household against his interests with agnates (cf. Maher, 1974) The conflict between the new ties of a conjugal relationship and the ascribed bonds of agnation enters into the course of most marriages among the Ait Ayash; its resolution through a long process of shifting allegiences is not inevitable.

Throughout the Protectorate period the Ait Ayash followed the customary law concerning inheritance. This specified that sons could demand their share of the paternal estate to set up a conjugal household. The tribal law derived from Muslim legal stipulations concerning allotment: sons received equal shares and daughters equal half-shares.

Since Independence the tribal codes have been abolished and with them the obligation of division of property during the lifetime of the parent. This has tended to increase men's age at first marriage. A widely ecountered arrangement is for sons on marriage to set up separate residence and work their alloted portion of the family fields without legal division. A daughter's portion of the estate remains under the guardianship of the closest agnate: the father, and later, brothers. The woman's share does not come under her control and is not transferred to the conjugal household after the death of the father. A woman at marriage remains, in significant aspects of her economic and social welfare, a ward of her male agnates. Her rights in the agnatic estate remain usufruct rights, without rights of disposition. What usually happens is that she receives a portion of the harvest from the fields worked by her agnates. In the present the brothers may opt to reimburse her and buy her share. But this decreases her material security in case of divorce. Her usufruct rights guarantee her a place in the natal household. The trusteeship of a woman's share is justified by agnates as it provides security during periods of marital failure. But it also seems that the prolonged loyalty of the woman towards her agnates keeps the conjugal attachment tenuous. This, in turn, is reflected in the limited liabilities which a husband assumes toward the woman as wife. A young woman needs to turn to her agnates for succor in sickness, personal expenses, and other burdens which the husband refuses to consider his own.

The wife is held responsible for the full complement of domestic services, while the accepted obligations of the husband are limited to the necessities of food, shelter and clothing. The young bride follows the period of confinement after the wedding with frequent visits to her parents. The man may view this as disloyalty to the conjugal bond. Men say they are forced to divorce a wife who begins to transfer goods

Figure 10 **Age at marriage in Ait Akhatar**

Marriage	Age of Men	Age of Women	Age Difference (years)
I. Age at first marriage (undissolved)*	23.5	16.2	7.3
II. Age at first marriage (dissolved)*	21.6	15.3	6.3
III. Age at last marriage‡	32	18.7	13.3
IV. Ages in marriage undissolved (I and III)	26.8	17	9.8

*sample: 18 marriages
‡sample: 25 marriages

from the husband's household to the house of her parents. This is to say, the woman can precipitate divorce, which only the man can legally demand, by indicating a stronger allegiance to her natal kin.

The groom provides a minimal economic investment for the services of a wife. There is agreement among informants that marriages, even in the recent past, did not involve large expenditures. The pre-nuptial celebration, *henna,* entailed gifts of clothing to the bride from the groom's kin. The *sdaq* (arab.) is the financial settlement made to the wife's agnates and, in large part, deferred until divorce. No bridewealth proper is offered to the woman's family for her removal and services and no dowry is proffered by the woman's kin for the new household. Marriage does not alter the economic status of the husband.

The ideal age for marriage of the girl is said to be sixteen years. For the man there is wider latitude, depending on the economic situation of his family. The reported ages at first marriages in Figure 10 reflect the ideal as much as they reflect as they reflect actual ages since there was widespread belief in the village that 16 years is the legal minimum age for girls, when in fact the minimum age established by the government since Independence is 15 years for females and 18 years for males. The Ayashi girl, and generally the rural Moroccan girl, leaves childhood and enters adulthood without experiencing a period of adolescence. In contrast, the young male experiences a prolonged adolescence, the more so as marriage is delayed. One of the rare studies on rural Moroccan youth based on interviews of 296 males supports the impressions gained during fieldwork (Pascon and Bentahar 1969). Marriage for both sexes serves as a rite of passage into adulthood, but with no firm expectation that the first union will be permanent.

148 THE AIT AYASH OF THE HIGH MOLOUYA PLAIN

Figure 11 **Marriage stability among the Ait Ayash men (85 males of Ait Akhatar)**

	Married men	%	Formerly married men	%	Row totals	%
No. of marriages contracted						
1	31	41.9	8	73	39	46
2	24	32.4	—	—	24	28
3	10	13.5	3	27	13	15.3
4	5	6.8	—	—	5	5.9
5	2	2.7	—	—	2	2.4
6	—	—	—	—	—	—
7	2	2.7	—	—	2	2.4
Column totals	74	100.0	11	100.0	85	100.0
No. of marriages dissolved by death of spouse						
0	68	92	8	73	76	89
1	6	8	3	27	9	11
Column totals	74	100.0	11	100.0	85	100.0
No. of marriages terminated through divorce						
0	36	48.6	2	18	38	44.7
1	21	28.4	6	55	27	31.7
2	10	13.5	1	9	11	12.9
3	3	4.1	2	18	5	5.9
4	2	2.7	—	—	2	2.4
5	—	—	—	—	—	—
6	2	2.7	—	—	2	2.4
Column totals	74	100.0	11	100.0	85	100.0

MARITAL INSTABILITY IN AIT AKHATAR

Figures 20 and 21 are based on a village sample of 85 men and 64 women. Divorces ended 49.4 percent of all marriages contracted among the men and 41.7 percent among the women. The men had contracted a total of 170 marriages, an average of two marriages per person. Nine marriages had ended through the death of spouse. Of the rest, 84 had ended in divorce. The total of 77 undissolved marriages indicates that three men have two wives each. Discounting the nine death-terminated marriages, divorce in the men's sample reaches 52 percent. Fifty-five percent of all the men had divorced one or more

Figure 12 **Marriage stability among the Ait Ayash women (64 women of Ait Akhatar)**

	Married women	%	Formerly married women	%	Row totals	%
No. of marriages contracted						
1	24	42	4	57	28	44
2	28	49	2	29	30	47
3	4	7	—	—	4	6
4	1	2	1	14	2	3
Column totals	57	100.0	7	100.0	64	100.0
No. of marriages dissolved by death of spouse						
0	53	93	5	71	58	91
1	4	7	2	29	6	9
Column totals	57	100.0	7	100.0	64	100.0
No. of marriages terminated through divorce						
0	27	47	1	14.3	28	44
1	26	46	4	57.1	30	47
2	3	5	1	14.3	4	6
3	1	2	—	—	1	1.5
4	—	—	1	14.3	1	1.5
Column totals	57	100.0	7	100.0	64	100.0

times. Eight-seven percent remained married. Of these, 42 percent were first marriages.

The women in the sample had accumulated a total of 108 marriages, giving an average of 1.7 marriages per person. From the total of marriages that were not death-terminated (102), 45 of them, 44 percent, had ended in divorce. Fifty-six percent of all the women had divorced one or more times. Eight-nine percent remained married, 42 percent in their original marriages.

The ages of the unremarried men given in Figure 24 suggest that most (eight out of 11) are likely to resume marital careers. All except one are either members of joint or extended households or have a widowed mother coresident for domestic services. The one exception maintained a solitary residence but continued agricultural associations with married brothers with whom he had shared a joint household two years earlier. The unremarried women of 20 years of age or younger in

150 THE AIT AYASH OF THE HIGH MOLOUYA PLAIN

Figure 13 **Age distribution and remarriages among the Ait Ayash (85 men and 64 women of Ait Akhatar)**

Present age	Married Men Number of marriages							Unmarried Men Number of marriages				Row totals
	1	2	3	4	5	6	7	1	2	3	4	
17–20	2	—	—	—	—	—	—	—	—	—	—	2
21–30	11	8	2	1	-	—	—	4	—	1	—	27
31–40	9	4	2	1	1	—	—	1	—	1	—	19
41–50	4	5	2	—	—	—,	—	1	—	—	—	12
51–60	3	2	3	2	1	—	1	1	—	1	—	14
61–over	2	5	1	1	—	—	1	1	—	—	—	11
Column totals	31	24	10	5	2	0	2	8	0	3	0	85

	Married Women							Unremarried Women				
14–20	7	—	—	—	—	—	—	3	—	—	—	10
21–30	7	11	1	—	—	—	—	—	—	—	—	19
31–40	6	10	1	—	—	—	—	—	1	—	—	18
41–50	2	5	1	—	—	—	—	1	1	—	1	11
51–60	2	2	—	—	—	—	—	—	—	—	—	4
61–over	—	—	1	1	—	—	—	—	—	—	—	2
Column totals	24	28	4	1	0	0	0	4	2	0	1	64

Figure 13 had returned to their natal households. The other four formed the solitary households of the village. Two are widows and two divorcées.

A young woman after divorce gains some freedom that is denied unmarried girls. She is viewed as more capable than her unmarried sisters in managing her life with a store of experience and little diminution of opportunity. In this sense, early marital failure is treated as a kind of nubility rite with minimal social consequences.

SELECTION OF SPOUSES

Marriage choices among the Ait Ayash can be characterized as open and lacking preferential patterns. Marriages in the majority of cases are not arranged by agnates without the active participation of the couple. I can state this more confidently concerning the men than the women. Direct questions on how one chooses a wife brought forth replies such as, "a couple decides they like each other and asks their families to arrange the marriage." The selection is left to the kin group only when a young man specifically requests agnates to seek out a bride for him. This was the case among a few men from joint or extended households who had to cope with the approval of the larger household. A number of brides sought by different young men were rejected as choices by their families because of the amount of bridewealth requested for them. This is a problem of recent years and one likely to escalate, after the pattern of urban practice.

Close cousin marriages, especially of patrilateral parallel cousins or of matrilateral cross cousins are viewed as good matches. The statistical incidence of such unions turns out to be low. The commonly cited Arabic preference for unions in the patriline, particularly in the ideal range of father's brother's daughter, is held by the Ait Ayash to be consonant with sound management of the patrimony. The economic advantages of close family endogamy held minimal relevance for most households because of their inadequate land holdings. Land-sufficient families took greater care in manipulating marriage alliances and in favoring endogamous unions.

A reflection of the Arabic marriage preference is seen in the practice of addressing spouse's parents by the kin terms, *'ammi* (father's brother) and *khalti* (mother's sister). The terms imply an equivalence of social roles not a prescriptive norm concerning marriage. Affinal relatives of any generation are subsumed in reference under the term *idgwaln* (pl. affines; *adgwal*, sing.).

Affinal bonds can be used for preferential economic ties between two groups, but affinity does not generally serve as an important alliance mechanism. A study of women in the region documents cases of marriages undertaken without any clear knowledge of the social and economic situation of the spouse's family (Maher, 1974). Such cases may not be common but they come close to characterizing the minimal significance attached to affinal ties by the kin groups of the couple. But any opportunities to upgrade the family's economic status by the manipulation of affinal ties are not needlessly missed. An illustration with a case from Ait Akhatar follows.

Qssou ou M___, at 23, married for the second time a girl of 16 from the town of Tounfit. The couple took up residence in the house of his parents and his two siblings, a girl of 12 and a boy of seven. Two years later the wife became pregnant for the first time and, as is the custom, she left to visit her parents. At the date of her anticipated return, a message arrived from her parents informing him his wife did not want to return because of his mistreatment of her. Qssou requested a member of the village jmaa to act as his spokesmen and mediator, and together they traveled to Tounfit to confront his affines. Before them, he denied any mistreatment of his wife and asked for her return. Her parents refused, and the two sides consulted a qadi. The judge wanted to hear the wife's version of the situation in private consultation. She denied any mistreatment from her husband and stated she did not want a divorce, but added that she was not reflecting her parents' view. The husband in his turn conceded that their domestic arrangements in his father's household were not ideal. He realized the burden his wife had carried in caring for his parents and young siblings and agreed to separate his conjugal family from the father's household when his wife returned. Her parents insisted that their daughter's statements reflected her intimidation and fear of physical abuse from the husband. The judge insisted the decision rested with the couple and not with the parents. He appointed a neutral observer, the muqaddam of Qssou's village, to report for a period of three months on the domestic situation and problems of the couple.

Subsequently, it became known that the parents had sought a divorce in order to arrange another marriage for their daughter. A merchant of Tounfit had made it known that he was looking for a second wife, a good indication of economic status, and had made preliminary inquiries concerning their youngest daughter, who was the woman in question. From their perspective, the opportunity for an alliance with a town merchant was preferable to a first marriage, compatible or not, in a poor household of a distant qsar. The pregnancy posed no particular problem, since they could foster their grandchild until the father claimed it.

At the end of fieldwork, the case had not been resolved. Qssou was pessimistic about the survival of his marriage. The wife's allegiance to her parents, he felt, would weaken her resolve to stay with him. The marriage foundered on the conflicting loyalties experienced by the woman as daughter and as wife.

RELATIONSHIP OF SPOUSES

Figure 14 indicates either the kinship relationship or place of origin of the wives of 101 men in Ait Akhatar. The categories (kinship of wife to husband) are given in terms of increasing social and kinship propinquity and concommitantly, decreasing physical distance between the spouses' kin groups. Those delineated for the Ait Ayash men are not mutually exlusive. A matrilateral cousin is likely to be from another tribe, but the fact that affinal links are already present is more relevant than geographical distance. In kin relations, patrilaterality takes precedence over matrilaterality, so there is no overlap. A total of 189 marriages were accumulated by the 101 men. Fifty-three individuals had only one marriage, and these are indicated both under "First"

DOMESTIC ORGANIZATION

Figure 14 **Degree of kinship of wife in first and last marriages of 101 men in an Ait Ayash qsar.***

Kinship of wife to husband	First marriage	Last marriage
(Among 65 Ait Ayash Men)		
Another region (non-kin)	2	2
Another tribe (non-kin)	23	23
Another Ait Ayash qsar (non-kin)	12	12
Same qsar (non-kin)	9	12
Same ighs in qsar	4	3
Matrilateral parallel cousin	1	—
Matrilateral cross cousin	5	4
Classificatory patrilateral parallel cousin	3	4
Patrilateral cross cousin	1	1
Patrilateral parallel cousin	5	5
	65	65
(Among 25 Settlers In The Village)		
Another tribe (non-kin)	7	6
Region of origin (non-kin)	2	2
Tribe of origin (non-kin)	2	3
Village of origin (non-kin)	2	2
Another Ait Ayash qsar (non-kin)	7	6
Same qsar (non-kin)	3	4
Classificatory patrilateral cousin	1	1
Patrilateral cross cousin	1	—
Patrilateral parallel cousin	—	1
	25	25
(Among 6 Tent Dwellers Registered In The Village)		
Same tribe (non-kin)	3	4
Classificatory patrilateral cousin	1	1
Matrilateral cross cousin	1	—
Patrilateral parallel cousin	1	1
	6	6
(Among 5 Shurfa Of The Village)		
Region of origin (non-kin)	1	1
Another Ait Ayash qsar (non-kin)	3	3
Same village (non-kin)	1	1
	5	5

*The 101 men had accumulated 189 marriages, of which those between the first and last marriages are not considered in the table.

The 65 Ait Ayash men had contracted 122 marriages; 31 men had had one or more remarriages. The 25 settlers had a total of 51 marriages; 14 individuals had remarried one or more times. Among the six Ait Morghad tent dwellers, two men had a second marriage. One sharif of the five had married four times.

and "Last" marriage. This means 48 subsequent marriages are listed under "Last" marriage.

Besides the low incidence of close kinship endogamy, the pattern of marriages suggests regional endogamy. A larger unit of analysis would be necessary to test for wider networks of social exchange. Among the recent settlers, marriage choices favor the women of the same tribal origins. The women listed under Another Ait Ayash qsar are also from families of the same tribal origin. The iqblin found in this group follow endogamy within their perceived social estate, which is distinguished from that of imazighen and that of the shurfa.

All marriages of the pastoralist households are with other pastoralist families. The tent-dwellers take wives from other tent-dwelling Ait Morghad families, not only on the basis of kinship identity, but also because village women cannot cope with the life of the tent. Village women do not marry tent-dwelling herders, just as townswomen will not tolerate a return to village life. On the other hand, Ait Morghad women are given in marriage to sedentary householders.

EXTENDED HOUSEHOLDS IN AIT AKHATAR

There are 12 extended households in Ait Akhatar. Only five have all the married sons coresiding with the father. Three of these households will be discussed below, one for the economic specialization that engenders cooperation between the coresidents, and the other two for the manipulation of marriages in the family by the senior agnates. The fourth household head with all his married sons coresident with him enjoyed the personal history of being the only son of a man without male siblings. He had inherited both father's and father's father's shares of the family fields, which had been divided on the marriage of his father. The family owns two ha of irrigated fields, a garden of eight fruit trees, and holds hereditary rights through continuous cultivation of four ha of dry fields in the Jebel Ayashi section of the tribal collective land. The fifth household is of a tent-dwelling Ait Morghad family registered in Ait Akhatar, whose reliance on animal herding makes its situation different from that of field dependent households.

The other extended households each have only one married son coresident, either because of the youth of other brothers (five households), or because brothers had refused parental control on marriage and had left the village (two households). Coresidence of two generations of married agnates may not be a sufficient criterion for indicating an extended household, although I include 12 households by this criterion. Continued authority over the reproduction units of male offspring and control over the family's real and movable property is fundamental. In two other cases where the sons have purchased the fields of the family, I have treated the coresidence of the parents or the male parent as filiolocal and included the households under the nuclear type.

Among the 11 village-dwelling extended households, three have insufficient land for family subsistence, and one of these owns no fields at all. Alternate economic activities, as within joint households, remain critical determinants of the cohesion of coresiding agnates who forego the risks of individual rewards for the security of the larger household. A specific case is given as illustration. The household of Muha A___ includes his three married sons, their conjugal families and a teen-aged son. The family of 14 individuals forms one extended unit of production and consumption, but maintains two separate residences because of its economic activities. The household head, who gives his age as 75, had settled in the Ansegmir valley during the Protectorate period. He was born in Tineghir, a pre-Saharan town, where his father had been an ironsmith. After an apprenticeship with his father, he moved north and established residence among the Ait Ayash. His skills enabled him to accumulate enough capital to buy irrigated fields, which are presently under the management of the eldest son. Muha has opened a smith's shop in the town of Midelt. Two married sons work as his apprentices and assistants; they are respectively 27 and 23 years old. The youngest son, 16 years old, is attending school in Midelt. The senior son, 34 years old, has been married for 16 years and has five children. The second son has married and divorced three times. He has one nine year old son, who is fostered by the grandmother. The third son has remarried recently for the fifth time and is childless. The parents, and all except the eldest son's conjugal family, reside in Midelt near the shop, but consider their permanent home the village of Ait Akhatar, which they visit at every opportunity. Only the oldest son devotes full time to farming. The agricultural land acquired by the skills of the household members provides the focal concern for agnatic cooperation. The success of the enterprise requires separate residences. But, the residential base of town permits the family to continue the education of the youngest son in the region's nearest secondary school. There was only one other 16 year old from Ait Akhatar at the lycée in Midelt. He is also a third generation member of an extended household, lodging during the nine month school term with his father's sister, who is married to a Midelt resident. The problem of town lodging prevented other students in the village from continuing their secondary education.

The second set of circumstances that propels the formation of extended households depends on the existence of family fields sufficient for subsistence production before division. Joint fraternal households similarly assess their coalescence as a way to avoid subminimal individual shares. With joint households there is more evidence of independent decisions to continue collaboration than there is in land-sufficient extended households. The authority of the senior agnate over property and over the reproduction units of the sons gives little choice to junior agnates concerning their economic security. I turn to the marriage alliances contracted by two extended households belonging to the wealthiest lineage (tighst) of the village to illustrate this point. The two extended households of two brothers, and a joint household of the sons of the third, deceased brother own the most land in Ait Akhatar. The elder senior, 78 years old, stands as a patriarchal figure over the three households, which are in principle, autonomous economic units.

Patrilateral endogamy, successive affinal ties (matrilateral ties) with families of similar economic circumstances in other settlements, and affinal links with physically distant families from other tribes, form the marriage patterns that are seen to protect property and the claims on it by affinal kinsmen. In no case has a junior male separated from the households to establish a nuclear conjugal unit. One married member had privately expressed the wish to break away from the father; this remained an idle wish because separation would mean effective relinquishment of future inheritance. Within the whole descent group all marriages, except the close endogamous unions and an exception to be discussed, have been contracted with families outside the village. The tighst fostered a sense of solidarity and concern that others in the village need not 'know their business'. Effective isolation from the other village families is maintained with respect to affinal alliances and is in part a response to political alignments that developed in the village since the local introduction of national political parties. The political alignments form two political parties. The political alignments form two blocs. Party "A" claims the attachment of the shurfa, all of the 'settlers', and more than half of the Ait Ayash families. Party "B" claims the remaining Ayash families. All the posts in the local administration, and more than half the seats on the communal council are filled by members of party "B". The descent group in question supports party "B". In spite of active campaigning for a political post, the family has not succeeded in placing one of its members on the council or in the post of shaikh or muqaddam.[2] Early political activity guided by Addi ou Bihi and ties of affinity with the family of the qaid under

---

[2] On festive occasions such as marriage celebrations, the villagers compose songs that touch on local personalities and events for the enjoyment of the party. Criticism that is awkward to express in ordinary circumstances is given full vent on such occasions. Songs about this extended family that were composed after the appointment of tribal shaikhs in 1967 were related to me by others. They poked fun at the family for 'eating their cows' (selling property) in their unsuccessful campaign to win a political post for one of their members.

the Protectorate has kept the tighst from local political participation and its rewards, even though the party it supported dominated in the elections of 1963.

The household heads of the agnatic group stood aloof from the other village families and involved themselves in local affairs indirectly. They did not participate actively in meetings at which household decisions that touched on common village interests were discussed. An aspect of their aloofness with respect to the village is shown in their affinal linkages. With one exception, of a son who maintained a separate dwelling from the main household, no local women had been taken as wives into the extended households. The wives are either kinswomen with rights to the estate or women from physically or socially distant groups. This minimizes demands by affines on the economic resources of the tighst and the pressures of conflicting family allegiances.

The marital alliances of three generations of the family are sketched in Figure 15, and indicate the patterns of affinal bonds maintained by the senior agnates for the succeeding generations. The wife of the senior elder had come from a prominent family of ighs "B" in Ait Akhatar. In a reciprocal exchange, a sister of the man had been given to wife's brother in ighs "B". A similar arrangement took place with the marriage of the second brother. He had married a sister of the qaid of the Protectorate period to whom his own sister was given as wife. Exchanges were continued with the same family in generation II. The deceased brother of the elders had married twice. His first marriage was with a woman from ighs "C" in the village. His second marriage was to a woman from another tribe (Ait Izdeg). His two sons from the second marriage maintained the third and joint household of the tighst. The oldest brother had married four times and divorced three wives because of childlessness. The fourth marriage (of one year's duration at the time of fieldwork) was with father's sister's daughter, that is, the daughter of the Protectorate qaid. She had been married previously and was already the mother of two children. His first marriage had been with a daughter of father's brother. She has remarried and produced children, so the responsibility for the lack of children in his marriages has long been established. His younger brother has married mother's brother's daughter, thus replicating affinal linkage to the Ait Izdeg family established in the preceding generation. In addition, one of their sisters has been given to mother's sister's son in the same Izdeg village. The only marriage in the third generation from this joint family is that of a thirteen year old daughter of the younger brother. She has been given to father's father's brother's son, 30 years old at the time. According to villagers, outside the family, the groom, the fifth of the six sons of the senior brother, stood to inherit

158   THE AIT AYASH OF THE HIGH MOLOUYA PLAIN

insert Fig 15

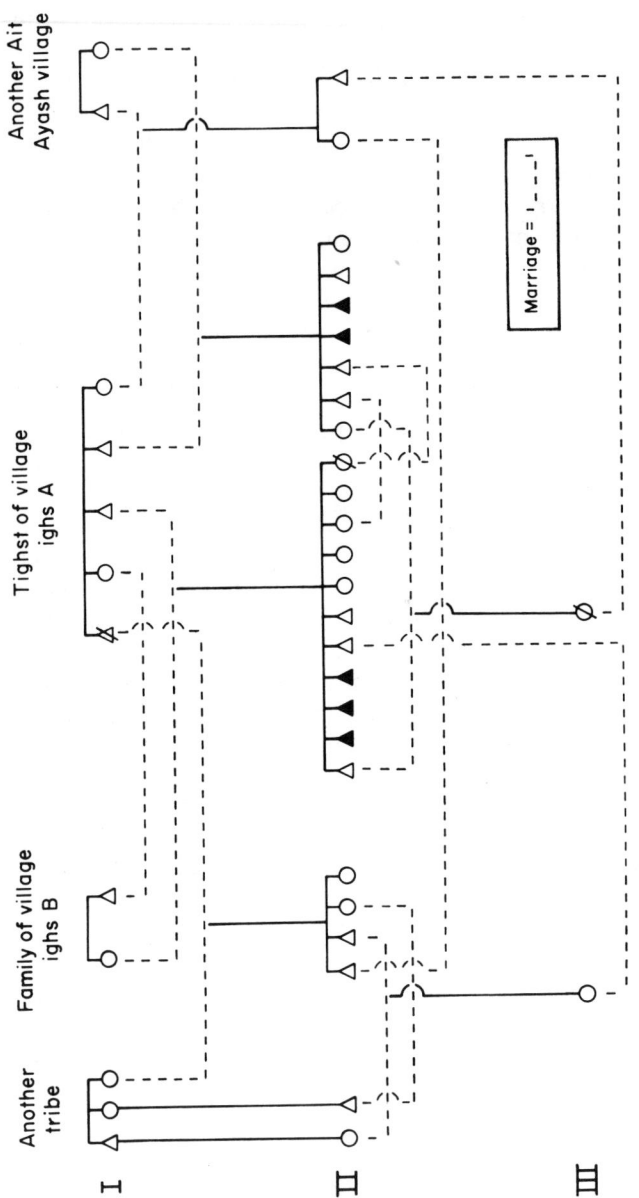

Figure 15 **Marriage alliances in an extended family (tighst) of Ait Akhatar**

Note: Genealogies and marital histories are incomplete. Generation III is not given except for the two women married respectively to FAFABROSO and FAFASISO (and/or MOFASISO). Shaded symbols in generation II indicate men married to women of non-village families.

one-third of the paternal estate by the arrangements of the father's will. This provision, which was impossible to confirm, was said to have been made in order to avoid division of the property into six shares, and the half-shares for the daughters, and to coerce the future cooperation of the brothers.

Four other sons of the senior elder were married. The first born had been given a daughter of father's brother. The second son had been married to an Ait Hadiddou woman and had divorced her after three years; he had a daughter now 17 years old. This man lived near family fields on the piedmont of Jebel Ayashi with his mother who had fostered his daughter. His mother had left her husband in a terminal separation some years before. The separation followed the suicide of a daughter who had been given in marriage against her will to a patrilateral parallel cousin. The mother left her husband at this time to live with the second born son. Since then, she has not spoken to her husband. She visits other members of her family during his absence from the household. The bizarre occurrence, in view of the strong religious prohibition of suicide and the ease with which divorce usually takes place, reoccurred in the family with the daughter of the first born son. She repeated her father's sister's act when a marriage with father's father's sister's son (of the qaid's family) was arranged for her.

The third son of this household was the only male member of generation II to have married within the village. This union, following two marriages with women from other tribes, was permitted because he lived separately from the extended family. He resides with his conjugal family in a house behind a shop which he manages in association with an absentee partner who has invested the capital for the business.[3] The shopkeeping requires his separate residence and keeps his wife from being brought into the extended domicile. Even so, the relationship between his wife's agnates and his own remains extremely strained. His father treats links with village families as threats to the integrity of the family's estate. The acceptance of the son's village marriage owes to the circumstances of the commercial venture that requires residential but not economic separation from the agnatic household.

The fourth son has married and divorced a woman from a southern town (Rish). A second union was contracted with a woman from another Ayashi village. He has no children from either marriage. The fifth son's marriage, at the age of 30, to his patrilateral parallel cousin's daughter has already been mentioned. The youngest son, at 24 years of age, remains unmarried. Of the five daughters, another besides the

---

[3]The partner is a former religious teacher of Ait Akhatar who has prospered after gaining a post as secretary to a judge and marrying the daughter of a former governor of Tafilalt. He has invested in various commerical ventures throughout the region. His village partner had befriended him when he had been the fqih of the village and extremely poor.

deceased has been given in marriage to a coresident son of father's brother. The other three are married, after two or more dissolved unions, into Ait Mgild families in Boumia, Midelt, and elsewhere; in each case into socially distant families.

The marriages in the extended household of the second brother replicate the pattern already given for the other brother's household: close endogamous unions, matrilateral links or use of established affinal links, or marriages with women from distant groups. For the sake of completeness I summarize the alliances in the second household. The first son married a daughter of father's brother. The second born, after the short union with the daughter of father's brother who took her own life, married a woman from the town of Rish. The third and fourth sons also married women from Rish. The last born, at twenty-four years of age, remains unmarried. A job has been secured for him in a governmental bureau in Rabat, through connections of the former qaid (mother's brother).

The marriages with women from the town of Rish were arranged by a close family friend who lived there. This circumvented affinal links with physically and socially proximate families which were seen as threatening to the solidarity of the agnatic group and its estate.

The extended households of the village represent either land-sufficient families before division or those families pooling skills and opportunities for productive activities other than irrigation farming. The latter arrangement does not take place in many cases because alternative activities, and capital and labor investment, are promoted as much between horizontal social units as between vertical kinship units. Contractual associations between autonomous households spread the risks of failure.

CHAPTER SEVEN

Conclusion

The local groups in the High Moulouya plain, a region with ecologically transitional characteristics, formed independent tribes and, at certain times, tax-paying tribes in the period before 1912. Their socio-political organization reflected environmental adjustments and their relationships with the politically unstable government of the Alawite dynasty. This study analyzes the socio-political organization of the Ait Ayash, a tribe of intensive agriculturalists, and its transformation through different political periods. The early history of the tribe reveals that the social group on the Ansegmir valley resulted from the break-up through government measures of a larger independent tribe in the early part of the 19th century.

The episodic interference of the makhzan on regional formations and the exploitative nature of the relationship between makhzan and tribes brought forth adaptive responses in the socio-political organizations of tribes, as exemplified by the Ait Ayash. The Ait Ayash relied for group recruitment on agnatic reckoning without the development of lineages, on ritual collaterality, and on contractual alliances. These adaptive mechanisms appear to be common features in the other tribal formations as well. Berber tribal organization stressed equality of male members and open recruitment both of which served to maintain flexible and viable social entities in an environment of political and ecological hazards. The Ait Ayash, whose subsistence production relied on intensive land use, treated irrigated land as individual, or private property. This shifts responsibility for allotting a nonextendable resource from the group to the individual householder. The tribes which used land extensively with seminomadic pastoralism practiced communal ownership of all land. Private ownership of irrigated land among the Ait Ayash regulated group size with respect to land without subverting cohesion through tribal membership. Land was sold only to other tribal members who were ascribed as such through patrifiliation or ritual agnation. Nonirrigated land remained communal property with joint use rights to members of the tribe. Another feature of the organization of the Ait Ayash was the corporate nature of the local-territorial settlements with respect to rights over persons. This contributed to the leveling of status differences, and limited stratification to that imposed by the makhzan during periods of governmental control.

The French Protectorate ushered in the modern period and destroyed the tribal framework as it extended the political and economic control of the central government over the countryside. The French administration chose, partially in the spirit of preserving indigenous institutions, to maintain certain ascriptive-status relations, such as the customary legal codes, and to recognize tribal collective lands by official registration at the same time that the status-bound economy of the earlier period was being rapidly replaced by a market-oriented economy. The administration of tribal groups through appointed chiefs limited the range of changes that were possible in the new political and economic conditions to particular decisions of particular chiefs. Among the Ait Ayash the opportunities for initiating new economic projects were refused by their chief. A moment for bringing about some local innovations was missed.

The advent of Independence led to a reorganization of rural structures. Rural communes replaced the moribund tribal structures. The new administrative unit has had little relevance to date on the life of the Ait Ayash. Their production activities have not changed. The region of the High Moulouya plain today is one of high unemployment and underemployment, despite its low-growth rate compared to other Moroccan regions. Modernization has made the option of selling one's labor in the market the preferred one. This is precisely the option that is unavailable. Traditional subsistence activities increasingly fail to provide an adequate livelihood for more and more households but still provide the impetus for village cooperation outside the trappings of modern administration.

BIBLIOGRAPHY

Abdel-Massih, Ernest T.
    1971a   Tamazight Verb Structure; a Generative Approach. Bloomington: Indiana University.
    1971b   A Course in Spoken Tamazight; Berber Dialects of Ayt Ayache and Ayt Seghrouchen. Ann Arbor: Center for Near Eastern and North African Studies, University of Michigan.
    1971c   A Reference Grammar of Tamazight; a Comparative Study of the Berber Dialects of Ayt Ayache and Ayt Seghrouchen. Ann Arbor: Center for Near Eastern and North African Studies, University of Michigan.

Abun-Nasr, Jamil M.
    1971   A History of the Maghrib. Cambridge: University Press.

Adam, André
    1968   Casablanca, essai sur la transformation de la société marocaine au contact de l'occident. Paris: Centre Nationale de la Recherche Scientifique.

Ashford, Douglas E.
    1961a   Political Change in Morocco. Princeton: Princeton University Press.
    1961b   Elections in Morocco; Progess or Confusion? Middle East Journal 15: 1–15.
    1967   National Development and Local Reform, Political Participation in Morocco, Tunisia, and Pakistan. Princeton: Princeton University Press.

al-ᶜayyāshī (Al Ayashi), Abū Salīm, see Berbrugger, ed.

Bachir, Said Ben
    1969   L'Administration Locale du Maroc. Casablanca: Imprimerie Royale.

Barth, Fredrik
    1959   Segmentary Opposition and the Theory of Games: A Study of Pathan Organization. Journal of the Royal Anthropological Institute of Great Britain and Ireland 89 (1):5–21.

Beaudet, G.
    1969   Les Beni M'Guild du Nord. Etude géographique de l'évolution récente d'une confédération semi-nomade. Revue de Géographie du Maroc 15:3–80.

Berbrugger, Adrien, ed.
    1846   Voyages dans le Sud de l'Algérie et des Etats Barbaresques de l'ouest et de l'est par El-'Aiachi et Moula-Ahmed. Sciences Historiques et Géographiques 9. Exploration scientifique de l'Algérie 1840 à 1842. Paris:Imprimerie Royale.

Berque, Jacques
    1953   Qu'est-ce qu'une 'Tribu' Nord-Africaine? Eventail de l'Historie Vivante—Hommage à Lucien Febvre. 1:260–271. Paris: Armand Colin.
    1955   Structures Sociales du Haut Atlas. Paris: Presses Universitaires de France.
    1958a   Al-Yousi. Problèmes de la culture marocaine au XVIIème Siècle. Paris: Mouton & Co.
    1958b   Droit des terres et integration sociale au Maghreb. Cahiers Internationaux de Sociologie 25:38–74.
    1962   Maghreb entre des deux guerres. Paris: Editions du Seuil.
    1966   The Rural System of the Maghrib. In: State and Society in Independent North Africa, ed. Leon Carl Brown, pp. 192–211. Washington, D.C.: The Middle East Institute.

Bertalanffy, Ludwig von
    1969   General System Theory. New York: George Braziller.

Bidwell, Robin
    1973   Morocco under Colonial Rule, French Administration of Tribal Areas 1912–1956. London: Frank Cass.

Blom, Jan-Petter
    1969   Ethnic and Cultural Differentiation. In: Ethnic Groups and Boundaries, ed. Fredrik Barth, pp. 74–85. Boston: Little, Brown & Co.

Bourdieu, Pierre
    1966   The Sentiment of Honour in Kabyle Society. In: Honour and Shame, ed. by J. J. Peristiany, pp. 191–241. Chicago: University of Chicago Press.

Bousquet, Georges Henri
    1950   Islàmic and customary law in North Africa. Journal of Comparative Legislation and International Law 32 (3–4): 57–65.

Bouverot, Commandant
    1920   Ras-Moulouya. Bulletin de la Société de Géographie du Maroc 1:31–35.

Brignon, Jean, Abdelaziz Amine, Brahim Boutaleb, Guy Martinet, Bernard Rosenberger and Michel Terrasse
    1967   Histoire du Maroc. Casablanca: Librairie Nationale.

Bruno, Henri and Georges Henri Bousquet
    1946   Contribution à l'étude des pactes de protection et l'alliance chez les Berbères du Maroc central. Hespéris 33 (3–4): 353–371.

Burke, Edmund, III
    1972   The Image of the Moroccan State in French Ethnological Literature: A New Look at the Origin of Lyautey's Berber Policy. In: Arabs and Berbers, ed. Ernest Gellner and Charles Micaud, pp. 175–199. London: D.C. Heath & Co.

Caillé, Jacques
    1953   La Mission du Capitaine Burel au Maroc en 1808. Paris: Institut des Hautes-Etudes Marocaines, Notes et Documents No. 13.

Carter, Meril G.
    1966   Feasibility study for a range management project in Morocco, ms. S.C.S. United States Department of Agriculture.

Castries, Henry, comte de
    1911a   La Zaouia de Dila et la Chute de la dynastie saadienne. In: Les Sources Inédites de l'Historie du Maroc, Première Série, Dynastie Saadienne, Archives et Bibliothèques de France, Vol. 3, pp. 572–583. Paris: E. Leroux.
    1911b   Les Moriscos à Salé et Sidi el-Ayashi. In: Les Sources Inédites de l'Historie du Maroc, Première Série, Dynastie Saadienne, Archives et Bibliothèques de France, Vol. 3, pp. 187–198. Paris: E. Leroux.

Cazautets, J.
    1965   Les Mariages consanguins dans la plaine du Loukkos. Revue de Géographie du Maroc 8:35–40.

Celerier, Jean
    1937   La croisée des routes en Haute Moulouya. Paris: Mélanges Gautier.

Chambergeat, Paul (pseud.)
    1961   Les élections communales marocaines. Revue Francaise de Science Politique 2 (1):89–117.
    1963   Les élections communales au Maroc. Annuaire de l'Afrique du Nord 2: 119–128. Aix-en-Provence: Centre National de la Recherche Scientifique.
    1965   L'administration et le douar. Revue de Géographie du Maroc 8: 83–86.

Cheneb, Mohammed ben
    1908   Etude sur les personnages mentionnés dans l'idjaza du cheikh 'Abd el-Qadir el-Fasy. In: Actes du XIV Congres International des orientalistes, Alger, 1905, Troisième Partie (Suite), Langues Musulmanes, pp. 168–560. Paris: E. Leroux.

Cherkaoui, Abdelaziz
    1968   Le Contrôle de l'Etat sur la Commune. Rabat: Editions La Porte.

Colin, Georges S.
    1938   Origine Arabe des grands mouvements de populations Berbères dans le Moyen Atlas. Hespéris 25: 265–268.

Coufourier, L.
    1906   Chronique de la vie de Moulay el-Hassan, translation of Al-Houlal al-Bahya (anon.). Archives Marocaines 8:330–395.

Couleau, Julien
    1968   La Paysannerie Marocaine. Paris: Centre National de la Recherche Scientifique.

Coursimault, Capitaine
    1917   La 'Ttatta'. Archives Berbères 2(3):261–264.

Couvreur, G.
    1968   La vie pastorale dans le Haut Atlas central. Revue de la Géographie du Maroc 13: 3–54.

Despois, Jean
    1964   L'Afrique du Nord. 3me ed. Paris: Presses Universitaires de France.

Dowling, James H.
    1975   Property Relations and Productive Strategies in Pastoral Societies. American Ethnologist 2 :419–426.

Drague, Georges (pseud.)
    1951   Esquisse d'histoire religieuse du Maroc, confrèries et zaouias. Paris: J. Peyronnet.

Dunn, Ross E.
    1972   Berber Imperialism: The Ait Atta Expansion in Southeast Morocco. In: Arabs and Berbers, ed. Ernest Gellner and Charles Micaud, pp. 85–107. London: D.C. Heath & Co.

Durham University
    1956   Report of the Expedition to French Morocco, 1952. n.p.: Durham University Exploration Society.

Emberger, Louis and René Maire
    1934   Tableau phytogéographique du Maroc. Première partie, Mémoires de la Société des Sciences Naturelles du Maroc 38. Rabat: Institut scientifique chérifien.

Emberger, Louis
    1930   La végétation de la région Mediterranéen. Revue général de Botanie.
    1939   Aperçu général sur la végétation du Maroc. Mémoires hors serie de la Société des Sciences Naturelles du Maroc, Rabat. Berne: Hans Huber.

Evans-Pritchard, E.E.
    1940   The Nuer. Oxford: Clarendon Press.

Favret, Jeanne
    1972   Traditionalism through Ultramodernism. In: Arabs and Berbers, ed. Ernest Gellner and Charles Micaud, pp. 307–324. London: D.C. Heath & Co.

Fogg, Walter
    1936   The economic revolution in the countryside of French Morocco. Journal of the Royal African Society 35: 123–129.

Foucauld, Charles de
    1888   Reconnaissance au Maroc (1883–1884). Paris: Challamel

Gellner, Ernest
    1969   Saints of the Atlas. London: Weidenfeld and Nicholson.
    1972   Patterns of Rural Rebellion in Morocca during the Early Years of Independence. In: Arabs and Berbers: ed. Ernest Gellner and Charles Micaud, pp. 361–374. London: D.C. Heath & Co.

Guennoun, Said
    1939   La Haute Moulouya. Renseignements coloniaux et documents de L'Afrique française 10–11: 209–224; 12: 225–240; 2–3(1940): 25–31; 4–5(1940): 42–48.

Guillaume, Augustin
    1946   Les Berbères marocains et la Pacification de l'Atlas Central (1912–1933). Paris: R. Juillard.

Hajji, Muhammad
    1964   al-Zawiyah al-Dilai'iyah. Rabat: National Printing House.

Harris, Walter B.
    1895   Tafilet, the Narrative of a Journey of Exploration in the Atlas Mountains and the Oases of the North-West Sahara. London: Wm. Blackwood & Sons.

Hart, David M.
    1967   Segmentary Systems and the Role of 'Five Fifths' in Tribal Morocco. Revue de l'occident musulman et de la Mediterranée 3: 82–92.

Henry, R.
    1944   Où se trouvait la Zaouia de Dila? Hespéris 31: 49–54.

Hoffman, Bernard G.
    1967   The Structure of Traditional Moroccan Rural Society. The Hague: Mouton & Co.

Ibn Khaldoun
    1925   Histoire des Berbères et des dynasties musulmanes de l'Afrique septentrionale (Kitab al Ibar) trans. Baron de Slane, 4 vols. Paris: P. Geuthner.

al-Ifrānī, Muḥammad al-Saghir ibn Muhammad (also al-Yafrānī, al-Ufrānī
              El Oufrâni, Mohammed Esseghir ben Elhadj ben Abdallah)
    1889   Nozhet-Elhâdi, Histoire de la dynastie saadienne au Maroc (1511–1670) trans. O. Houdas. Ecole des langues orientales vivantes Publications, series 3, vol. 3. Paris: E. Leroux.

Irons, William
    1975   The Yomut Turkmen: A study of social organization among a central Asian Turkic-speaking population. Museum of Anthropology, University of Michigan. Anthropological Papers 58.

Jacques-Meunié, D.
    1958   Hierarchie sociale au Maroc présaharien. Hespéris 45: 239–269.

La Chapelle, F. de
    1931   Le Sultan Moulay Isma'il et les Berbères Sanhaja du Maroc central. Archives Marocaines 28: 7–65.

Laoust, Emile
    1930   L'habitation chez les transhumants du Maroc central:
    1932   I, La tente et le douar; II, La maison; III, L'igerm.
    1934   Hespéris 10: 151–253; 14(1932): 115–218; 18(1934): 109–196.
    1949   Contes berbères du Maroc. 2 vols. Paris: Larose.

Leach, Edmund
    1954   Political Systems of Highland Burma: A study of Kachin social structure. Cambridge: Harvard University Press.

Leo Africanus, Joannes (Al Hassan ibn Mohammed al Wezaz al Fasi)
    1963   The History and Description of Africa, trans. John Pory. Reprint of Hakluyt Society, First Series 93. New York: Burt Franklin.

Lesne, Marcel
    1967   Les Zemmour: Essai d'histoire tribale. Revue de l'occident musulman et de la Mediterranée 3: 97–132.

Lesur, Capitaine
    1920   Notes sur la Zaouya Sidi Hamza. Bulletin de la Société de Géographie du Maroc 1:141–147.

Lévi-Provençal, Evariste
    1922   Les Historiens des Chorfa. Paris: E. Larose.

Lewis, William H.
    1961   Feuding and Social Change in Morocco. The Journal of Conflict Resolution 5:43–54.

Linarès, Fernand
    1932   Voyage au Tafilalet avec S.M. le Sultan Moulay Hassan en 1893. Extrait du Bulletin de l'Institut d'Hygiène du Maroc, Nos. 3–4.

Magnin, Jean
    1952   Notes sur les alliances traditionelles dans le Moyen-Atlas septentrionel. Anthropos 47 (5–6): 784–794.

Maher, Vanessa
    1974   Women and Property in Morocco. Cambridge: Cambridge University Press.

Marcy, G.
    1936   L'alliance par colactation (Tâda) chez les Berbères du Maroc central. Revue Africaine 2 (2): 957–973.

1939 La problème du droit coutoumier Berbère. La France Mediterranéene et Africaine 1: 7–70.

Marthelot, P.
1961 Histoire et réalité de la modernisation du monde rural au Maroc. Tiers Monde 2 (6): 137–168.

Martin, J., H. Jover, J. Le Coz, G. Maurer and D. Noin
1967 Géographie du Maroc. Casablanca: Librairie Nationale.

Mennesson, E.
1965 Ksour du Tafilalt. Revue de Géographie du Maroc 8: 87–92.

Middleton, John and David Tait, eds.
1958 Tribes without Rulers. London: Routledge and Kegan Paul.

Midelt (Morocco). Archives du Bureau de Cercle de Midelt.
1925–1969 Miscellaneous Papers and correspondence (uncatalogued).

Montagne, Robert
1930 Les Berbères et le makhzen dans le sud du Maroc. Paris: F. Alcan.
1931 La vie sociale et la vie politique des Berbères. Paris: Editions du Comité de l'Afrique française.

Morocco, Service Central des Statistiques
n.d. Resultats de l'enquête á objectifs multiples (1961–1963),
(1967) vol. 2, Agriculture traditionelle. Rabat: Cabinet Royal.

Mouette, G.
1683 Histoire des conquestes de Moulay Archy, connu sous le nom de roy de Tafilet, et de Mouley Ismaël ou Seméin, son frère et son successeur à présent régnant . . . . reprinted under title of: Histoire de Moulay er-Reshid et de Moulay Ismail. In: Les Sources Inédites de l'histoire du Maroc, Second Series, Archives and Libraries of France 2 (1924):1–201.

al-Naṣiri, Aḥmad ibn Khalid (also al-Salāwi, Ennâsiri Esslâoui, Ahmed ben Khaled)
1906 Kitab elistiqsa li-akhbari doual elmagrib elaqsa. In: Part 4, Chronique de la dynastie Alaouie du Maroc, 1631 to 1894 trans. E. Fumey. Archives Marocaines 9 (1906):1–399 and 10 (1907):1–424.

Nicholas-Mourer, H.
1963 Les collectivités locales dans l'administration territoriale du Royaume du Maroc. Annuaire de l'Afrique du Nord 2: 126–160. Aix-en-Provence: Centre National de la Recherche Scientifique.

Nicolas, Georges
1961 La sociologie rurale au Maroc. Tiers-Monde 2 (8): 527–543.

Noin, Daniel
1965 Types d'habitat dans les campagnes du Maroc. Revue de Géographie du Maroc 8:101–108.
1970 La population rurale du Maroc. 2 vols. Paris: Presses Universitaires de France.

Pascon, Paul
1977 Le Haouz de Marrakech. 2 vols. Rabat: Centre Universitaire de la Recherche Scientifique.

Pascon, Paul and Mekki Bentahar
1969 Ce que disent 296 jeunes ruraux. Bulletin Economique et Social du Maroc 31 (112–113): 1–43.

al-Qādirī, Muḥammad ibn al-Ṭayyib
(Al-Qadiri, Mouhammad ben At-Tayyib)
1913 Nachr al-mathani trans. A. Graulle and P.
1917 Maillard. Archives Marocaines 21:1–400 and 24:1–464.

BIBLIOGRAPHY

Rabinow, Paul
 1975 Symbolic Domination, Cultural Form and Historical Change in Morocco. Chicago: The University of Chicago Press.

Raynal, René
 1952 La terre et l'homme en haute Moulouya: Quelques exemples d'évolution récente des genres de vie. Hespéris 39: 487–500.
 1960 La terre et l'homme en haute Moulouya. Bulletin Economique et Social du Maroc 24 (86–87): 281–346.
 1961 Plaines et piedmonts du basin de la Moulouya (Maroc Oriental). Rabat: Faculté des lettres de Rabat.

Renaud, H.P.J.
 1934 Un prétendu catalogue de la bibliotheque de la grande mosquée de Fès, daté de 1268 Heg. 1851–1852 J.C. Hespéris 18:76–99.
 1939 Recherches historiques sur les épidemies du Maroc, IV. Les pestes du milieu du XVIII-e siècle. Hespéris 26: 293–319.

Sahlins, Marshall
 1961 The Segmentary Lineage: An organization of predatory expansion. American Anthropologist 63: 322–345.
 1965 On the Ideology and Composition of Descent Groups. Man 65:104–107.

Schorger, William D.
 1969 The Evolution of Political Forms in a North Moroccan Village. Anthropological Quarterly 42: 263–286.

Segonzac, Edouard, Marquis de
 1903 Voyages au Maroc 1899–1901. Paris: Armand Colin.
 1910 Au coeur de l'Atlas, mission au Maroc (1904–1905). Paris: Emile Larose.

Terrasse, Henri
 1950 Histoire du Maroc des origines à l'établissement du Protectorat français. Casablanca: Editions Atlantides.

Villeneuve, Michel
 1971 La situation de l'agriculture et son avenir dans l'économie marocaine. Paris: Librairie Générale de Droit et de Jurisprudence.

Vinogradov, Amal Rassam
 1974 The Ait Ndhir of Morocco: A Study of the Social Transformation of a Berber Tribe. Museum of Anthropology, University of Michigan, Anthropological Papers 55.

Voinot, L.
 1939 Sur les traces glorieuses de pacificateurs du Maroc. Paris: Lavauzelle.

Waterbury, John
 1970 The Commander of the Faithful, the Moroccan Elite: A Study in Segmented Politics. London: Weidenfeld & Nicolson.

Zartman, I. William
 1964 Morocco, Problems of New Power. New York: Atherton Press.

al-Zayyānī, Abū al-Qāsim ibn Aḥmad
 (Ezziani, Aboulqasem ben Ahmed)
 1886 Le Maroc de 1631 à 1812, trans. O. Houdas. Extracted from Al-tarjaman al-muarib an duwal al-mashriq wa al-maghrib. Paris: Ecole des langues orientales vivantes.

GLOSSARY

OF TERMS

NOTE ON TRANSLITERATION

The transliteration of Moroccan Arabic and Berber terms and names is given in a simplified system without the Arabic ʿ*ayn* (ʿ), the Arabic *hamza* (ʾ) and diacritical marks. The Arabic speaker will recognize the correct form, while the general reader can approximate the pronunciation without undue complication. The ʿayn, hamza and diacritical marks are included for reference only in forms within parentheses in the glossary, following some forms used in the text. The parenthetical forms employ the system found in the *International Journal of Middle East Studies*.

Tamazight Berber words in the glossary are indicated by a b. after the word. All others are Moroccan Arabic. The plurals of some words are given after the symbol /. Variant forms are given after the symbol ~.

Glossary

abra (ᶜabrâ)	b.	a unit of dry measure which is regionally variable (from arabic ᶜbr = to weigh)
abrid	b.	road, way
adoul (ᶜadl)		notary public and secretary to a judge
agourram/ igourramen	b.	saintly person of Berber origin
ait	b.	people of, descendants of
akhatar/ikhatarn	b.	elder, notable, large
akhumas/ikhumasn	b.	sharecropper, agricultural laborer
alim/ ulema ~ ulama (ᶜâlim/ ᶜulamâɔ)		savants, custodians of canon law and theology
almou/ilmouten	b.	meadow
amalou	b.	in the shade, the northern mountain slopes, the wet regions
aman		safety, peace, truce
amazigh/imazighen	b.	Tamazight-speaker, tribesman of Berber origin, free man
amazouz	b.	spring cultivation
amenzou	b.	winter cultivation
amghar/imgharn	b.	tribal chief, notable
amgilla/imgillan	b.	co-juror
aqbli/iqblin	b.	'southerner', one without tribal affiliation
ari (ᶜari)	b.	mountain
asamar	b.	in the sun, the southern mountain slopes, the dry regions
ayyelid ~ aglid	b.	king
azaghar	b.	winter pastures, plain country
baraka		blessing, religious charisma, the benign influence of a saint
baroud		war, gunpowder
blad ~ bilad		countryside, region
blad al makhzan		land of government
blad al siba		land of dissidence
bour		plowland, dry farming
dahir (ẓahîr)		royal edict
dir		zone between mountain and plain
dirham/drahim		official Moroccan currency; abbrev.: DH.; the dirham is divided into 100 francs; one dirham equals 20 U.S. cents (1969).
diya		blood payment
douar		rural settlement; circle of tents
fellah		peasant, farmer

173

fqih/fuqaha		religious teacher
gamila	b.	unit of dry measure
gish ~ jish		army; status of tribes which provided military service in exchange for land
habous		land in mortmain held by a religious institution; religious or pious endowment
halfa		esparto grass, Stipa tenacissima
henna		reddish-orange dye and cosmetic, pre-nuptial ceremonies
ighrem/igherman	b.	walled settlement, village
ighs/ighsan ~ ikhs	b.	bone, tribal fraction, clan
iyr/iyran ~ igr	b.	field
iyran daw n' tergwa	b.	'fields under the water channel', irrigated fields
izmazz	b.	fine
izref	b.	customary law
izri	b.	white wormwood, Artemisia herba-alba
jihad		holy war
jmaa/ijmaa (jamâ'a)		assembly, tribal council
jmaa l'qarawiya		rural commune, an administrative unit since 1956 replacing tribal units
khalifa/khulafa		deputy
khams-khumas	b.	five-fifths, a confederation of tribes
leff		alliance, political moiety
makhzan		government of Morocco
melk ~ mulk		private property
moussem		an annual pilgrimage to a saint's tomb and a festival held in his honor
mshaikhat		division of a rural commune
mujahid		fighter in a holy war
mukhazni ~ mkhazni		gendarme
mumttil/ mumttilin		representative
muqaddam/muqaddamin		local agent of the administration
murabit/murabitin		saintly person, mystic, 'marabout'
naiba		a tax-paying tribe under the control of the central government
nasf		half, a moiety
ou	b.	filiation marker, belonging to, son of
qadi		religious judge
qaid/quyyad (qâɔid)		administrator, civil or military officer
qanoun		law, rules, tribal code of laws and fines
qasba		fort
qebala	b.	south, also east
qsar/qsour		walled fortified settlement
raiss (raɔis)		leader, president
ryal	b.	monetary unit used in the countryside which corresponds to no actual coinage; from Spanish real; twenty ryal equal one dirham
sdaq		bridewealth
shafaa (shuf'a)		preemptory rights of agnatic kin
shaikh/shioukh		elderly and venerated man, chief, local agent of the administration

GLOSSARY

sharia ~ shraa (al shari‛a)		the law of Islam consisting of Prophetic revelation, tradition and sayings
sharif/shurfa		descendant of the Prophet
shih		white wormwood, Artemisia herba-alba
siba		dissidence
souq/aswaq		market
sufi		mystic in Islam
tada		alliance
tagella	b.	collective oath
tajin~dajin		stew
takessa	b.	protection
taleb/ tulba (ṭâlib)		religious teacher
tallis		a double sack for grains, a muleload
tamazight	b.	berber language
tamazirt	b.	territory
tamghrost	b.	animal sacrifice
taqbilt/tiqbilin	b.	tribe
taqbut	b.	woolen cape
tawala~tawallat	b.	communal herding of domestic animals
tergwa~tarja	b.	irrigation canal
tertib		tax on production
tighst/tighsatin~	b.	little bone, extended family, patrician segment
triq sultan		the sultan's road, the main trade route
urf (‛urf)		customary law
zawiya/zawaya		religious establishment under a brotherhood or a murabit

PLATES

Plate 1. Mausoleum of Sidi Abdullah ou Hamza (d. 1750) constructed by the sultan Sidi Muhammad (1757–1790) who had studied with the Hamzawi fqih. Sidi Abdullah was the fouth sheikh of the zawiya Hamzawiya. The green tiles from the fallen roof are now placed (for the baraka of the saint) over the gravesites in the adjoining cemetery.

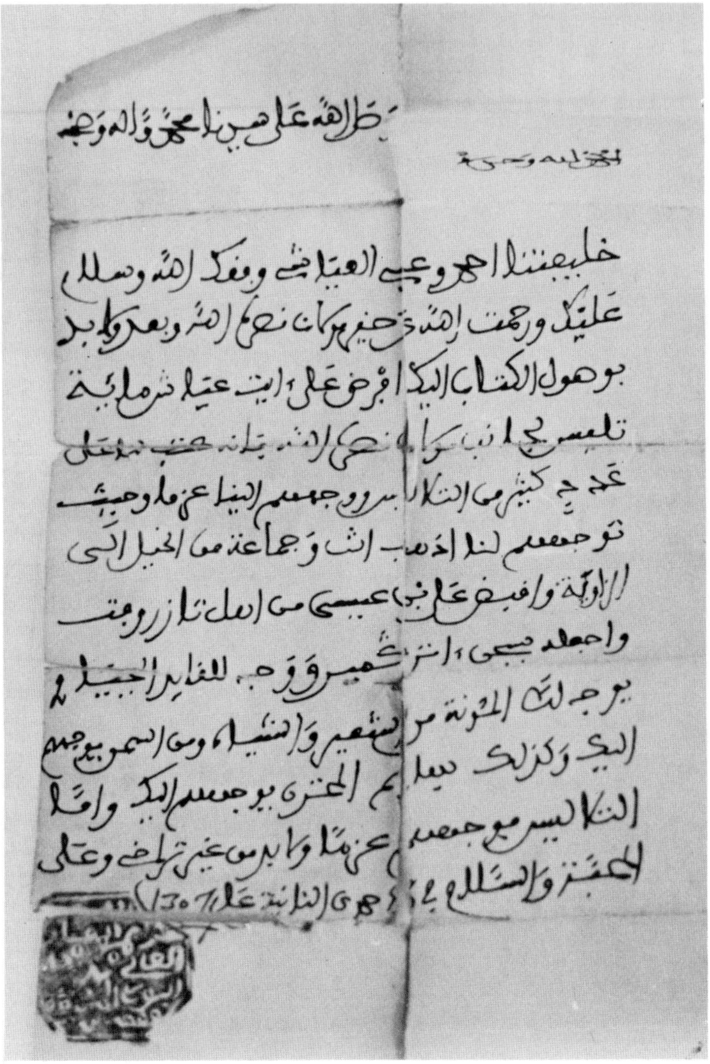

Plate 2. Letter of qaid Mhand ou Talb to the Ait Ayash, 1889. Source: Private collection of an Ait Ayash family.

Plate 3. Aerial photograph of two Ait Ayash villages.

Plate 4. Members of an extended family of the Ait Ayash.

Plate 5. Ait Ayash group circumcision. Each cane represents one boy.

Plate 6. Schoolboys standing beside an abandoned and crumbling qsar.

Plate 7. Contemporary Ait Ayash village houses.

Plate 8a. Threshing wheat at Ait Oumghar. The threshing grounds are in the center of the village.

Place 8b. Winnowing wheat.

Plate 9. Measuring wheat. A portion of the wheat is set aside for charitable distribution.

Plate 10. A market of the High Molouya plain at Kerroushen.

Plate 11. Construction of a mosque by cooperative village effort.

Plate 12. Some members of an Ait Ayash extended family.